THE
OPPRESSED
MIDDLE

THE
OPPRESSED
MIDDLE

Politics of Middle Management

Scenes from Corporate Life

EARL SHORRIS

ANCHOR PRESS/DOUBLEDAY
Garden City, New York
1981

Brief excerpts from this book appeared in an entirely altered form in *Harper's*. This Anchor Press edition is the first publication of THE OPPRESSED MIDDLE: Politics of Middle Management, Scenes from Corporate Life.

Anchor Press edition: 1981

ISBN: 0-385-14564-0
Library of Congress Catalog Card Number: 80-717
Copyright © 1981 by Earl Shorris

To Sylvia Sasson Shorris

Contents

Preface

There are no villains in this book. It is about victims without crimes or criminals. In twenty-five years as a worker and a manager, I have found few people to dislike, none to hate; no one I have met in business has committed an error of which I am incapable.

This is a conservative book in that it seeks to preserve the freedom we have in America and to extend it. This is a radical book in that it seeks a change in the structure of society. I intend no less than to destroy the comforts of fearful people, for which I suffer no guilt and offer no apology.

No business secrets are revealed in the following pages; I have avoided the teasing pleasures of gossip, not for a lack of tales to tell, but for fear that gossip would function as a distracting balm. In place of gossip I have substituted forty examples told in the form of fictions (Chapter 7). Each of the fictions was invented to exemplify one of the tactics of totalitarianism. Each is followed by a brief analysis and comparison to the tactics used in organizations commonly recognized as totalitarian. It was my hope that these fictions would prove to be more affecting than the abstract language of economics, sociology, psychology, or philosophy; they are meant to let the reader exist in them for the time it takes to read a few pages.

The people I have known in business will not find themselves in this book. To portray them and their privacies would be a betrayal with no purpose but to harm them, and I owe them no harm. Indeed, I hope this book will be helpful to them, for it is intended that way, like the mirror and the balance leading us to new considerations of ourselves.

Many people have helped me in my attempt to understand the politics of business. I choose not to thank them by name here, for that might well lead to the notion that they, in their roles as managers, were more likely than others to use the tactics described in the following pages.

The idea for this book came to me during a discussion with Louis T. Hagopian in which he described what he considered an unfair management practice. Lewis H. Lapham asked difficult questions about definitions and suggested readings that led to the hypothesis put forward in Chapter 8. Anthony Shorris suggested revisions in the manuscript, as did James Budenhdzer. Loretta Barrett edited in manner most fierce and most friendly. I am especially grateful to them.

Plan of the Book

At the core of this book are the forty examples of Chapter 7. They are preceded by the thesis of the work (beginning with Chapter 2), including a series of definitions and an attempt to place the work in historical, economic, and philosophical context. A few pages of speculation follow the examples.

The reader whose interest is confined to the examples of Chapter 7 risks misunderstanding the view of man that caused the writing of this book. The standards implied by criticism are stated in the earlier chapters as the possibilities for man.

The work of Hannah Arendt on totalitarianism has served as a guide throughout the book. The interested reader will be well served by going to the source.

As a human being, a creature whose
own reason subjects him to certain duties, everybody is a *businessman.*

Kant
On the Old Saw: That May Be Right
In Theory but It Won't Work in Practice

FROM LETTER IX
THE FIRST EUNUCH TO IBBI AT ERZERUM

Weighed down by fifty years of effort and anxiety, I groan
when I realize that during all of my long life, I have not enjoyed one serene day, not one tranquil moment.

Tired of the debasing services I was forced to perform, I
reasoned that I was sacrificing my passions for the sake of ease
and wealth. What an unhappy decision that was! Preoccupied
by what I would gain as compensation, I failed to realize the
extent of my sacrifice.

I remember always that I was born to command them, and
when in fact I do so, I feel as though I have once again become a man.

Although I guard them for another, I feel a secret joy when
I make them obey. When I deprive them of everything, I feel
as though it were I who had exercised the prerogative.

I make myself into a barrier that cannot be removed; I put a
stop to whatever plans they may make; I arm myself with re-
fusals; I bristle with scruples; I never stop talking of duty, virtue, decency, and modesty. I drive them to despair. . . . Then
I complain of the severity I am forced to use. I pretend that I

have no motives other than their own interest and my great affection for them.

Never for a moment am I certain of my master's favor, so many are the enemies who possess his heart and wish my ruin. When they are with him, I am not heard; at those times, nothing is denied them and I am always wrong.

How many times have I been in favor when I went to sleep, only to find myself in disgrace when I awoke?

Montesquieu
The Persian Letters

THE
OPPRESSED
MIDDLE

1

Introduction:
What Works in Practice May Not Work in Theory

I

In March 1953, a group of scholars met in Boston to discuss what many believed was a new form of political organization, totalitarianism. Among the participants were some of the best minds of the time: Hannah Arendt, David Riesman, Karl Deutsch, W. W. Leontief, George F. Kennan, Erik Erikson, and Carl Friedrich. They did not arrive at a definition of totalitarianism satisfactory to the group, nor were they able to bring the noun beyond its use as the description of a political entity, a kind of society. There was very little discussion of the methods of totalitarianism outside the totalitarian state. They were caught in the concept of totality, pioneers seeking to understand a new and terrible phenomenon, concentrating on basics, as pioneers must.

While he was preparing for that discussion, David Riesman

taught at the University of Chicago, where I was one of his less distinguished students. It astonishes me now that when we sat around that boat-shaped table, speaking of Weber and Veblen, it did not occur to Riesman that the great social scientists had failed to recognize the adumbrations of a new form of social and political organization.

The 1950s were the years of sociology. For me, as for so many others, the excitement of those years came in the discussions with Riesman, the visits to his office, the classes with Reuel Denney, his collaborator on *The Lonely Crowd*. In a far corner was Richard McKeon, whose Aristotelian concepts dominated the organization of the curriculum, but whose mind was too subtle and too discomfiting for the time. We rushed from McKeon's philosophy to the personal niceness of Riesman and to his sociology. There would have been no fun in carrying McKeon's depth to Riesman's wonderful gossip of the way we lived, so we never did.

Hannah Arendt's trilogy had been published, but it is only since then that her work has had its effect, illuminating much of modern history by carrying to it many of the ideas one might have learned at McKeon's feet. The theory of totalitarianism was advanced some ten years later by Hans Buchheim in a book not widely known in the United States, and yet another decade passed before Arendt put forth the notion of the banality of evil in her work on the Eichmann trial.

Most of the theoretical work, the thinking, was done prior to World War II. After the war, with a few major exceptions, the literature of totalitarianism has been confined to history. The available detail is now enormous, but the understanding of the roots and methods of totalitarianism has been advanced but little. The concept has not been applied in discussions of China, the Philippines, Cuba, Chile, Cambodia, etc. Both theory and history assume that totalitarianism was born in the Reichstag fire and died with Stalin. The only working definition of totalitarianism thus becomes the detailed history of

Nazi Germany and Stalinist Russia, and if no other definition can be made, totalitarianism is a danger against which society cannot protect itself, comparable to a disease that cannot be diagnosed until the patient has died.

By the middle of the 1960s the word itself became an embarrassment. The jejune mutterings of an insincere revolution misspelled "fascism" and applied totalitarianism to whatever displeased the children. An obviously unjust war and the possibility of a useless death literally frightened students out of their wits. Invective needs obscenity, and fascism and totalitarianism are obscene; the students said whatever was practical. It required no thought to oppose the Vietnam War, and they were desperate.

The problem with the misapplication of obscenity is that words lose their meaning. Lyndon Johnson, for all his failings, was not a fascist and Richard Nixon, despicable though he may be, was not a crazed murderer. Totalitarianism does not suddenly emerge full-grown and total nor does it, except in its final throes, have spectacular symptoms. Arendt's description of Eichmann reveals far more about the system in its thoughtless, stolid, clerical reality. Whether war, murder, and concentration camps are necessary components of totalitarianism will be discussed later, as will the question of the possibility of totalitarian traits. Meanwhile, it may be sufficient to say that the word should not immediately call up visions of storm troopers or purge trials, nor should it be construed as an hysterical denunciation. Totalitarianism denotes a form of political or rather apolitical organization, a diminishing or absence of freedom. It does not advertise itself for what it is; in fact, the longer it remains concealed the stronger it becomes.

II

The social science industry performs daily examinations in minute detail of all aspects of man. Citizens are pinched and poked individually, in small groups, and by the statistically significant thousands. Like hordes of tourists, the social scientists roam the country, learning the monuments, mountain ranges, restaurants, hotel accommodations, and climate. Also like tourists, they begin and end their work as strangers, reporting to their friends and colleagues a secondhand view of life. Their work generally lacks the systematic proofs of science and the intuition of art. They produce a presumptuous journalism of man and society; they do not know; they are students removed to the distance of gods.

At its best social science is a risky business. Unlike the historian, the social scientist cannot describe the life he considers at the end of its season; time is not his ally nor distance his instructor. He begins *in medias res,* seeking out perfect hearsay, forgetting the amusing truth of secrecy: if men wished to tell their secrets, they would not be secrets.

When the social scientist stays long in simple societies, he begins to penetrate the illusions the societies create as protection from strangers. Interesting theories emerge, the layers of the palimpsest are more easily visible, less confusing, neolithic man reveals modern man as the laboratory implies the world. But the sheer size of modern society makes it less easy to comprehend, and complexity itself operates as a barrier, shielding men from their observers.

From the godly remove of the social scientist politics go unseen, too subtle, too secret, too entwined in complexities that hinder observation. To understand politics requires the hindsight of history or the sensibility of the engaged person. One who stands in the center of the world and avoids contact with his surroundings follows other paths.

The application of social science to the use of man began early in the century. Now, in the winter of the century, the literature is rich and sophisticated. The social scientist, employed by managers and leaders, bears a distinct resemblance to the capitalist of Marxist political philosophy. For him man has become a means, a thing to use in the making of things. As an efficiency expert the social scientist works at skinning pennies off the souls of employees. The ethical aspects of his job are obscured by his efforts at objectivity, by his own need to produce something useful, his own role as tool.

In the extreme, Stanley Milgram, studying obedience or more accurately the ethics of ordinary citizens, subjected innocent human beings to a painful and demeaning experience under the guise of social science: in studying the ethics of his subjects he forgot to consider his own. Gods may behave in that way, for they are beyond politics, victims of Atē and her spell of moral blindness. In such circumstance, they cannot recognize the politics of the life around them: men are reduced to things, and things cannot be as complex as equals; those who participate in the use of men are prohibited by their own need for self-preservation from considering the meaning of their work.

Totalitarianism, as trait or totality, escapes social scientists because of their innocence, as it must have escaped Heidegger when he spoke in defense of the educational policies of the National Socialists. Neither engaged nor gifted with the distance of history, social science sits in the middle ground where Atē rules.

III

After the war, strange people came to our town. The first of them was a girl with pale red hair, blue eyes, and a bosom. She was older than the rest of us, she was sixteen. All the boys were in love with her and her soft red hair and her bosom and her accent, which was not the Old Country accent of our grandmothers but the sound of sophistication, of a woman, as if a beautiful actress had slipped from our dreams into the real world of tennis shoes and two pubic hairs. We loved her and we were terrified of her. She wore perfume.

Because I was the youngest, she sometimes smiled at me, and now and then she spoke to me. Perhaps she thought I was still too young for leering. Perhaps she thought I was too young to share in the general awe of her. Once or twice we spoke about books. I was trying to read *Crime and Punishment*. She wanted to hear about Sonia but not about the murder. I quoted for her, "It is not before you I bow down but before the suffering of all humanity." She laughed softly. Her voice was lower than mine.

One afternoon, more than a year after our discussion of Dostoevski, I found her alone in the recreation room attached to the synagogue. She was standing next to a phonograph, listening to records and humming the tunes. Her hair had darkened, setting off the whiteness of her skin to greater effect.

For lack of anything to say I asked her if she was from Germany.

"It depends," she said. "The place where I am from is sometimes Germany, sometimes Poland."

"Can you dance the polka?"

"From the time I was a little girl."

"Teach me."

She found a recording of a polka and put it on the phonograph. We walked to the center of the room. She told me the steps. We walked through them. We were dancing. We skipped and whirled and laughed, dancing to that record and another and another until we were exhausted, laughing, and embarrassed with perspiration. We sat on a bench together to catch our breath. She fanned herself with her hand. I slid down on my spine and looked up at her shining face and her hair, which was even darker now, curling in dampness. She opened the buttons of her dress at the wrists and rolled up her sleeves. On the inside of her forearm were blue numbers.

She saw me staring at the numbers. There were tears in my eyes. She kissed me on the cheek. We said nothing. We always smiled at each other after that, but we never spoke.

A family came to our town from Poland after the war. There were rumors that they had escaped from the Nazis by hiding in caves and living on soups made of roots, insects, and rodents. The parents were selfish and acquisitive. The woman had three gold teeth and the man had a nose like a pale potato. She was aggressive, he was lazy, the children had bad manners. After a year, they moved away, perhaps to California. Everyone was glad to see them leave, they had not become a part of the community.

My son and I traveled through East Germany, Poland, and the Soviet Union in 1970. I was working as a journalist, visiting writers, editors, and officials. He was thirteen years old, and he had read the Communist Manifesto in preparation for the trip. Most of the people we met were pleasant, helpful, even hospitable. I enjoyed the trip and the work. By the time we reached Moscow he was terrified. Many years passed before I understood the difference between careful observation and the permeability of a child.

For a time a Soviet journalist and I were friends. We knew each other's families. We exchanged confidences. He is a very successful journalist, with friends in high places. His loyalty to his country and to the Communist Party is unquestionable. I cannot conceive of him as a villain.

A Jew, born in 1936, I expect the understanding of totalitarianism to be my birthright, a sensitivity carried in the genes, the ability to smell evil on the wind, survivor's sorcery. But it is not so, I am a second-generation parvenu, more American than Jew, nevertheless a Jew, nevertheless surprised by the failure of my ethnicity to alert me to evil in distant places. I was as blind as any tourist, even though I visited the synagogues in Leningrad and Moscow and saw the prejudice against my people and the abuse they suffered. No system was revealed to me by what I saw. My son, who did not look so hard, saw more.

What had the girl with red hair taught me but that heroines exist and are romantic? The numbers were the color of the veins beneath her white, almost translucent skin. They were not real to me, they did not say how or why they came to be there on her arm after dancing. I was new in her country; she taught me the polka, not politics.

Did my friend, the Soviet journalist, try to explain totalitarianism to me? He spoke with such humor of himself. If he is a man of angers, he turns them all to wit. He was well traveled in America, he made jokes of comparison between his country and mine. Perhaps he offered clues. If so, I did not hear, I cannot remember. Russia is a caricature to me, and I have been there, my grandparents were born there, I prefer to drink tea from a glass.

The family that lived in caves disgusted me. I never invited the children to my home. That is how far travelers live from totalitarianism, even when it is murderously evident, even when the traveler is a Jew.

IV

In the middle of this century two important books about race relations were published in America: Gunnar Myrdal's *An American Dilemma* and Ralph Ellison's *Invisible Man*. Myrdal, a Swedish economist, came to the problem without prejudice or preconceptions; there is no race problem in Sweden. Ellison came to the problems of blacks as a black man. Myrdal discovered or reiterated the economic basis of racism. Ellison produced a work that events of the next decades proved to have been prescient.

Myrdal said plainly that he sought objectivity, to write without making value judgments. Were Gunnar Myrdal a man of lesser quality, an *ad hominem* defense of objectivity could be made, but in this case it was clearly the method and not the man that was lacking. Racism breeds subtleties beyond the ken of the observer. Like any form of oppression, it breeds secrets of survival: variant language, double entendre behavior, an entire sub-culture. A clear example of the forced insincere behavior of oppressed people can be found in the Hebrew song "Kol Nidre," sung traditionally on the Eve of the Day of Atonement. The Jews of Spain during the Inquisition, forced to profess Christian beliefs to avoid the auto-da-fé, gathered once a year to say in their prayers that all religious vows they had made contrary to their own beliefs were null and void. How like the black maid who tells her despised white mistress she is kind and beautiful! How like the employee who tells the feared employer his errors are strokes of genius!

Dissembling, lying, petty thefts become the ways of survival of the oppressed. They live in secrets, not in opposition to but in fear of their oppressors, they are made into something other than themselves in pursuit of life, they do not rebel, they exist.

The classic response to oppression has been to withdraw from the world, to abandon politics for religion, the body for the soul, reality for thought. For Boethius, languishing in prison, waiting to die, freedom existed in the mind and philosophy was consoling. Anyone can thus be secretly free, as long as his freedom remains his secret. Jews who told the Inquisition their true beliefs enjoyed torture and death for the exercise of their freedom. American blacks who told slaveholders of their freedom enjoyed whippings, imprisonment, or death. Nor was there any more latitude in the world for rebels in Nazi Germany or Stalinist Russia or Maoist China. The oppressed suffer secretly, they give the appearance of comfort or acquiescence, they are quiet until they are told to shout agreement with their situation.

When the oppressed permit their secret life to be penetrated by an outsider, they risk their survival in the real world of appearances. That choice leads to suicide or revolution. No other options are open to them. It is not surprising then that oppressed people are quiet. Even Immanuel Kant, he of the categorical imperative, when criticized by Prussian authorities for his writings and lectures on religion, chose to apologize and thereafter remain silent on the subject. Perhaps he meant the maxim of his will in that response to oppression to always hold as a universal law, for silence or secretiveness has certainly been very close to a universal response to oppression.

The first rule of totalitarianism is silence, and the isolation it implies. The traveler in a totalitarian society cannot see or hear silence. Isolated himself, he cannot recognize isolation. The surface of nascent totalitarianism appears normal. From the outside one cannot recognize totalitarianism until it reaches the bizarre stage of expansion by force, repression by overt terror, unmitigated madness. The earlier stages can only be experienced subjectively.

William L. Shirer recognized the internality of the effects of totalitarianism in his *Rise and Fall of the Third Reich:* "No one who has not lived for years in a totalitarian land can possibly conceive how difficult it is to escape the dread consequences of a regime's calculated and incessant propaganda." Perhaps as a result of having lived in Germany during Hitler's rise to power, Shirer's portrayal of the regime contains a sense of great outrage, very unlike the almost forgiving objectivity of John Toland's biography of Adolf Hitler.

Hans Buchheim describes totalitarianism as "extraordinarily incomprehensible to all outsiders." He begins his book *Totalitarian Rule:* "The concept of totalitarian rule cannot be determined by purely logical means. It was explicated and clarified only by our own bitter experience with this form of government." He believes that even those under totalitarian rule understand it only gradually.

Although one can theorize about totalitarianism, the recognition of it comes in the practical world, wherein one experiences fear, isolation, the loss of internal space, and ultimately, the disappearance of self. As Aristotle knew, ". . . Political writers, although they have excellent ideas, are often impractical men," and the creation of totalitarianism takes place in mundane, often seemingly insignificant ways. The only theory of National Socialism comes from the incoherent works of Adolf Hitler and his publicists, and the theory of Stalinism has so little relation to the reality of Stalinist Russia that it cannot even be considered as germane as the insane anti-Semitism, crude psychology and scatterbrained geopolitics of *Mein Kampf.* The theory of Maoism, as it operated in reality, cannot be found even by reading between the lines of Mao's works. Only Plato's *Republic* can be considered a true theory of totalitarianism, and one must question whether that was Plato's intent in the work.

It may, in fact, be that totalitarian states do not arise according to plan or intent, but are created by contingent responses and events. Or it may be that the desire for certain ends leads societies unsuspecting into totalitarian means.

Trotsky, perhaps with a wink, explained how economic depri-
vation leads to bureaucracy. He spoke of a shortage, people
wanting the goods in short supply, and needing someone, a policeman, to keep order in the queue for the goods.

Totalitarianism may arise in similar fashion out of a wish
for efficiency, for comfort, for security, for order itself. It
seems a bit simpleminded to say that governments do not
come to power by promising evil, but it is true. The promises
that rational men recognize as evil cannot be so perceived by
those who must support the proposed regime or the regime
will not come to power. Hitler's promise of genocide, in his insane thinking, was not the promise of evil acts, but the promise
to rid Europe of evil. The good intentions of Mao are indisputable, the means by which he sought to make reality of his
good intentions are another matter.

Henry Ford, an American hero, was an immoral, unethical
man, who sought to use totalitarian methods to achieve what
he believed were good ends. Ford was a professed racist, pub-
lisher of *The Protocols of the Elders of Zion,* and a believer in
the leader principle. Ford was so certain of his own unique
claim on the understanding of virtue that he sent company investigators to the homes of his workers to determine whether
they were living properly. Those whose standards of morality,
cleanliness, child rearing, etc., did not conform with Ford's
were advised to change their ways or be dismissed. His vision
of his customers was also that of the leader: they were all to
drive Ford automobiles of the same size, style, and color, a
principle Hitler embraced when he asked Porsche to design the
Volkswagen. Ford's employment practices were destroyed by
the unions. His hegemony over the automobile market came to
an end when Alfred Sloan offered different kinds of cars in
different colors.

The great entrepreneurs of the late nineteenth and early
twentieth centuries, risen from mere mortals to industrialists,
shared much of Ford's vision of his role among men. Cal-

vinism gave them leave to adopt the leader principle: their very success proved them the elect of God and man, they had to carry out their mandate. If nothing else, generosity demanded that they make men over in their own image. They might have made greater efforts in that area if the rationalization of work had not been more interesting and more profitable than the rationalization of men.

In Germany, Russia, and China, another point of view, not so much opposite as different in the ordering of priorities, led to totalitarianism: the rationalization of men took precedence over the rationalization of work. Both approaches hold that the increase of man's material possessions raises his standard of living and furthers his progress toward the new golden age of goods.

Rationalization of work peaked some time ago in America; little more remains to be accomplished, automation having superseded mere rationalization of tasks; the new goal has become the rationalization of man. To that end business and government have begun to use the methods of totalitarianism, which will no doubt come as a surprise to them, for it is not their intention. No less than Plato, had he seen the advice he offered in the *Laws* put to use by Hitler and Stalin, they would be horrified to think themselves party to the genesis of monstrous government; nevertheless, they have, however unwittingly, adopted the methods of totalitarianism.

It will not be difficult for anyone who has spent some years in business at the middle management level to recognize the methods described in this book: they are common practices, some of them are advised by industrial psychologists, many are advocated by the authors of textbooks and pseudo-textbooks on management, others have come about through the search for efficiency and the very structure of modern corporations. They exist in various industries to a greater or lesser extent. A few corporations have evolved into organizations that are more authoritarian than totalitarian, although they may be in the process of changing. One might think it necessary for a corporation to be very large to use totalitarian methods; it is not so; totalitarian organizations can be as large as China or as small as the harem of Montesquieu's *Persian Letters*.

No magic is required to compare the methods of business to those methods that are generally described as totalitarian. One merely needs the experience on one side and the reading of a few books on the other; the similarities then become obvious. If those more adept at political science than I have not recognized these traits, it is because they have no experience with them—few middle managers in corporations are political scientists. Those who practice the social sciences would be less likely to recognize these methods as totalitarian: first, because they are also tourists, relying on secondhand information, with no more experience, in most instances, than political scientists; and, second, because the methods of social science do not lead to the understanding of politics.

After more than twenty years in business, I had no understanding of the similarity between the methods of totalitarian government and business practice until the chief executive officer of a small corporation described a situation to me that he thought unfair. Using Hannah Arendt's description of totalitarianism, I began compiling a list of its methods and comparing them with business practices with which I was familiar. There was a difference of degree, and I believe, there is a great difference of intent; but the congruences are too numerous to disregard, the dangers are too great to ignore.

For the businessman who reads this book it will be difficult to accept the term totalitarian with regard to business practices. For the political scientist it will be difficult to accept the business practices described in this book as real and common. I have conducted no surveys, mailed out no questionnaires, psychoanalyzed no technologists or middle managers. As Aristotle advised, ". . . It is . . . foolish to accept probable reasoning from a mathematician and to demand from a rhetorician scientific proofs." The reader will have to be satisfied with putting the thesis of this work to the tests of reason and credulity.

V

Finally, one must question whether the thesis, if proved, is of any but academic value. Erich Fromm, asking a similar question in *Escape from Freedom,* found this answer from John Dewey: "The serious threat to our democracy is not the existence of foreign totalitarian states. It is the existence within our own personal attitudes and within our own institutions of conditions which have given a victory to external authority, discipline, uniformity and dependence upon The Leader in foreign countries. The battlefield is also accordingly here—within ourselves and our institutions."

Forty years have passed since Fromm's book was written. Half the world lives under totalitarian rule, democracy is uncertain in India and the gift of technology increases the possibility of totalitarianism in many Third World nations. We must now ask, without the paranoia of the Cold War or the rage of the Vietnam years, whether any large societies can survive as democratic societies, indeed whether men are willing or even able to live in freedom.

In his daily life of survival, his business, man is most vulnerable to requirements of conforming, for every failure of adaptation to the requirements of business threatens his security. When the structure of business necessitates acceptance of certain totalitarian methods, what can men do but change themselves into creatures that find such a life acceptable? After that change, neither a foreign power nor a fifth column is needed for government to become totalitarian, the citizens are prepared to fall willingly into the depths of oppression, as Dewey, Fromm, and so many others have thought, for men who have shed their human sense of self-worth can participate in their own destruction.

According to Hannah Arendt, men do the work of totalitarianism unthinkingly; the evil of that work is banal, but evil nevertheless. In business, men do not arrive at totalitarian methods because they are evil, but because they wish to do the good in what seems to them the most efficient way, or because they wish merely to survive, or with no more evil intent than the desire to prosper. We may find that those in business and government who would oppose totalitarianism most vigorously, were they aware of it, are the very people who now prepare this society for a totalitarian end. It is possible that the origins of totalitarianism lie neither in the aberrations of history nor in the failures of economic systems to maintain living standards, but in man himself. If so, the primary task of freedom is no less than for man to overcome his own nature, to do his business in a way befitting a creature capable of transcending himself.

2

Happiness, Boredom, and Fear

If a government were founded on the principle of benevolence toward the people, as a father's toward his children—in other words, if it were a paternalistic government (imperium paternale) with the subjects, as minors, unable to tell what is truly beneficial or detrimental to them, obliged to wait for the head of state to judge what should constitute their happiness and be kind enough to desire it also—such a government would be the worst conceivable *despotism*. It would be a constitution that cancels every freedom of the subjects, who retain no rights at all.

Kant
On the Old Saw: That May Be Right
In Theory but It Won't Work in Practice

We have invented happiness, say the last men, and blink.
Heidegger

The most insidious of the many kinds of power is the power to define happiness. It is the dream of merchants, despots, managers, and philosophers, because whoever defines happiness can control the organization and the actions of other men: he not only assigns aspirations and desires, he constructs the system of morals by which the means of achieving happiness is judged. Whoever defines happiness is a philosopher with the option to be a king.

The opportunity for the taking of power comes from the inability, so far, of any merchant, despot, manager or philosopher to define happiness once and for all, to make happiness as solid as a stone, a measurable, comparable, universal happiness. Wittgenstein asked, "What is the objective mark of the happy, harmonious life?" And answered, "Here it is again clear that there cannot be any such mark, that can be *described*. This mark cannot be a physical one but only a metaphysical one, a transcendental one." Happiness then belongs to worlds beyond man, to heaven or to thought. Yet the work of those who seek power consists of defining what cannot be described, and what cannot be described surely cannot be attained. Then what is the meaning of happiness and how can something indescribable and unattainable be useful?

A currently fashionable theory of man postulates that he behaves according to the dictates of his genes, implying that men could and even should be satisfied with their lot in life. The politics of this theory put forward by a man who professes admiration for the ant* notwithstanding, there would seem to be

---

* E. O. Wilson, *Sociobiology*, Harvard University, 1975. The history of ideas is marred by outbreaks of neatness. These outbreaks are neither dangerous nor without use in our agonizing, slow progress toward understanding who and what we are and how we may live best, unless they are adopted as the sole acceptable basis for human actions. Heraclitus now appears to have been a better physicist than Parmenides, but the conflict between the two views of matter was a greater contribution than either theory alone would have been. Mechanical theories, like Wilson's, are not without precedent: as Newtonian physics provided the impetus for the Enlightenment, newly discovered principles of genetics have given rise to sociobiology. The perspective of history makes the grand theories of Voltaire, D'Alembert and their circle into amusements. Sociobiology will merit less interest. To make

ample historical evidence of man as a creature of his own dissatisfaction. If one accepts the thesis that language more than any other attribute defines man, a materialist view makes sense: to paraphrase Lévi-Strauss, society must have preceded language, for it would be of scant use for man to devise language to speak to himself or to the trees. We can hypothesize that society evolved from man's dissatisfaction with danger and loneliness and that language evolved from his dissatisfaction with the loneliness and frustration of a society based on the minimal communication of grunts, gestures, and facial expressions. One might add to the Hegelian notion of man creating himself through thought and the Marxist notion of man creating himself through labor the possibility of man creating himself through dissatisfaction.

By itself, dissatisfaction of an animal nature could be easily solved: ample food, shelter, safety from predators, and regular breeding would do nicely. Animals do not require either society or language to satisfy themselves. A social contract that evolved from animal dissatisfactions makes no sense; the family unit would suffice, there would not be sufficient benefits to merit the relinquishing of food and freedom to participate in a social contract. Human dissatisfaction must be of another order, relating to the mind as well as the body, to the ability of man to imagine something other than his current existence, no matter how well it satisfies his animal needs, to a concept born of his mind rather than his genes.

Human dissatisfaction must be the result of the imagining of its opposite, which we call happiness or blessedness. What man first imagined cannot be known, since the fossil remnants of ideas require writing, at least in the form of glyphs or pictographs, but we can guess that it had something to do with

---

a mildly interesting metaphor into the guiding principle of human behavior, as Mr. Wilson has done, is an intellectual disaster.

death, for nothing else limns so clearly the uncertainty of the future.

In *The Ancient City,* Fustel de Coulanges constructed a course from the mystery of death to ancestor worship to war between cities to religion and the rise of the nation state. The abstract, unattainable state, the metaphysical in Coulanges' construction, lay in death; it was a short step from burying ancestors in the doorway of a house to the invention of gods. Similar development can be read in Egyptian antiquities and in accounts of Aztec life and religion.

At first, religion used the gods for earthly needs; they were but another, more sophisticated form of magic—the shaman concerned himself with cures, hunts, and fertility. But the shaman himself was a sign of the more abstract notion of happiness. He was the neurotic of the tribe, proclaiming himself superior by virtue of physical deformity or behavioral eccentricity. He was also the culture bearer of the tribe, singer of songs, storyteller, reciter of ritual. With the advent of the shaman, man further distinguished himself from the rest of the animal kingdom, because culture was metagenetic—language carried information that could not be imprinted on the gene. Beyond the world lay the imaginable world, heaven and happiness; the shaman had something to promise to the man with a full belly, good health, a safe dwelling, and numerous progeny.

With happiness at his disposal, the shaman held enormous power. For the sake of happiness, men, acting under the direction of shamans, made sacrifice to the gods of their food, their possessions, their young, and even themselves. A bizarre utilitarianism can be discovered in the practice of human sacrifice: there could be no other reason to send a young man or woman to a useless ritual death but to petition the gods for the greatest happiness for the greatest number. The system of morality based upon happiness as defined by the shamans permitted ritual murder as part of the means of achieving happiness.

The effect of the definition of the end upon the use of certain means becomes clearer by substituting an alternate definition of happiness: if happiness were defined by the number of one's living relations, few would consent to the loss of even the most distant cousin for the purpose of bringing rain: one would be more likely to cut off a finger or sacrifice a sheep than to give up a fourth cousin. On the other hand, if happiness were defined as racial purity, one might accede to the wish of the definers of happiness to consider it a moral act to destroy a racial minority within the nation.

From its connection with death and abstraction, happiness gained a power greater than magic, because it bridged the real and spiritual worlds. The Greek words *makarios* and *olbios* can be translated as either happiness or blessedness, similarly the Latin makes no distinction. "Happy are the meek . . ." is every bit as correct a translation of the Beatitudes as "Blessed are the meek . . ." Heaven and earth meet in a single concept. The Aztec youth and the Christian martyr are able to go happily to their deaths, captives of a moral system determined by the definition of happiness current in their time.

The power of all religious leaders depends entirely upon their ability to define happiness; they can give nothing else in return for fealty. Secular leaders gain other strengths, but they must also define happiness or lose their power. In a democratic society, where leaders are frequently replaced, the power of happiness is obvious. In monarchies, oligarchies, aristocracies, and the various forms of despotism, the power of the leader or leaders lasts so long as the leader's definition of happiness outweighs the dissatisfaction of the led. When the dissatisfaction of the people becomes too great, another definition of happiness will be found and a system of morality constructed to permit the destruction of the state. One may find examples from Rome to the Reformation to the Russian Revolution; history merely becomes the replacement for heaven in recent times, which is not to say that heaven cannot also replace history.

To maintain the state the king must also be a philosopher; if he lacks that ability, he must either have an invincible army at his back or be destined to a brief reign. Of course, kings themselves need not do the thinking. A king may be of the kind of Mohammed or Lenin or he may hire Aristotle or Locke or Hobbes to do his defining and construct his system of morals; the only necessity is that the defining of happiness and the administration of power be conjoined.

The willingness of philosophers to serve kings gains as much validity from history as the daring of philosophers to oppose kings. Plato spent a portion of his life looking for a king to serve, Aristotle found Philip of Macedon, Vico had a difficult time keeping up with the shifts in power, contemporary American liberals have demonstrated great moral agility in the scramble to become neoconservatives. Opposition to kings may be traced from the prophets to Socrates on through Christ, Luther, and Marx to the increasingly isolated Americans, like John Rawls.

Whether the philosopher serves, opposes, or gives the appearance of doing philosophy for its own sake, he seeks to achieve power by defining happiness; the bad odor in which Machiavelli was held for so many years had less to do with his advice to princes than with his lack of talent for the very sort of dissembling he advocated. Without ambition, moral or political philosophy would be nothing more than persiflage, an amusement for academics. The desire for power so influences philosophy that to attempt to understand works of philosophy outside their historical context often leads to gross, even comic misinterpretation.

The enforcing aspect of happiness is its impossibility. Were happiness achievable it would be of no use to philosophers or kings, for a person who had achieved happiness could no longer be depended upon to behave in a prescribed manner; instead, his reward found, he could be entirely independent of the commandments, no one could be more free than a happy man. However, those who use happiness to achieve power need have no fear of losing their followers to freedom. To paraphrase Wittgenstein, the concept has use, but no meaning. Happiness, continuously renewed in its struggle with human dissatisfaction, is infinite. Like imagination, it proceeds from reality, remaining by definition beyond the grasp of reality.

Philosophers have been aware of the impossibility of achieving happiness since they first began to speak of it. No matter what his state of existence, man can always find reason for dissatisfaction, like Augustine, who could find sin in the most saintly act. Thus there are no descriptions of happiness. One may look for them in the Bible, in the Greeks, the Scholastics, and in the moral and political philosophers. Happiness is heaven on earth. Happiness is in Aristotle's words, "something final and self-sufficient . . . the end of action." Something, but what? T. S. Eliot had to make do at the end of *The Wasteland* with the Sanskrit word "shantih," defined as "the peace which passeth understanding." John Rawls writes that "a person is happy when he is in the way of a successful execution (more or less) of a rational plan of life drawn up under (more or less) favorable conditions, and he is reasonably confident that his intentions can be carried through." For all of Professor Rawls's care in the writing of his *Theory of Justice* and his political sense of needing to define attainable goals, the language he uses to describe happiness is as abstract as the word he seeks to describe. The attempts of well-intentioned men to limit the powers of others as well as their own powers by describing happiness are no more successful than Socrates' essaying of justice in the *Republic;* much of interest happens along the way, but the question remains unanswered.

Happiness has always been defined by unhappiness. We know a great deal about hell, but precious little of heaven.

Happiness has always been defined by the road one must follow to achieve it, as in the Decalogue or the sayings of Chairman Mao.

In the absence of absolute happiness, relative happiness has always been defined by example, as in the trappings of kings, popes, and movie stars.

In the mythology of every society a Golden Age has been invented to prove the possibility of happiness, as in Eden or Diderot's noble savage.

Since the beginning, all men have been dissatisfied, but only a few have had sufficient imagination to invent happiness as a device to aim dissatisfaction.

II

In recent times, philosophers have declined to define happiness, choosing instead to analyze the interiors of philosophy, giving over their power to merchants, managers, and despots, who have become the political philosophers of the twentieth century. These three may be distinguished by the temporal quality of their definitions: the merchant deals with the immediate future, the manager with the future, and the despot defines happiness in the historical future. Merchants have worked in the same way for thousands of years, managers have appropriated the role that belonged to the ruling nobility, and despots have replaced the great organized religions.

The merchant works his definition in the gray area between human and animal dissatisfaction; in the most basic of his work, he describes happiness as food, shelter, and sexual attraction. In poor or simple societies, the merchant needs no more than animal necessity translated to human desires to succeed. One merchant may extol the happiness one finds from a full belly, while another defines happiness as protection from the discomfort and danger of winter. The merchant to the poor competes for a better place on the indifference curve of happiness.

Affluence changes the merchant's problem. Even the pur-
veyor of food, clothing, or shelter cannot survive by selling animal happiness, for his customers can satisfy their needs with
but a small fraction of their wealth. The merchant to the
affluent must define happiness in human ways. He must make
leisure, ostentation, sloth, comfort, acquisitiveness, wasteful-
ness, subtlety, and social competition through displays of material wealth the definition of happiness. The natives of the
Pacific Northwest practiced this form of happiness in its most
obvious form by purposely destroying their material possessions in a potlatch. Veblen's notion of conspicuous consumption describes another aspect of the happiness defined by the
merchant to the affluent.

Since all modern societies are dependent upon a division of
labor, everyone must sell to everyone else at all times or large
segments of the society will sink into poverty and social disen-
franchisement. Those who advocate a definition of happiness
other than that of the merchant to the affluent risk their own
expulsion from affluence, or more likely, that of others. A person who opposes changes in fashion, for example, risks the
employment and therefore the social enfranchisement of retail-
ers, garment manufacturers, millworkers, truckers, and farm
workers.

Consequently, everyone must behave as if he were a merchant, and every merchant must define happiness in a way that
makes his goods necessary. The affluent nation thus becomes a
nation of merchants, all of whom must define happiness to
each other in the same way, none of whom may dare to stray
from the consuming definition. In a wealthy nation a consumer advocate may rise to the position of a priest of happiness, demonstrating by his moral outrage at poor quality merchandise the validity and the goodness of the moral system
constructed by the merchant nation, a system based on the act
of consumption as a social good and permitting almost any
means to achieve increased consumption.

In a society of merchants the manager serves as the enforcer of the moral system built upon the merchant's definition of happiness. He proves the system in two ways: the manager enjoys more of the signs of happiness, by the merchant's definition, than those he manages; and he has power over the lives of those he manages. For some the divine right of kings has been replaced by the Calvinist theory of the elect; for others the very organization of society, simply because it exists, has the agreement of all those in the society based upon one version or another of social contract theory. No matter which justification of the manager's position one accepts, the man who refuses to acknowledge the general order of society implies by his refusal either revolution or anarchy; he is an outlaw, an opponent of happiness as other men know it.

The manager, like the nobleman of earlier times, serves as the exemplary merchant: since happiness cannot be defined, he approximates his definition through the display of symbols, such as expense account meals, an expensive house, stylish clothing, travel to desirable places, job security, interesting friends, membership in circles of powerful people, advantages for his children, and social position for his entire family; he defines happiness by the trappings of the manager's life. While many of the foregoing aspects of the manager's life reach his subordinates only vaguely, his power over them bears directly on their lives, daily iterating the definition of happiness by which he controls them. His power may be illusory, but to an underling it feels real; and the structure of the business world makes it appear to be real.

Although the addition of power strengthens the manager's definition of happiness, he suffers in comparison to the merchant because of the temporal distance between actions and the rewards of happiness that the manager enjoys. A worker may trudge along the road to the manager's definition of happiness for ten or twenty years before arriving at the place he had accepted as Eden, only to find that yet another step remains, and after that another, and another. Like other definitions of happiness, the example of the manager can never be achieved, not even by the manager, for no manager can rule absolutely and no absolute ruler can be secure.

The manager's definition of happiness operates most cruelly on its adherents through the use of fear and teasing. The corollary moral system uses fear of dismissal, demotion, and the more subtle weapon of stasis amid an upward flow, to coerce belief and behavior. At each small step upward a further proof is offered of eventual happiness through the giving of small rewards in the form of increased power or wealth. The aspirant is pushed and pulled toward his dream of managerial happiness, constantly having to renew his faith in the definition given to him by his managers to overcome the disappointments that dominate his life.

In the twentieth century a new kind of despot has arisen. He is no longer content to rule in the manner of a king, preferring instead the role once assigned to priests. The new despot differs from ancient priests only in that he promises history rather than heaven in his definition of the happiness of the distant future. Since history has no time and heaven has no place, neither has happiness any reality: both are unattainable, both are connected to the conception of death that engenders metaphysical thinking.

For all that these definitions run counter to man's sense of incredulity, they still have enormous power because of the eternal nature of their promise and the punishment they set forth as the alternative to acquiescence in the moral systems built upon them. Perhaps more important, they are the only definitions that offer perfect happiness: communism, nirvana, a master race, Valhalla, heaven.

The despot or leader himself offers the most perfect example of both wealth and power. As the manager of all other managers the despot holds title to all wealth and all power, he lacks only immortality to be a god. Within the society ruled by the despot one must either believe that a man so rewarded by the world is the true symbol of happiness in his very persona or concede an irrational world, with neither order nor purpose, chaos. To oppose the despot while living within his system is to abandon the meaning of existence, for the apparatus of despotism, using modern technology, can crowd out all alternatives.

While the temporal value of the despot's happiness falls short of that of either the merchant or the manager, the eternal nature of the definition and the encompassing of both the merchant's definition, according to goods and social status, and the manager's definition, according to power and wealth, affords the despot's definition a magisterial quality rivaling heaven itself.

The road to historic happiness may be as difficult as the road to heaven, calling for self-denial, even martyrdom, but one who accepts history, like one who accepts heaven, may consider the direction itself a kind of happiness and suffer shame and guilt for failing to carry out the duties of the aspirant. Finally, the moral system of the despot accords him a power of proof, once he achieves control, that cannot be equaled by either of the lesser definitions of happiness: neither the merchant nor the manager is able to murder those who dispute the correctness of his vision.

This ultimate power of the despot, linking him to the characteristics of a god, is demonstrated by a curious bit of literary criticism. Thomas Mann's foreword to Kafka's novel *The Castle* interprets a novel about exclusion and bureaucratic omnipotence as a metaphoric explanation of man's relation to the divine. One need not go far beyond Mann's interpretation to give theological justification to the despot's right to define happiness for man and to will the death of any man who chooses autonomy.

How can it be that men continue to succumb to externally imposed definitions of happiness? How can Heidegger have supported the Nazis? Why did otherwise reasonable men permit Stalin to come to power? What causes us to emulate movie stars? How could Chou have supported Mao's executions? Why do we desire color television receivers, French cuisine, suburban life, blue eyelids, disco music, and gold? How is it that we permit hungry children to see advertisements in which food is prepared to the taste of a perverse cat? How has the world been so often convinced that murder leads to happiness?

The argument that one could not have human society without mutual acceptance of a definition of happiness does not hold. Society must precede or arise with language, and language must precede a social contract based upon human happiness. A society of free men is possible; for a moment of human history a noble savage, autonomous but civilized, must have existed. We can only speculate, based upon the weaknesses of contemporary man, as to why men abandoned the power to define happiness for themselves, and having once abandoned that power, do not now attempt to regain it.

Man is an anxious, fearful creature, unable to distinguish between solitude and the loneliness he abhors more than anything but death. He is a competent animal, but as a man he does not know what to do. He is too busy to think. He knows he is dying. He dreams, and cannot understand his dreams any more than he understands what preceded his birth or will follow his death. He desires lassitude, excitement, pain, pleasure, survival, death, society, solitude. His inability to fly troubles him. Peace and power intrigue him, enabling him to make great sacrifices for peace, which he then willingly sacrifices to gain power. Love, which is of his invention, corrupts his selfishness, annoys his whims, and fetters his instincts. He prefers Parmenides to Heraclitus, but he cannot decide, because the world will not wait. He named time and he laments the short time of his life. No man has been born free since the beginning, but every new birth is a beginning. Autonomy seems a disconnection, freedom seems a vacuum. He wants more than he needs. He can imagine everything but nonexistence and happiness. In his search for meaning, he settles for happiness, which he has named but not known. He wanders, and wandering frightens him because his time is so short. He accepts direction, and hurries.

Blind acceptance of direction, which is to live according to an external definition of happiness, has no alternative but freedom, and what does freedom offer but risk? To avoid risk, men endure oppression, deluding themselves into believing they are happy and free.

III

Delusion, like magic, requires confirmation. Alone, the witness to magic will question his senses, but magic or a miracle performed before a crowd succeeds because the people in the crowd reinforce each other's belief in the truth of the act they witnessed. If one among the crowd has certain credentials to attest to his ability as an observer, his agreement in the truth of the miracle or the magic greatly increases the belief of the others. Thus scientists and psychologists are called upon to verify demonstrations of extrasensory perception or other dubious phenomena. Finally, a scientific paper, adorned with learned borrowings from ancient languages and designed to be incomprehensible to the crowd, proves conclusively to the scientists, the miracleworker, and the crowd the reality of the delusion.

In the modern world a delusion about work and happiness enables people not only to endure oppression but to seek it and to believe that they are happier because of the very work that oppresses them. At the heart of the delusion lies the manager's definition of happiness: sweat and dirty hands signify oppression and a coat and tie signify happiness, freedom, and a good life. According to the rules of verification, it could not be otherwise. The credentials for verifying the delusion belong to the wealthiest, best-educated, most powerful people, and they do not sweat at their labors, nor do they dirty their hands or wear blue collars.

Verification of the delusion gives self-respect to the expert; without the delusion, his life would be unendurable, he would have no choice but to suffer desperate sorrow or to revolt. If the grass were always greener on the other side of the fence, a society based upon the division of labor would be in constant turmoil or drowned in depression. Delusion permits men to "make the best of a bad situation" or to "keep a stiff upper lip" or to "take the bad with the good," thus maintaining a stable society. Those with the best credentials and loudest voices (writers, journalists, professors, managers, and to a lesser degree in this instance, politicians) have the most thoroughgoing delusions; they define happiness and save themselves as best they can by their definitions.

To seek the reality of the situation poses certain difficulties: those who examine life presume the very credentials that lead men to verify delusions. The psychologist, the journalist, and the anthropologist cannot, for example, find the life of the blue collar worker better than the life of the person who works with his mind, unless they are willing to attack their own lives. The structure of the merchant's world demands self-defense from the rich. Neither capitalist nor socialist society offers an alternative. Even the primitive tribe cannot survive without envy of the chief.

The public expressions of self-defense in modern society are well known. One reads often of the "blue collar blues" and of the glorious lives of those who enjoy "expense account lunches." Films portray the grimness of blue collar work and the fun of various kinds of white collar and managerial work. Michael Maccoby has named the new manager "the gamesman," implying by the name a quick, skimming sort of life, a life in which the consequences of failure are not serious. In language and form, most distinctions between white collar and blue collar work have their origins in eighteenth- and nineteenth-century revolutionary writing, especially in Marx, whose view of the worker's life has survived the union movement, child labor laws, and occupational health and safety regulations. Imagine Marx's astonishment at a steelworker or an auto worker enjoying supplementary unemployment benefits, medical and dental insurance, and the prospect of comfortable retirement at the age of fifty or fifty-five after only thirty years of labor!

The nature of work has not changed importantly: one can still distinguish between the maker and the laborer. Society still fails to achieve justice or equality in every nation, under every government. Poverty has not been eliminated, wars are still fought. What has changed greatly since the end of the nineteenth century is the organization of work. The change came in two stages: first, the rationalization of work itself, and then the rationalization of those who do the work.

In the first stage, the rationalization of work, the organization of work continued in the authoritarian manner of preceding centuries: the relationship between the man and his superior did not change, only the tasks of which labor is made changed. In the second stage, the rationalization of those who do the work, the tasks may or may not have changed, but the relationship between the laborer and his superior changed completely: the laborer had to be made over to fit the task. If the distinction between authoritarianism and totalitarianism is the difference between limiting freedom and abolishing it, these two stages of the organization of work stand not as analogues but as examples.

Blue collar workers, who suffer boredom when performing highly rationalized, repetitive tasks and still often work in unhealthful or otherwise dangerous situations, are managed by authoritarian methods. The managers of blue collar workers are concerned with physical acts: digging coal, attaching nuts to bolts, soldering transistors into place. They are also concerned with time: the duration of each act and the duration of the series of acts that constitute the workday. As long as the acts required by the manager are performed properly within the allotted time, the manager has no quarrel with the worker. In the case of unionized workers, management accepts an adversary relationship with labor and negotiates within that structure the limits of the workers' freedom: the content and duration of work, holidays, vacations, overtime requirements, rest periods, and other work rules. A worker's thoughts during his workday and his thoughts and actions outside the workplace do not concern management. By its very nature the union does not permit rationalization of the man; and when the work is sufficiently rationalized, the rationalization of the man is not required. The merchant's definition of happiness is all that is needed to cause men to acquiesce in the limitation of their freedom under an authoritarian system.

The tasks of white collar workers can be rationalized to some degree, but the tasks of managers are all but immune to rationalization; only the white collar workers and the managers themselves can be rationalized. Authoritarian methods, limiting the manager's freedom, can affect his work but little, for he is required to think as the business requires both at the workplace and away from the workplace. Totalitarian methods, aimed at abolishing freedom and recreating man as a part of the organization, must be applied to the manager to rationalize him.

No union separates the manager or even the white collar worker (in most instances) from the organization. An adversary relationship between middle management and senior management is unacceptable. Decisions made by the manager must be organization decisions, he must reason according to the tenets of the organization, putting the needs of the organization before the needs of his subordinates.

Unlike blue collar workers, white collar and management employees do not suffer poor working conditions, nor do they complain of boredom in their jobs, although some white collar work can now be differentiated from blue collar work only by the mode of dress of the worker—a result of the ever increasing rationalization of clerical tasks. White collar workers and, to a far greater extent, middle managers suffer fear rather than boredom; and the diseases of stress have more than replaced the dangers of working with heavy equipment or toxic chemicals.

The manager's definition of happiness creates the moral system in which white collar workers and some managers live, but the despot's definition, with its ultimate promises and religious demands, has greater effect upon the middle manager's life. In return for historic happiness the middle manager agrees to the abolition of his freedom, he becomes part of the organization, and he accepts the notion that any sin against the organization may cast him out of heaven and into the limbo of the unemployed. To endure a road to happiness that abolishes his freedom and fills him with unmitigated fear, he allows himself to be deluded about his happiness; and having the credentials of education, wealth, and power, he deludes himself, he expels the meaning of his life from himself and places it in the organization. If the population were counted by the number of politically distinct units or persons in the nation, middle managers and many white collar workers would not exist.

3

A Hand Both Invisible
and Inefficient

The changeable nature of social organization has been known
since the earliest histories of man: in the Bible the organization grows from little more than an extended family to a
tribe to a monarchy, but it was not until Plato that all the
forms of social organization were described as forms of government and related to each other in a circular and pessimistic
continuum. From the perspective of history all governments
are short-lived, part of a process in which forms oppose other
forms only to be opposed by yet other forms, a situation that
might lead one to acceptance of the Hegelian description of
the process as dialectical, but only if one believed the process
were linear, evolving toward some ultimate perfection of form,
rather than circular. The formal exception to this process, according to Lévi-Strauss, is tribalism, which in his mind is the
natural state of man, the place where the process might have
stopped had it not been for the accident of literacy. To Karl
Popper, however, tribalism is the worst situation of man, the
least free, the most closely related to modern totalitarianism.
    The best exception to the circular process described by

Plato, if its duration proves it truly an exception, is consti-
tutional democracy as practiced in the United States. The government has survived difficult periods, including great social
and economic changes, but it has always enjoyed the protection of isolation and seemingly unlimited natural resources,
and until recently it has been the most powerful and most
efficient producer of both commodities and manufactured
goods. However, the economic character of America, based on
internal and then on international expansion, is changing: the
replacement of the long entrepreneurial era by an era that will
demand careful management of resources puts a new kind of
stress on the nation.

For the moment, Adam Smith's notions about perfect competition have caught the fancy of both the political left and
right, but the fallacy of putting the point of no return too far
up on the marginal cost curve will soon return the nation to
the direction it has been following for nearly a century, continuing the concentration of industry. The economies of scale,
the value of transfer lines, the efficiencies of single mission
plants, the enormous costs of research and development, and
the capital investment required to improve productivity pre-
clude the possibility of a return to eighteenth-century economic
organization.

The new national and international economic situations,
combined with a revolution in the nature of work comparable
to the industrial revolution, place new demands upon business
and government that can lead to profound changes in the political organization of business, the business of government
and the nation. In reviewing these stresses and the demands
they create, it may be useful to keep in mind a bit of advice
from Diderot: "Mistrust the man who comes to bring order.
Order is always a means of getting control of others. . . ."

Glut

According to rumors attributed to various statisticians, the nation has achieved "zero population growth," which may or may not mean that the number of people living in the country will not increase, depending upon how many die, and when they die. Other factors, such as immigration, the counting in the census of many of the nation's poor, and the admission to the status of humanity of those who immigrated illegally may also affect the rate of population growth. Some form of universal medical care may extend life for many people and even lower the infant mortality rate in the United States to that of other industrialized nations, having an additional effect on population. Finally, a lack of employment opportunities may decrease the number of women in the work force, encouraging some women to reconsider the merits of child rearing. No matter how many of these situations occur, however, the worldwide trend of slow population growth in middle-class nations seems unlikely to change. Expansion of internal markets through population growth cannot be relied on to encourage industrial expansion.

An alternative to population growth would be to raise the 25 to 50 million Americans living in poverty to middle-class status through job opportunities or transfer payments. Given the current mood of the population, the abolition of poverty seems unlikely. It is more likely that the poor will become poorer as budgets are lowered and transfer payments reduced, further reducing the size of the internal market, producing a bittersweet irony: the long-term result of greed will be impoverishment of many of the greedy.

Meanwhile, the internal market sinks toward stability and decline because it is glutted. David Riesman's observation of a quarter of a century ago, in which he gave the shift from a production-oriented economy to a consumption-oriented economy as one of the reasons for a change in the national character, may have to be revised as the economy becomes saturated with goods. The two-car family sustained the growth of the automobile business for several decades, but the three-car family, like the two-hair dryer family, the two-washing machine family, the two-instant camera family, the two-refrigerator, two-vacuum cleaner, two-tea kettle, two-toaster family seems unlikely. No matter how brilliantly products are marketed and advertised, a person can ride but one bicycle at a time or use one blow-drying device per head. The invention of disposable goods put off the fall to the replacement level of some markets, but the notion of disposable automobiles, washing machines, hair dryers, telephones, or typewriters seems a bit extravagant even in America.

Markets have reached or are nearing their optimum size in America, which is not to say that new products will not open new internal markets, but to certify the end of rapid growth within the national market for many industries. Two alternatives then arise: either businesses expand internationally or they achieve expansion through the elimination of less efficient or less imaginative competitors. The third alternative, survival without expansion, remains theoretically possible, but even without consulting Marxist economics, one can dismiss this alternative for lack of examples in either capitalist, socialist, or mixed economies.

Competition

Twenty-five years ago, the cry of the Third World radical was, "You buy our raw materials at the lowest price, Yanqui, and then you sell us your manufactured articles at any price that pleases you. You rob us here and you rob us there!" There is no doubt that the industrialized nations continue to rob the underdeveloped nations whenever and wherever possible, but the situation has changed quite a lot in a quarter of a century: Third World nations now attempt to rob other Third World nations, limiting the pickings for the industrialized thieves; and quite recently, Third World nations have discovered how to rob even the most highly industrialized nations. Finally, the industrialized nations rob each other at an accelerated pace.

The effects of the democratization of thievery on a world scale are well known: cartelization of raw materials and agricultural products, most notably oil; dumping of manufactured goods in foreign markets, as in the selling of Japanese automobiles and television sets in the United States at prices that do not reflect the cost of manufacturing; protectionism by tariff or by more subtle barriers; the fall of the U.S. dollar and the absurd rise in the price of gold resulting from the huge U.S. trade deficit, which is almost universally attributed to the price of OPEC oil, but is, in reality, tied more closely to the import of manufactured goods and the preference of U.S. corporations for transnational operations rather than export; the storage of money in the newly rich Third World nations due to their unwillingness or inability to distribute sufficient amounts of wealth to their people to create new markets for manufactured goods; government ownership or subsidy of manufacturing organizations with export capability.

In the United States the effect of foreign competition has been to shrink further already saturated markets for U.S. manufacturers. In the automobile market alone, foreign manufacturers have achieved a share worth over $25 billion annually. In the electronics market, foreign domination is even greater; not only do foreign manufacturers hold a large share of the market, foreign contractors or labor produce most of the parts and components for products marketed under the names of U.S. manufacturers. Markets for many other categories, from cameras to baseball gloves, are dominated by foreign goods, forcing U.S. makers either to seek other markets with new products or to go out of business.

A further complication is the cost of energy to operate most of the manufactured goods owned and sold in America. One must approach the oil business with a Cartesian view: some things about the business are dubious and everything about it is dubitable. The world's supply of crude oil is unknown, as are the proven reserves and the probable reserves and the possible reserves and the reserves that might be found if someone explored the 90 per cent or more of the earth's surface that has not been explored for oil. Neither can it be understood why only the puniest of efforts has been put into the development of the various alternative sources of energy, ranging from the conversion of coal to oil and gas, to solar power, to fusion, to the extraction of oil from shale. Many theories of conspiracy have been advanced, none of which seems to have any validity except the theory of the conspiracy of stupidity.

Whatever the reason, the fact of the high price and relative unavailability of energy promises to decrease the market for many kinds of manufactured goods to below the replacement level. Newly designed, energy efficient products will have some vogue in a few markets, but without increased availability of energy at reasonable prices or a reversal of the laws of thermodynamics, there is an excellent probability that markets for manufactured goods will decrease and remain depressed long enough and deeply enough to affect the basic organization of American business and government.

Productivity

The method of raising the standard of living in the goods as goodness school, to which the entire modern world belongs is to increase productivity: let each person produce 2x instead of x and everyone will be twice as well off. Economic logic carries the idea through to doubling the worker's pay as his productivity doubles, enabling him to buy twice as much of the goods produced by the other workers whose productivity has also doubled. Obviously, this is the point of view of the employer, who sees himself paying just a hair less than double wages to the worker whose productivity has doubled. The worker, on the other hand, sees himself collecting just a hair more than double wages for doubling productivity. Each side argues that if the other wins the extra bit of wealth out of productivity, disaster will follow: the left says obscene profits lead to unemployment and depression, the right says exorbitant wages lead to inflation. Recent events have produced a heretofore undreamed-of compromise ingeniously named stagflation.

Neither side will under any circumstances abandon its belief in productivity as a panacea. Employers have embraced Taylorism, the rationalization of work, since the beginning of the century, and for the last half century, Elton Mayo's notion of human relations, leading to the rationalization of the worker. Unionized workers have offered only mild objections to either method of increasing productivity, and unorganized workers, of course, have no means of objecting, except by quitting the work, becoming ill, or dying.

The problems created by increased productivity in glutted sectors of the economy have been considered only in relation to farm products. Unfortunately, no labor bank program comparable to the soil bank program has been devised, the possible exception being the halfhearted attempts of Keynesian economics. As each worker who produces goods for a glutted market, functioning at or below the replacement level, increases his productivity by 100 per cent, the labor of another worker in that sector is no longer required. The failure of demand need not lead to the Marxist nightmare, but it forces changes to accommodate the situation.

New kinds of work must be found to employ people to enable them to consume what the more productive workers produce, but the new kinds of work must be immune to the danger of great increases in productivity and they must not
produce goods that can be stockpiled.* The new work must be
of a kind that cannot be completed or it will not absorb the
slack in the system created by productivity and slow population growth. In the case of man in a glutted society, economic
necessity rather than ontological absurdity demands the creation of Sisyphean tasks: nothing comes to have as much value
as something, the highly productive give birth to the need for
the utterly unproductive, the Marxist view of the objectification of man takes on a bizarre aspect as the producer of nothing finds himself existing as the product of his labor.

Unemployment

Despite changes in the form and application of labor, improved productivity in a nation at or near saturation creates
the need either to export large amounts of manufactured articles or to learn to cope with a high rate of unemployment. No
accurate estimates of the true number of unemployed in
America exist, because the poor and the racial and linguistic
minorities are not counted accurately in any form of census
and because no formal means exists to count those who no
longer seek employment. Even so, the estimated level of unemployment has risen, and we have begun to accept as reasona-

* According to the Bureau of Labor Statistics, output per hour
almost doubled between 1950 and 1978, from 61.0 to 119.2 (1967=
100). In the manufacturing sector alone, the increase was slightly
greater. Hourly earnings of production or nonsupervisory workers on
private nonagricultural payrolls as of September 1979 were only 104.8
in constant dollars (1967=100).

ble the inability of the economy to absorb six million workers during a period of high growth. The true number of unemployed may actually be half again or even twice that number.

The effects of cybernation contribute to unemployment by increasing productivity; low population growth increases unemployment by releasing a greater number of women without children to the job market and by reducing the size of the market in some categories while barely maintaining it in others; and the shift to transnational operations in a nation that was built upon more overt forms of economic imperialism reduces the opportunities of employment in the production of goods for export.

A further, and perhaps more serious, diminishing of employment opportunities results from double employment: pensioners taking full-time jobs, moonlighting, and middle- and upper middle-class married women working not for need but to have a career. Because of the tax structure, far less income is left for consumption of goods and services in the double employment situation than would be available were each job or pension held separately.

Government relieves some of the problems of a glutted society by employing great numbers of people in useless or inefficient work and then employing more people to study the inefficiencies of the first group. Fortunately, the group devoted to eliminating inefficiency must be supported by sufficient people in accounting, maintenance services, etc., to more than compensate for any people dismissed because of inefficiency. Thus bureaucracy, like the creatures of the lower phyla that are capable of regenerating lost parts, can be depended upon to survive the assaults of those who do not recognize its value to a glutted society.

The danger in relieving unemployment through government first surfaced in the Classic Maya civilization of the sixth to ninth centuries. As the Maya theocracy grew, it became increasingly difficult for those outside the theocracy to grow enough corn, tomatoes, chiles, cacao, and hairless dogs to feed the priests and their staffs. When the civilization reached the point at which the workers no longer had sufficient food to sustain both the theocracy and those who were blessed and governed by the theocracy, themselves, they abandoned the grand cities and the Maya civilization came to an abrupt end.

Any economy based on waste faces the same end unless it contains some mechanism to balance production, consumption, and waste. Had the Maya, for example, leavened waste with compassion or a sense of justice, aiding those who lived on the poorest land to retain their health and to produce more, the leading astronomers and mathematicians of the first millennium might have survived.

Barring a disaster comparable to that of the Maya, employment in government serves to lessen the power of the buyer in the labor market, but not to eliminate it. When people who hold bona fide graduate degrees that would enable them to perform useful work, were the work available, must support themselves by doing odd jobs, the employed have reason to be fearful, and the conditions of employment will reflect the fear of the employed, as supply and demand affect price in simplistic economics.

Shrinking Unions

In 1945, union membership reached its peak: 35.2 per cent of all non-farm workers were members of unions. By 1977, the percentage had fallen to 23.8 per cent.

In the two-year period, 1976–78, the AFL-CIO lost 500,000 members.

When farm workers are included as part of the labor force, the number of workers belonging to unions is less that 20 per cent.

Sophisticated, high technology companies, following the example of IBM, have successfully resisted union organization of their employees.

Women, who now represent over 40 per cent of the work force, appear to be particularly resistant to union organizing: only 16 per cent of working women belonged to unions in 1978.†

Employment in manufacturing, where unions have traditionally been strong, will continue to decline.

Corporations have learned to defeat union organizers. Over the last five years unions have lost as many collective bargaining elections as they have won. The methods most commonly used to defeat union efforts at organizing workers have been codified in simpleminded fashion by M. Scott Myers of Coral Gables, Florida, formerly an "organizational psychologist with Texas Instruments" and "professor of public administration for the University of Southern California in Tehran." He has published his methods in a book, *Managing Without Unions,* and it is reasonable to assume that the book would not have been published if there was not some market for it.

Finally, with the exception of a few unions, most notably the United Auto Workers, the union movement has begun to resemble George Meany and Jimmy Hoffa rather than Samuel Gompers. Few young workers, raised to seek another vision of happiness, wish to see themselves in the image of George Meany, and the corruption of the teamsters will wound the union movement until the end of this century and perhaps beyond.

---

† An opposite theory holds that few women belong to unions because of the kinds of occupations open to them—white collar work, domestic work, various kinds of service work—and the low level of union organization of those occupations. It is more likely, however, that the high percentage of women in those occupations has contributed to the failure of union organizers.

The Shift from Manufacturing to Service

The great reversal has been completed: seventy-five years ago, service workers made up 30 per cent of the non-farm work force; the rest were production workers. Now, 70 per cent of all non-farm work is service, and the remaining 30 per cent are production workers. As manufacturing productivity increases, the imbalance will continue to move in the direction of service.

Daniel Bell has labeled this change a part of *The Coming of Post-Industrial Society,* but there would seem to be other requirements than the shift from production to service work. The true distinction may have been pointed out by John Kenneth Galbraith, who noted with amusement that a toilet is counted in the Gross National Product but a teacher's education is not. Without a change in the method of valuation, there can be no true change in society. Industrial society borrowed its methods from agrarian society, assigning value to manufactured articles in the same way that value had been assigned to food: agribusiness can be organized along the lines of manufacturing businesses, one may trade in real estate, commodities, stocks, or bonds. There is no market in knowledge, the price of gold does not fall because Bok and Rossovsky attempt to make an educational institution of Harvard College, the price of gold does not rise because graduates of New York and Chicago public high schools can't read. Iran is no less wealthy in the eyes of the world because the Ayatollah Khomeini leads his nation to the blessed state of ignorance and superstition.

Post-industrial society requires a worldwide change in the system of valuation, one that is not likely to occur in the next century, if ever. Man himself must come to have economic value based on what he can think; a teacher must be worth at least as much as a toilet, a poem must be worth as much as the paper it is written on. One begins to imagine philosophical assessors, bureaus of literary and musical standards, a moral assayer's office in every city, Euroideas, the First National Bank of Quantum Mechanics. The notion of post-industrial society seems utopian in the true sense of the word.

That economic society will continue to be based on things rather than thoughts seems certain, although a real change has taken place. The result of the shift to service has been to create a great class of economic aliens, people whose utility can be challenged. Even now, the cry of "Big Government and Bureaucratic Waste" warns the service workers of their lack of place. They are a confused and frightened class, as exemplified by members of the American Federation of State, County and Municipal Employees, who consistently vote against the tax increases that would enable them to be paid the wage increases they demand.‡

The social and political roles of this class of economic aliens have not yet been defined. As a class it is still inchoate, uncertain of its interests, lacking formal leadership. The test of the class will come during a period of severe economic problems when the class of service workers will seek to become less vulnerable by organizing against production workers. However, since the vast number of service workers in various kinds of civil service jobs tends to stabilize the economy, making the likelihood of a true depression very remote, the character of the service worker within an organization rather than the organization of service workers bears the most serious study.

‡ The leadership of AFSCME, which supports tax measures that will make more money available to increase employment, pay, and benefits for its members, has not been able to convince its members of the validity of its position. On the other hand, union members voted against Proposition 13 in California, apparently accepting the argument that a massive reduction in property taxes would cause a reduction in employment of state, county, and municipal workers.

How does an economic alien, a maker of nothing, maintain himself as a whole, political person?

Knowledge Workers

Perhaps more than any other group in society the knowledge worker has been the object of attempts to rationalize man himself. The issues facing managers of knowledge workers have few precedents: university research has no end but learning, it is pure; only in religious organizations does the mind get harnessed to a goal, and there the goal is confused with altruism, making possible a kind of management by morality, with the promise of salvation in the next world. Managing thought is a skill yet to be learned by free men.

If a man works with his mind to develop new technology, what part of his mind may be controlled and what part left free? Can he live half controlled and half free? Can thinking be anything but free? That is, if it is not free, is it thinking? In truth, a satisfactory explanation of thinking does not exist. Thus knowledge workers perform a task that has not been satisfactorily defined, yet must be rationalized if it is to be used according to the prevailing rules of efficiency.

In knowledge work perhaps the place of thinking is not great but small. It may be that most of what has been called knowledge work (technology, education, and science) does not involve thinking at all, but merely the application of scientific methods to new problems: e.g., thinking produces a theory of relativity but sophisticated labor produces a landing on the moon. If so, the hierarchy of the knowledge society described by Daniel Bell gives first place to the most sophisticated worker rather than the deepest thinker. Then the knowledge worker is more akin to the service worker than to the genius; he has a different kind of skill, one that does not require the use of his hands.

The vision of a near perfect society of knowledge workers and their moral managers originated with Saint-Simon in the early nineteenth century, influenced Marx, and comes to a momentary end in Daniel Bell, who theorizes that a technocracy will make men more, rather than less, political, in the narrow sense of politics as a synonym for greed. So far, knowledge workers have neither been more political nor, with some exceptions, more difficult to manage than other workers. Since they do not think in the metaphysical sense, they are possessed of no more interior freedom than other workers; "the consolations of philosophy" are not for them; and their political freedom remains in the world of actions, where they take neither more nor less advantage of it than other men. It may be that they are more, rather than less, vulnerable to management techniques than other workers, because their work requires greater involvement.

For a long time, the product of knowledge workers, technology, was expected to keep the economy from "maturing," a euphemism for the diminishing of growth that comes with saturation, but the effect of technological change has been quite unlike the futurists' expectations. Productivity has increased in the manufacturing sector, based on simple technology and wide application of the principles of rationalization of work and workers, but society has changed very slowly, the new markets have not opened, service work has been used to absorb the slack in the demand for labor. Furthermore, knowledge work has proved no more stable, perhaps less, than blue collar or white collar work: as each technological fantasy expired, great numbers of knowledge workers found themselves unemployed. The aerospace industry expanded, failed, and suffered severe unemployment; aerospace companies have sought government loans to remain in business, making them part of the economically necessary waste rather than the pioneers of new markets and new growth. The nuclear power industry faces a similar, if not worse, future. The computer, which still serves mainly as a replacement for the slide rule, the accounting department, and the basement records storage room, has not led to a revolution in any area but records retention and retrieval in a society that already suffers from the retention and retrieval of too much useless information. Virtually all the technological changes of the second half of the century have had to do with increasing speed: the telephone is faster than the mail, the jet plane is faster than the ship or the train, the computer is faster than the clerk. The major effect of these time-saving devices has been the necessity of finding ways to waste time.

The knowledge worker, who by his job description might seem another Galileo, Newton, or Einstein, is but a sophisticated clerk, unsure of his future, generally disappointed, deluded by his own sophistication into acceptance of a definition of happiness that makes him the most eminently manageable of all workers.

Size

In many kinds of business it has become increasingly difficult for small companies to compete. Entrepreneurs continue to surface and survive, even prosper, but the world belongs more to the Fortune 500 and more and more to the Fortune 50. The reasons for the concentration of industry are not difficult to divine. The cost of entry in most industries is now virtually prohibitive: a billion dollars will not start a major oil company or build a steel mill capable of competing with U. S. Steel, nor can one hope to compete with General Motors, ITT, Du Pont, AT&T, IBM, or Boeing with such a small investment of capital. Government regulation exacts a high cost from large companies, but some environmental and health and safety regulations are all but prohibitive for smaller companies. Foreign competitors are often government owned or subsidized, enabling them to enjoy economies of scale, availability of capital, and efficiencies of stability that can be matched only by the largest U.S. corporations. Despite the complaints on both the left and right that business has grown too big, the point of no return keeps pushing farther and farther out and the prospect of a nation of small, fiercely competitive businesses now suggests economic suicide.

Through growth, merger, and acquisition, corporations have reached enormous size, managing billions of dollars in assets and sales and tens of thousands, even hundreds of thousands of employees. Organizations of such size require great numbers of middle-management, white collar and technical workers; for one third of a company's employees to be included in the foregoing categories would not be unusual. The day of the boss, the foreman, and the worker disappeared long ago. Management personnel, techniques, and organization are now considered among the most important assets of a corporation.

While the managers of these giant companies make marketing and technical decisions of great importance, their value to the companies lies more in their ability to manage large numbers of people and great amounts of capital. Misallocation of resources, marketing errors, and to a lesser degree financial miscalculations can be tolerated by any large organization, whether it is privately or state owned, but the maintenance of the organization, the task of management, must be carried out with reasonable effectiveness or the corporation will deteriorate and perhaps be destroyed through bankruptcy, merger, or acquisition.

Large organizations follow a simple and almost universal pattern: the closer one moves to the apex of the management pyramid the greater his concern with the organization and the less his concern with the actual making of the product or delivery of the service. The first line supervisor divides himself equally between the organization and the product or service; his supervisor devotes more than half of himself to the organization.

Knowledge workers, those whose tasks cannot be rationalized, must belong at least as much to the organization as first line supervisors, for they are required to supervise themselves by exercising the self-discipline necessary to concentrate on their work. Karl Marx, in the famous passage on architects and bees in *Capital*, failed to understand the distinction between work and rationalized labor. "What distinguishes the worst architect from the best of bees is this, that the architect raises his structure in imagination before he erects it in reality. At the end of every labor process, we get a result that already existed in the imagination of the laborer at the commencement." Later in the same paragraph he concludes of the worker: "The less he is attracted by the nature of the work, and the mode in which it is carried on, and the less, therefore, he enjoys it as something which gives play to his bodily and mental powers, the more close his attention is forced to be."

Marx gathered his ideas about the nature of labor from reports of British industrial studies; he had no personal experience to draw upon. A day in a factory would have taught him that a worker performing a repetitive task need not have raised the structure in his imagination at the commencement. In fact, workers in some kinds of single mission supply plants are unaware except in the most general way of the structures that will be made of the parts they produce. Production workers daydream or think about problems entirely divorced from their labor. It is the knowledge worker and the manager who are forced to give close attention to their work, whose place in the organization and whose form of work deny them even the internal freedom of the daydreaming factory worker or the philosopher in his prison cell.

The Invisible Hand

> Every individual intends only his own
> gain, and he is in this, as in so many
> other cases, led by an invisible hand to
> promote an end which was no part of his
> intention.
>
> Adam Smith

Two theories of the origins of totalitarianism are included in
this book. One theory (see Chapter 8) considers totalitarian
systems, like Plato's republic, as homologues of the structure
of the mind. The other concentrates on the traits most commonly associated with totalitarianism as tactics used to manage people in business and government. The latter theory is a
case of the invisible hand at work; i.e., at first glance it appears that someone has imagined a pattern and guided events
to fit it, but upon closer inspection neither the pattern nor the
patternmaker can be found, and the work must be credited to
an invisible hand.

As Adam Smith would not have expected the invisible hand
of perfect competition to function in a socialist country, so the
invisible hand that originates totalitarian tactics cannot function except under the proper conditions. A family farm does
not use totalitarian methods in its operation, neither does a
neighborhood candy store. Authoritarianism, which merely
limits freedom, functions well in small manufacturing operations and in organizations using temporary or migrant
workers. High growth and overemployment make it difficult to
impose totalitarian tactics on workers at any level, because a
worker who feels the pressures of such tactics can easily
change his place of employment. Unions are the single greatest

deterrent to the use of totalitarian tactics, because a union, no matter how corrupt or ineffective, is an ongoing revolt against management, signifying freedom.

It would be relatively easy to attribute the adoption of totalitarian tactics to size per se, but the evidence to the contrary is too great to permit that oversimplification. The largest units under a single manager have been military forces, which have always been managed by authoritarian methods. Even in Nazi Germany, where totalitarianism dominated virtually every aspect of life, the military followed authoritarian procedures so rigidly that it was more resistant to totalitarianism than any other sector of society. Less is known about the Soviet Army, although the fate of Leon Trotsky, the military leader of the Russian Revolution, may be an indication of the dissident nature of the army under Stalin. In the United States, Great Britain, France, and other democratic societies, armies have reached enormous size without losing their authoritarian nature. Only when the police are described as the army does an army become totalitarian, and that is not an example of a totalitarian army, but of the perversion of language common to totalitarian societies.

Size is a requirement in business and government, but the invisible hand cannot work if it has only one finger. Carl Friedrich says that Christian convictional certainty and democratic antecedents are necessary to the formation of totalitarian societies. Other writers, particularly J. L. Talmon in his study of eighteenth-century thought, find that a messianic element must be present for democracy to deteriorate into totalitarianism. Technology has been identified as another factor. But these writers, like Hannah Arendt and Hans Buchheim, have concentrated on totalitarianism as a form of society; in their analyses totalitarianism springs full-blown into the world.

Arendt finds the roots of totalitarianism in imperialism and anti-Semitism, Buchheim finds the danger in the limitless promises of technology, rather than in technology itself. To them the hand is visible, guided by something akin to evil, although neither of them would consent to the use of a mystical concept in describing politics. Their explanations are satisfying to the moral sense, but they are not very useful in that they do not describe the disease in its early stages of growth, when it may still be arrested.

In the first nine sections of this chapter some of the conditions in America that affect the organization of work are briefly described. The quantified details of each are available from the Bureau of Labor Statistics, but they are really unnecessary for the purpose of this book. Most of the conditions are obvious and well known. What is not known is how they are maneuvered, combined, recombined, exacerbated, and ultimately employed by some invisible hand to create a totalitarian atmosphere inside organizations.

None of the conditions described in the last chapter are entirely new to modern civilization, but they have never been combined as they are now. The knowledge worker, who may seem peculiar to the last half of this century, differs but little from the churchman of earlier centuries, whose work was devoted to the expansion and codification of metaphysics. International competition for trade goods makes better sense to most scholars than the abduction of Helen as the reason for the Greek attack on Troy. The rise in productivity during the industrial revolution may never be equaled. Although we have no statistical information that is entirely reliable, it is reasonable to assume that during the Athenian democracy, service workers outnumbered production workers. All through history nations have gone to war to find new markets; glut, as Marx observed, is the spur of imperialism. Full employment has been a rarity in human history; the poor, as the saying goes, have always been with us. The decline of union membership dates from 1945, only 155 years after a group of shoe workers in New England protested the rationalization of their work and began the labor movement in America; for most of history men have worked without the protection of unions.

It is impossible to determine whether all or only some of the conditions present in America now necessarily lead to totalitarian tactics. Laboratory conditions cannot be established nor can economic and social subtleties be programmed into a computer to determine the outcome of all the possible combinations. However, some aspects of totalitarianism require certain preconditions. If there is a *sine qua non,* it is that men must accept an external definition of happiness, an act that in itself relinquishes man's freedom to determine his own meaning. Without acceptance of an external definition of happiness, many of the fears that cause men to give up their freedom would not exist. One who did not consider the material aspects of upper middle-class suburban life part of happiness, for example, might not be fearful of losing his job or failing to be promoted to a higher position. Would a man lie, if he thought honesty was a more important element of happiness than the money or position he could gain by lying? Probably not. There would be no incentive to lie. But a man who considered money and position of value to his happiness and that of his wife and children might lie under the guise of sacrificing his morality for the greater moral issue of aiding his loved ones. Talleyrand said that a man with a wife and children will do anything for money. Hannah Arendt argues that the family man "was the great criminal of the century," because "for the sake of his pension, his life insurance, the security of his wife and children, such a man was ready to sacrifice his beliefs, his honor, and his human dignity." The cause of this moral failing by so many men can be traced directly to the kind of fear engendered by conditions of high unemployment and glutted conditions that hold no promise of greater employment. Arendt wrote: "Each time society, through unemployment, frustrates the small man in his normal functioning and normal self-respect, it trains him for that last stage in which he will willingly undertake any function, even that of hangman." His moral self is shattered, not out of fear for his life, but out of fear that he will no longer be able to pursue happiness as it has been defined for him. The managers of frightened men, being frightened themselves, employ totalitarian tactics in what seems to them to be their own defense.

For a society to suffer the moral breakdown that permits men to exercise totalitarian tactics requires great and continuing pressure. International competition for trade and for basic resources provides that kind of pressure. The relative standard of living, one measure of the hope of happiness in America, has fallen. Oil belongs to the Third World, efficiency to the Germans and the Japanese, coffee to the Brazilians, platinum to the Africans and the Russians, tin to the Bolivians, cheap labor to the South Koreans and Taiwanese, diamonds and gold to South Africa; America exports wheat, corn, and soybeans. American economic hegemony has ended; the possibilities for failure have never been greater.

While size does not cause the use of totalitarian tactics, it enables them to be used. The percentage of managers in the U.S. work force has doubled in this century and in the same period the percentage of white collar workers in total has nearly tripled. Organizational size in government and business permits the large number of managers and white collar workers, and creates the layers of management and complexities of organization required by users of totalitarian tactics. Under those difficult circumstances, the use of totalitarian tactics may arise in lieu of any known alternative methods.

The management of knowledge workers presents even greater problems than the management of managers since it has even less history. Both categories demand careful supervision because of their potential for extension throughout an organization: managers have a spreading pyramid of employees below them and knowledge workers may affect great numbers of people by extending themselves through fostering new ideas and technologies; by virtue of sophisticated information management and communications systems both groups have instantaneous access to virtually all the employees of even the largest corporation. Freedom for them poses enormous risks for the leader of an organization: each manager, each knowledge worker is a potential revolution.

Under these basic conditions, every individual, intending only his own happiness as defined for him, is led by an invisible hand to participate in the use of totalitarian tactics, which was no part of his intention.

The Inefficient Hand

The excuse given for the use of totalitarian methods in business is always an echo of Mussolini's promise to make the trains run on time—efficiency. Mussolini expected to achieve efficiency through the most extreme form of authoritarianism; totalitarian methods move much more deeply into the lives of men. Neither fascist nor totalitarian methods have proved highly efficient over any length of time, however, for reasons that were apparent to Mill by the middle of the nineteenth century when he concluded his essay "On Liberty":

> The worth of a State, in the long run, is the worth of the individuals composing it: and a State which postpones the interests of *their* mental expansion and elevation to a little more of administrative skill, or of that semblance of it which practice gives, in the details of business; a State which dwarfs its men, in order that they may be more docile instruments in its hands even for beneficial purposes—will find that with small men no great thing can really be accomplished; and that the perfection of machinery to which it has sacrificed everything will in the end avail it nothing, for want of the vital

power which, in order that the machine might work more smoothly, it has preferred to banish.

Schumpeter delivered the twentieth-century version of that concept in *Capitalism, Socialism, and Democracy,* moving from the state to the corporation, foreseeing the end of capitalism in corporations without vitality, men and organizations so fearful, so bent on safety and security that they die of inertia. Although he was a conservative and he could prove the survival of capitalism by the laws of economics, Schumpeter recognized the end of the entrepreneurial spirit that had made capitalism succeed as a quiet capitulation to socialism. He accused the managerial mind and spirit of betraying the system he admired.

From the vantage point of Mill or Schumpeter the inefficiency of big business using what are described here as totalitarian tactics comes in the death of heroes. Like Carlyle, they find the world moved by heroes, risk-takers, great men. Schumpeter, in fact, wavers in that belief: he wishes for heroes, but finds that men are determined by the world in their time, much as Marx and Engels thought. Without heroes, men who overcome the times, businesses founder, changing too slowly, shirking innovation, drowning in a slough of social and economic fears.

Else Frenkel-Brunswick, following Freud, has theorized that total identification with the group, the thoroughgoing collectivism of totalitarian systems, leads to a reduction of intellectual abilities. She gives as an example the Nazi and Stalinist rejections of Einstein and his ideas, and goes on to show how a society rigidly adhering to irrational dogma may execute technology efficiently enough but fail to develop in the physical as well as in the social sciences. Growth, for a society or business in that situation, must be limited to repetitions at greater speed or on a larger scale, because fundamental change, predicated upon intellectual achievement, is prohibited at the source and in the execution.

In his biography of Stalin, Isaac Deutscher described the inefficiency of totalitarian management: "It instilled a grotesque fear of initiative and responsibility in all grades of the administration; it reduced every official to a cog; it often brought the whole machine to a standstill, or worse, by sheer force of inertia, it made the machine move in the wrong direction whenever the man at the top failed to press a button in time." Hannah Arendt described Stalin's policy of removing successful managers suddenly and without cause.

Misallocation of resources for ideological reasons under both Nazi and Stalinist management ranged from the bizarre to the comic. Hitler, desperate for troops, fuel, rail transport capacity, and munitions following the disastrous defeats on the Eastern Front, persisted in using his resources to carry out his policy of genocide, although his failure to permit the Wehrmacht generals to wage a militarily sound war of attack and strategic retreat on the Eastern Front, again for ideological reasons, may well have made misallocation of resources in the later stages of the war merely academic. Stalin's rigid support of Lysenko's crusade against the geneticists ultimately resulted in the Soviet Union having to import wheat from the West, where careful application of genetics had bred new strains that produced bumper crops.

Growth under totalitarian methods of administration has been vastly overestimated. Hitler's economic plan was novel enough, but not entirely realistic; he lifted Germany out of its depressed state with debt spending, which he planned to repay by conquering the world and paying the national debt off with whole nations. In China the failure of Maoist methods led to the opening of diplomatic and trade relations with the United States. Admirers of the Soviet Union point to the industrialization of that country in half a century as evidence of the practicality of Stalinism; however, no estimate can be made of where the Soviet Union might stand vis-à-vis the United States if its development had taken place under a democratic regime. Compared to West Germany and Japan its postwar growth has been unspectacular. Most of the growth has come from development of its vast natural resources and the implementation of relatively simple technology. The Russian space program, like that of the United States, resulted from sweat rather than genius: from Sputnik to the moon landing, both programs relied on applications of known technology; no advance in basic science was required, nor was one achieved, by design or accident, on either side. Although his dissident status may color his views, Roy A. Medvedev gives a fairly clear picture of the inefficiency of Soviet industry in the opening chapter of *On Socialist Democracy:* more than a fourth of all Soviet citizens still work in agriculture, production of consumer goods lags far behind the West, productivity in every sector has increased but is still only a fraction of that of Japan and the West, and the Five Year Plans have consistently failed to meet their goals.

The three-thousand-horsepower diesel engines used in drilling operations in central Russia are built in La Grange, Illinois, by General Motors, and the main frame computers in the cooled rooms of the Ural Mountains were designed in Armonk, New York, by IBM. All of Russia has eaten wheat from Kansas and Canada. Medvedev concludes that the dismal future of the Soviet Union could be overcome by replacing the smothering tactics of totalitarian management with the freedom of thought and argument of democratic processes. His thesis suggests an interesting irony: Medvedev believes socialism has failed for much the same reason that Schumpeter said would bring socialism to America. Inefficiency belongs neither to socialism nor capitalism, but to the tactics that make men into less than their possibilities. M. P. Follett, in a paper given in 1925, prescribed a sensible antidote: "What heightens self-respect," he said, "increases efficiency."

Tragic Utilitarianism

Most of the moral activity of the world consists of searching for scapegoats and villains, seeking the misunderstanding that will avoid serious disruption of the status quo. Evil is the best of villains, because it locates the enemy in its dark place, enabling all of us to presume we are good but not so perfect that we are incapable of defeat by the evil that rises up from some netherworld of the psyche to make us its helpless instrument. In this pleasingly clear misunderstanding, evil has form, will, and power; it is a thing, a noun; we can make moral war on it.

Once the concept of evil loses its status as a noun and becomes merely descriptive, it loses much of its usefulness: a different genesis of actions is implied, the question of contingency arises, and moral philosophy becomes variegated and difficult. Worse, the probability of actions being determined by a complex admixture of history, economics, and psychology arises; and we resort to explanations based on dialectical inevitabilities or fate. One could, based on any one of these misunderstandings, explain the use of totalitarian tactics in business management as evil, a demon that possesses managers, inflicting its will to abolish freedom on other managers and white collar workers through the hierarchy of business organization; or one could find that totalitarian tactics are the antithesis of freedom, promising a synthesis sometime in that future that will be challenged by some other antithesis, and so on, until paradise is achieved; or one could make the chief executive of a business the fate of those employed by him, his activities the will of God or Allah; or one could use the psychohistorian's methods and find the chief executive's employment of totalitarian tactics the result of his relationship with his mother; or as is commonly done, the senior managers of business could be adjudged villains, immoral, selfish, greedy, cruel, stingy, ambitious, deceitful, unconscionable, lacking in every virtue, rich in every vice.

The Greeks had yet another view, one that makes sense in our time if we are willing to substitute circumstance for fate. The hero of Greek drama struggled against his fate. It was his strength and his willingness to struggle that made him heroic, and it was the flaw in him that caused his failure that made him tragic. By recognizing the circumstances in which the modern executive finds himself, we can begin to develop an understanding of the tragic construction of the man's life. He begins his life by accepting another's definition of happiness, tricked by the gods into believing that happiness can be attained. The world changes, happiness eludes him, fear makes demands of him—for success, efficiency, growth, security, power. He succumbs to his fate, which is to employ totalitarian tactics, to attempt to abolish freedom in pursuit of his unattainable goal.

The flaw that causes him to succumb is that he does not love freedom enough to be free himself or to allow other men to be free.

Evil has no part in it. The noun is absurd, the adjective more properly describes the insane weakness of fearful men. Tragic acts and tragic men pervade the world of business and government. They are the routine of the organization, automatic responses to a world that seems to have gone off course, at once too large and too small, mired in human failing.

The tragedy of the executive comes in his attempt to rise above human weakness, to rationalize men by excising their humanity, to make of men a machine that will benefit mankind. He subscribes to a grandly utilitarian moral system, believing that growth will improve the standard of living for all, that the success of his organization will trickle down through society until the poorest of the poor receive some benefit. The payment of taxes, the enormous payrolls, the purchases of mountains of supplies and raw materials, the products of the organization are in his mind the instruments of the spread of happiness; and the multiplier of happiness is efficiency.

The tragedy of totalitarian management is that the efficiency of totalitarianism is a myth, and the use of oppression to create happiness is not utilitarianism, it is a self-defeating sophistry. The abolition of freedom gains nothing, the best of bargainers make the worst of bargains.

Velocity

In Greek tragedy the hero always comes to realize his flaw. It produces his downfall, he becomes aware, he suffers, he may blind himself or commit suicide. The modern executive may never know the tragedy of his life or the failure of his policies; not because he is a fool or an immoral man, but because he has been blinded by time to the moral issues of his work.

The changes of this century have been changes in speed: electronic communications take place at the speed of light, computer technology has struggled to reduce the time of a single operation from three billionths of a second because computer users complained of the slowness of the device, productivity increases the value of every instant of production. Max Weber found the preciousness of time at the heart of the Protestant Ethic. His discussion of the value placed upon time came at the beginning of the century, presaging the direction of technology and the organization of work. But Weber understood then how emphasis on the value of time would affect the way men think:

Not leisure and enjoyment, but only activity serves to increase the glory of God, according to the definite manifestations of His will. Waste of time is thus the first and in principle the deadliest of sins. The span of human life is infinitely short and precious to make sure of one's own election. Loss of time through sociability, idle talk, luxury, even more sleep than is necessary for health . . . is worthy of absolute moral condemnation. It [Baxter's *Christian Directory*] does not yet hold, with Franklin, that time is money, but the proposition is true in a certain spiritual sense. It is infinitely valuable because every hour lost is lost to labour for the glory of God. Thus inactive contemplation is also valueless, or even directly reprehensible if it is at the expense of one's daily work. For it is less pleasing to God than the active performance of His will in a calling.

How a life without contemplation affects the moral character of a man has been discussed at length by Hannah Arendt in *Eichmann in Jerusalem* and again in *The Life of the Mind*. For Arendt the cause of immoral or evil acts is thoughtlessness, a life without contemplation. She uses Eichmann as her example, pointing to his ability to quote a rough approximation of Kant's categorical imperative without ever having realized that by murdering others he wished for the murder of himself.

Business executives do not participate in mass murder, neither do they think, and by thinking recognize the value of freedom and the moral consequences of their acts—they work. They operate at great velocity, increasing their velocity with ambition and every extension of responsibility. One must have a certain velocity to win responsibility, the velocity must be increased beyond the required level for one job to earn promotion to the next, and finally one must maintain his velocity to hold on to his executive position.

Contemplative velocity is a contradiction in terms; velocity is action. When velocity occupies a man's life, he has no time for contemplation: he cannot think because he is always acting. Even when he gathers information (learns), he is acting. He learns only what is necessary to the maintenance of his velocity, his life is edited by its speed.

At great velocity one may act in ways that would, if contemplated, be inimical to his beliefs, offenses to his own moral sense. Thus velocity causes moral error in the same way that undue haste causes technical error. The executive who institutes the methods of totalitarianism in his organization commits a moral error because he has no time for thinking. He is a man of economics who makes a tragedy of his life because he so desires to economize his time that he believes he cannot afford to think.

4

Without Politics
or Possibility

Silence. Time has shelved the voices of moral outrage: Simone
Weil, André Malraux, Albert Camus, Ignazio Silone, Hannah
Arendt.

Nostalgia. After decades the innocent dead and their mur-
derers are both reduced to interesting bones: a revisionist biography of Stalin has been published in America, the West
Germans elected a former Nazi their President, the holocaust
provided the setting for commercials on television, Albert
Speer toured America to promote his book, Leni Riefenstahl's
Triumph of the Will has been accorded the status of a master-
piece by lovers of film. Nostalgia is a revolution in sensibility;
if history could not be made into entertainment, we would
have great difficulty in getting on with our business.

Dismissals. Reality, abstracted and categorized, becomes
peculiar, making dismissal as much an option as integration.
Anyone who finds the world as it is displeasing has the where-
withal to renovate reality. All visions of the future can be
proved certain by selecting the applicability of the past. The

truth, even if it could be completely, perfectly known, has no value unless it can be integrated to give it meaning. We live fictions.

Among the pleasing fictions is the picture of oppression as a beastly, bloody thing, easily recognized by the jackboots it wears and the instruments of torture and death it carries in its hands; like any poisonous substance in an orderly world, oppression must bear the stamp of the skull and crossbones. Accordingly, totalitarianism must have a certain gross anatomy or it cannot be recognized. Without concentration camps, mass murder, and a demented despot in complete control of an entire nation, there can be no act or system that is totalitarian. Any comparison of systems lacking that gross anatomy to totalitarianism is metaphor, hyperbole, or invective and not political science.

The ability to dismiss totalitarianism rests upon the common definition of it by description. Carl J. Friedrich, for example, lists five traits possessed by all totalitarian societies: "1. An official ideology. . . . 2. A single mass party consisting of a relatively small percentage of the total population (up to 10 per cent). . . . 3. A technologically conditioned near-complete monopoly of control . . . of all means of effective armed combat. 4. A . . . near-complete monopoly of control (in the same hands) of all means of effective mass communication. . . . 5. A system of terroristic police control. . . ." Hannah Arendt's *The Origins of Totalitarianism,* which is unquestionably the definitive work on the subject, also defines by description, although Arendt gives a theoretical basis for each part of the description. J. L. Talmon offers a brilliant but questionable view of the origins of totalitarianism in the ideas of Rousseau, Hobbes, the Jacobins, et alii, using the French Revolution to describe its manifestations. Buchheim's *Totalitarian Rule* relies less on description, but he too uses his experience as a German during World War II as the hard ground of his theory. Using the concept of description as definition, any reasonably well done history of Nazi Germany or Stalinist Russia could serve.

In fact, the general understanding of totalitarianism is based on history rather than ideas, with Nazi Germany functioning as a paradigm, even a synonym. There are some advantages in that, for theorists always run the risk of missing the point entirely, as Karl Popper did in *The Open Society,* a thoroughly confused work that culminates in praise of social engineering, which is distressingly close to what Hitler and Stalin had in mind.

The disadvantage of empiricism reduced to the comparison of raw data is that one deals with a language devoid of verbs, the world according to Parmenides. If we think that way, we must expect totalitarianism to exist only as a complete system, sprung full-grown from the head of a monster, implying a theory of history as the work of individual men, gods with mortal bellies. History, the data placed in time, disputes the notion of the sudden emergence of totalitarianism in complete form, and one of the commonly recognized qualities of totalitarianism, the impossibility of its achievement, concurs.

There must be seeds, proper soil, and a period of growth before the florescence. There must be some discernable course. Like anything else, totalitarianism must be composed of identifiable parts or motions. The confusion about it stems from its name. Since it can never be completed, it can never be total, it is a process, action, movement, the river of Heraclitus rather than the immutable sphere of Parmenides.

Totalitarianism is the process of destroying autonomy. It is a tautology, lacking authority in history, culture, or the consent of men; its power is the authority for its power. It is maddening and limitless, like facing mirrors, in which the one contains the many as infinite likenesses. Totalitarianism is apolitical, stateless, lawless, restless, a process that cannot stop until it has destroyed the autonomy of every man on earth or has itself been destroyed. It feeds on fear, which it converts to terror. It has no past. Its only weapons are lies proved in the unknowable future. It wills that its will becomes the world by the destruction through inclusion of everything but its will.

The concept of autonomy belongs to the beginning of man's discovery of himself as a reasoning creature. The word was common in Greece in the fifth century, having meaning both for men and for cities. It meant independence, to be able to live under one's own laws, to exercise one's own free will. The separation of man from his environment that first enabled him to wonder is implied in autonomy. It is the distinguishing characteristic of man in his humanity. Intellect is connected to it and so is culture. In an example of the man writ large, Coulanges described the basic characteristic of the ancient Greek city: "Every city held fast to its *autonomy:* this was the name they gave to an assemblage which comprised their worship, their laws, their government, and their entire religious and political independence."

In the *Orations of Himerius,* autonomy takes on an additional meaning: the poet's license. The quality that Pericles would leave intact to cities applies to the poet's right to establish rules, to invent fictions, to be the mythmaker. Plato, in the *Republic,* often described as the paradigmatic totalitarian state, calls this autonomy in the poet lying, and banishes poets from the republic. More than two thousand years later, Freud clarified Plato's motives. "Myth," he wrote, "is the step by which the individual emerges from group psychology."

The autonomy of cities prevented the making of nations. The autonomy of men prevented the making of the perfect organization. Group psychology, which is at the heart of totalitarianism, ceases to function when men become autonomous, for autonomous men do not love the group alone, they do not identify wholly with it; beginning with the making of myths, conflict arises, men form classes, mitigating (in Freud's terms) the dread of the Primal Father. Autonomy distinguishes the person from the frightened, dependent child. To Durkheim it is the essence of humanity: "To be a person is to be an autonomous source of action."

The great theorist in the meaning of autonomy was Immanuel Kant. For all his prim, Prussian coldness and the difficult formalism of his moral philosophy, Kant is the greatest lover of man. As Jaspers said, "Kant does not start from God, being, the world, the object, or the subject, but from man, for man is the area in which the rest become reality for us." Everywhere in his work Kant assumes the autonomy of men. They could never know "the starry heavens above" if they were part of them, and they could never know "the ethical law within" if there were no possibility of acting except as all men act. Without autonomy there could be no sensibility and therefore no reality. "Autonomy lies at the root of the dignity of human and of every other rational nature," he wrote in the *Metaphysical Foundations of Morals*, where earlier on he explained the meaning of dignity: "In the realm of ends everything has either a price or *dignity*. Whatever has a price can be replaced by something else which is *equivalent;* whatever is above all price, and therefore has no equivalent, has dignity."

Kant raises man above even the high place accorded him in Mosaic law. The concept of an eye for an eye rejected any thing (beast, money, goods, land) as the equal of man, but Kant argues that man, having autonomy, has a will of his own: there can be no equivalent, not even another man. Were it not for Rousseau, whose writings had a profound effect on his thinking, Kant might have suffered all his life from the elitism that affected his early years. But by 1762, long before his major work on morality, he thought, "I myself am by inclination a seeker after knowledge; I thirst for it and well know the eager restlessness of the desire to know more and the satisfaction that comes with every step forward. There was a time when I thought all this was equivalent to the honor of humanity, and I despised the common herd who know nothing. Rousseau set me right." He thought by then that he would be "far more useless than a common workingman" but for the possibility that philosophy might help "to establish the rights of humanity."

It was autonomy he defended, the notion of man as an end in himself, able to seek his own happiness, a creature of immeasurable worth, free. But it is not a perfect world, the rights of man are never safe. Kant describes the meaning of villainy: "Whoever transgresses the rights of man intends to use the person of others merely as means without considering that as rational beings they shall always be regarded as ends also. . . ." The practical imperative: always to treat man as an end, a creature with dignity, which is rooted in autonomy.

To discover the practical imperative of totalitarianism one need only invert the Kantian notion: Always treat man as a means, never as an end, denying his dignity, destroying his autonomy.

Kant saw the end of man as man's own happiness. In *Mein Kampf*, Hitler wrote: "As soon as egoism becomes the rule of a people, the bonds of order are loosened and in a chase after their own happiness men fall from heaven into a real hell." What worried Hitler was not egoism, which actually conspired in bringing the Nazis to power, but autonomy, which is the foundation of man's resistance to dehumanization, the source of his cantankerous originality, and the root of his stubborn dignity.

Autonomous men are recalcitrant, difficult creatures, willful, which is how they are free and why they hold tenaciously to their freedom, acting on it positively when they can or making themselves free by refusing to act except under the idea of freedom. By retaining their autonomy they retain the right to consent, to make contracts, to assign power, to create civil society, to be political.

"Free consent," said Hannah Arendt, "is as much an obstacle to total domination as free opposition." Free consent, which can be given by autonomous men only, is the most basic political act. It enables men to negotiate a social contract that includes a degree of reciprocity between the government and the governed. The giving of consent implies the withdrawal of it, placing limits on power, allowing the recalcitrance of man its opportunity; it permits man the exercise of his will, because his continuing consent is itself an act of will, an exercise of freedom.

Materialist criticisms of the social contract make a comedy of it, asking for the date of the signing and the names of the signatories. But there is a contract in effect in all societies, whether by free consent or by force. The question is of the conditions under which the contract is maintained, whether it allows men to thrive in their political nature or forces them into apolitical loneliness, whether it fosters the cantankerousness of man or crushes him into a docile thing.

Only totalitarianism disputes the Aristotelian concept of man as a political animal, for the nature of totalitarianism, its will to perfection, cannot tolerate the uncertainty of politics. Hitler found uncertainty intolerable: "One of the worst symptoms of decay in Germany of the pre-War era was the steadily increasing habit of doing things by halves. This is always a consequence of uncertainty on some matter and of the cowardice resulting from this and other grounds. This disease was further promoted by education." The halves of politics contrast directly with totalitarianism. An organization of political men, each one jealous of his autonomy, is dangerous. It can reach wrong decisions, it can decide to destroy itself and form another organization. It can split into several organizations or combine with another organization. The political propensities of man are as natural as the pluralistic and contingent chemistry of the physical world—the analogue of chemical bonding in man is language.

Political man, because he is free and cantankerously original, is himself unpredictable and forms unpredictable organizations. Simplistic statistical methods may be used to determine the outcome of an election a few days in advance of the actual voting, but such predictions are of themselves useless, although they can be turned by fools or despots to the creation of statistical man, an insidious tool in the making of mass man. In societies of free men the future is remarkably contingent, as has been demonstrated in America, where every prediction of the future, including the future of technology, has proved the unpredictability of political men.

Originality, both in science and in political actions, makes prediction impossible. What seer of the nineteenth century could have predicted magnetic bubble memories or California? What English futurist, returning home from World War II, could have predicted the Beatles or Margaret Thatcher? Neither Andrew Jackson, Abraham Lincoln, Harry Truman, nor a peanut farmer was destined in an orderly world to become President. Political man is indomitable, utterly unpredictable, and always practical. The American reputation for ingenuity, now faded, resulted from the political character of American society, composed of autonomous, therefore self-reliant and practical men.

When men engage in politics, they develop a great interest in the here and now; they care not at all for impossible schemes or grand views that will be proved out long after they are dead. Political men, acting on their autonomy, believe they can have some effect on their own lives. Autonomy gives man the ability to feel himself alive now; it makes him impatient.

Unfortunately, because men feel their autonomy and act in the world they are not necessarily moral. Politics is no guarantee of goodness or even of good sense: political men may injure others or even themselves, they may choose injustice or despise peace, they may be good in some things and not in others. The only certainty about political men is that they are unpredictable and too impatient to be impractical. Furthermore, the political nature of man makes him the potential originator of change. He has language to put him in contact with other men, he is not alone, he is man most human and most dangerous.

Lévi-Strauss wrote: "Whoever says man says language, whoever says language says society." Because man has language he has the courage to be free, to defend his own autonomy by forming autonomous societies of participants. Because he has language he is not alone, unless language loses its meaning. The moment language becomes the instrument of deception the most profound loneliness comes over men: they can no longer speak or hear, they are isolated from each other, from society, and even from themselves in that their own thoughts, made of words, can no longer be relied on.

In loneliness men lose their courage to resist domination. Atomized, unable to form groups, no longer part of any class or movement, incapable of politics, men float, sad and silent, vulnerable to sweeps of force. In loneliness the hope of happiness dies, man can no longer conceive of himself as an end, he submits to the destruction of his humanity by allowing himself to become no more than the means toward some end other than his own happiness. In his atomized existence man no longer feels the sense of limits of politics, which attaches him to at least some others in compassion and collusion; he competes, fiercely, like a hungry carnivore set loose in a herd of some other species. That dreadful old saying, *homo hominis lupus,* becomes the maxim of his existence: atomized, man really is a wolf to man.

It is this society of atoms, deceived, silent, lonely, men without politics, that totalitarianism seeks to create on its route to complete domination. Men with no connection to each other, deprived of any sense of their autonomy, their own humanity, can be swept along like so much dust. A mass is composed of atoms. There is no necessity for the atoms to be equal, but they must be disconnected, there must be no molecules of politics inside the mass. ". . . Transformation of classes into masses," said Arendt, "and the concomitant elimination of group solidarity are the condition *sine qua non* of total domination."

Mass man, the lonely wolf, has no place in the world. He lacks dignity. If he disappears, he will not be missed; another can replace him; only autonomous men are without equivalents. It is in the very nature of the wolf, as Cicero described him: "If we each of us propose to rob or injure one another for our personal gain, then we are clearly going to demolish what is more emphatically nature's creation than anything else in the whole world: namely, the link that unites every human being with every other. . . . everyone ought to have the same purpose: to identify the interest of each with the interest of all. Once men grab for themselves, human society will completely collapse."

A mass is not human society, human rules of morality are not binding on it. The ultimate effort of totalitarian movements in the creation of atomized mass man was, as Arendt described it, death without note, the unmarked grave, the mass execution, the failure to notify friends or relatives. Mass man is, as she said, superfluous. He does not credit himself with the right of resistance, not even resistance to his own death. He goes to his slaughter in silence, more docile than the bleating lamb, which in its last moments can recall at least the simple connections of the flock that verified its existence.

Arendt recalled Nechayev's doomed man: "[He] has no personal interests, no affairs, no sentiments, attachments, property, not even a name of his own." Ortega y Gasset described the mass as "all that which sets no value on itself—good or ill—based on specific grounds. . . ."

A distinction between atomized and mass man comes in the use of him. Atomized, man lives in moral chaos and social anarchy. He is the lone wolf, the stranger. In the conversion of him to mass man, which is but one early step on the course of totalitarianism, he ceases to be an alien anywhere, he is absorbed. All pluralism ceases in a process of terrible compression: atomized men are made into a thick, immobile mass; so tightly packed are they within the dark walls, both internal and external, that freedom of movement, even of thought, becomes impossible. The constrictions blur out individualism, the ceaseless revolt of originality stops, nothing more can be begun. Totalitarianism ensures its continuance through the elimination of the danger of unpredictable human life. With the making of the many into the content of the mass, no longer separable into discrete elements, totalitarianism realizes the stolid *one* of Parmenides' sphere. Now the world becomes predictable, the same river in the same place. Statistics need no longer be used as a tool in deception and reduction to the form of the mass, statistical man exists; he can be predicted, and when the predictions are made imperfect by some quirk of nature—disease, infertility, genetic change, madness—that could not be foreseen, the behavior of man can be changed to conform with the predictions.

At both ends of the organizational spectrum man lives in a state of anomia, which Durkheim described as "normlessness," caused by industrialization, the end of traditional rules and connections that can be overcome only by the division of labor, which he thought of as a new kind of connection in which specialized men become interdependent, like the specialized cells of an advanced living organism. The Greek word *anomilitos,* from the same root as *anomia,* means "having no communion with others, unsociable, uneducated." *Anomia* has a more radical sense than Durkheim gives it; the word means "lawlessness, lawless conduct." When the civil society of political men, those who act in the *polis,* ceases, and men become unsociable, silent, and alone, a state of lawlessness occurs. The laws of society, growing out of the free consent of autonomous individuals, have no place either in anarchy or totalitarianism. The atomized man, who has lost his lawful existence by no longer having the connection to others in which law can function, when converted to mass man has no tradition of lawful relations with which to protest the limitlessness of totalitarianism. As Arendt and others have pointed out, totalitarianism lays claim to lawfulness in the structure of control, but law without consent of those bound by it has no meaning as law and becomes the rule book of oppression.

Much has been made of the violence of totalitarianism, both physical and psychological, and there is no doubt that it does violence to man, his language, and his civil society. Anomia plays a role in the violence of totalitarianism, but it is not the cause of it; anomia is the apolitical state in which violence cannot be inhibited by society. The violence of totalitarianism comes from its reduction of man to a state of necessity.

The concept of necessity in English comes from the Latin, where its overtones are narrow. In Greek, necessity (*anangke*) serves also as the word for force, constraint, compulsion, violence, and duress. Aristotle felt the need to eliminate "the sense of violence" from the word when he used it in the context of the necessity of being in the *Metaphysics*. Apparently, the Greeks understood very well the connection between necessity and violence. The requisite that a citizen be a man of leisure indicates that necessity had passed from his life and he could avoid violence in his thought and behavior. Freedom to the Greeks could only exist after the conquest of necessity, which demeans man, causing him to have to live with force and violence, his very existence under duress. In that condition he could not be political; under the pressure of necessity he resorted to violence.

It led to the elitism of the Greek city state, the democracy of the leisured class, but it served also to define the nature of politics, to separate the violence of uncivil society from the cultured, creative, free, and thoughtful life of the *polis*. Under the rule of necessity autonomy is impossible since one who is constrained cannot also be independent; neither is politics possible; the relations between men are violent, man is a wolf to man. The difference in the behavior of the rich and the poor in modern society bears out the Greek theory of necessity. The rich may be no more moral than the poor, but they do not often commit crimes of physical violence, except for occasional crimes of passion. In totalitarian societies necessity has always been the excuse for violence; Hannah Arendt gave the example of the guard at a Nazi death camp who said he worked there because he had been unemployed and was willing to do anything to avoid continued unemployment.

The change from the necessity known to the Greeks to the modern form was recognized by Simone Weil in her *Analysis of Oppression*. "What is surprising," she wrote, "is not that oppression should make its appearance only after higher forms of economy have been reached, but that it should always accompany them. This means, therefore, that as between a completely primitive economy and more highly developed forms of economy there is a difference not only of degree, but also of kind. . . . At these higher stages, human action continues, as a whole, to be nothing but pure obedience to the brutal spur of an immediate necessity; only, instead of being harried by nature, man is henceforth harried by man."

To create necessity in men in developed societies a definition of happiness must be imposed that goes far beyond man's needs according to nature. The Kantian notion of the end of man being "his own happiness" must be perverted by making happiness unattainable and so foreign to man as he might choose happiness, if he lived in dignity, as to make his idea of himself as an end a deception. This is violence done at the very foundation of his humanity.

Then totalitarian methods can create the duress of necessity where it does not exist in the natural order, where men are not cold or hungry or in fear of death from wild animals or savage neighbors. This is the making of the man Arendt calls bourgeois, but who may be more correctly called violated, for the imposition of a definition of happiness is exactly that, violation, intrusion, the forcible theft of a man's autonomy. Once violated, men become weak, frightened, and cowardly. The natural sense of necessity, having to do with the basic elements of life, turns into the fear of losing one's opportunity of finding the unattainable happiness. The violated man lives on a treadmill, his values become ludicrous, he races against an abstraction in service of necessary happiness. He cannot know who he is, because he does not know what he wants or where he is going. He fears nothing more than stopping, he does violence to anyone or anything that threatens his pace on the treadmill, for the pace itself has become necessity—anything that slows his velocity does violence to him. Like a madman hoarding imaginary riches in the form of old newspapers or rags, he defends himself against the loss of nothing. The real world of politics and practicality has been taken from him, he lives abstracted, mass man; an early death is his only resistance against oppression, his sole remaining unpredictability.

Suicide, it has been argued by Camus, Arendt, and others, remains man's last freedom. Arendt claims that the final conquest of man in the death camps was the removal of the opportunity for suicide. Perhaps that was so, but the emphasis on the death camps as the major symptom or definitive trait of totalitarianism so limits the definition that one may arrive at the erroneous notion expressed by Walter Lacquer in his political dictionary: totalitarianism as the word used to describe Nazi and Stalinist domination.

If one considers the death camps as the absolute nadir of human acts, but not as the definitive trait of totalitarianism, another view of suicide as freedom even under totalitarianism can be considered. The goal of oppression is the suicide of the oppressed. Under totalitarian rule physical suicide, the death of the body, is not an issue, because the death of the personality by suicidal relinquishment of autonomy has already taken place. As Rousseau said, "Slaves lose everything in their chains, even the desire of escaping from them. . . ." Oppression is not defined by inaction, but by the inability to act. The suicide of a person under totalitarian rule does not express the cantankerous originality of freedom, it merely completes the submission of the person to the murderous will under which he previously had lost his real, human life. Since man cannot exist in the abstract as man, his suicide in the abstract is not an act of freedom, which is exclusively human.

The horror of the death camps overshadows the question of how totalitarian rule destroys freedom. Arendt tells of the crowding: "By pressing men against each other, total terror destroys the space between them; compared to the condition within its iron bond, even the desert of tyranny, insofar as it is still some kind of space, appears like a guarantee of freedom.

"It [totalitarian government] destroys the one essential prerequisite of all freedom which is simply the capacity of motion which cannot exist without space." She goes on to describe the physical crowding in the boxcars used to transport the innocent to the camps, the crowded conditions in the camps themselves, the slowing of the killing to maintain the crowding.

There is a danger in understanding crowding in the literal, physical sense as a totalitarian tactic. Boethius, languishing in prison, tortured, eventually bludgeoned to death, was able to write *The Consolation of Philosophy*. In the guise of the nurse of his childhood, Philosophy comes to his prison cell to advise him on the freedom that is contemplation. Philosophy tells Boethius of a freedom quite different from the freedom of the political world, the active freedom of the Greeks. The old nurse places freedom in the mind, taking it out of the world.

Totalitarianism aims at destruction of the freedom to act in the world "by pressing men against each other" and at destruction of the freedom to think. It wishes to prevent the visit of the old nurse by occupying the mental space in which she can exist. To accomplish that it crowds the mind with fears and anxieties that make thinking impossible. The victim of totalitarianism lacks the interior space required to contemplate his own situation, to make moral judgments, even to will his own freedom, as Rousseau said of the slave.

The process has been misnamed "brainwashing." Were that the case, were the slops of oppression washed out of the mind, the freedom to think would be enhanced rather than destroyed; nothing could be more conducive to the solitude admired so by Cato, nothing could make the mind of man more efficiently free. The moral disruption required by totalitarianism would be far less likely to occur in a "clearheaded" person. Brainwashing comes about through the crowding of the mind with lies, fears, anxieties, impossible expectations, and sheer detail. Given a sufficient amount of information to learn, no matter of what kind, and a sufficient number of processes, however simple, to perform on the information, the mind has neither time nor space to think of anything else; in other words, it cannot think at all.

Morality is not automatic. Kant thought it required painstaking scrutiny of oneself. A man with a crowded, hurried mind has neither the time nor the space for morality; he falls back into instinct and obedience, he ceases to be autonomous for lack of time and space to know his own will, let alone to exercise it freely. The crowded mind is enslaved because the room to be free has been forced out; a machine remains, a thing that cannot begin itself, not a man.

All of this crowding, both of the mind and the body, occurred in the death camps, but the oppression of the mind could have been accomplished—and was to a large extent—without prisons or slave labor or mass murder; it would have been more difficult, but the use of propaganda, the debasement of language, the creation of fear, and the revival of necessity could have produced much the same effect, although not always so quickly and not always to the same degree. It must be recalled that totalitarian methods were not used exclusively against the Jews in Europe; the German people were also debased, enslaved, reduced to inhuman creatures. With all that has been written about the debasement and suffering of those who were sent to the death camps, the point is often lost: the victims die innocents, it is their assassins who are made into unthinking beasts, the slaves of an unattainable dreamworld. The Jews, Catholics, Communists, Gypsies, and others who were murdered by the Nazi machinery were not part of a totalitarian system and might never have acceded fully to the system, as has been demonstrated by the dissident Jews in the Soviet Union. The requisite atomization of these people might well have been thwarted by their powerful group identity, which is precisely why they were murdered. They were the enemies of the system, the crimes against them were truly war crimes.

The thousand-year Reich destroyed itself before the cannibalistic nature of totalitarianism was clearly manifest in Germany. Under Stalin a society had already begun to feed on its own members, as demonstrated by the purges and the show trials. In Maoist China the purges and upheavals were even more severe, although the extent of the killing remains a secret, known to the outside world only through the scatterings of information brought out by refugees. Ernst Röhm, leader of the crowd of homosexual gangsters who were instrumental in bringing Hitler to power, said, "All revolutions devour their own children." He exhibited remarkable prescience, for not long afterward he and the rest of the leaders of his paramilitary group were murdered on Hitler's orders. Understanding of totalitarianism is subjective: Röhm could not save himself, but neither could he avoid knowing what lay ahead for him; only the outsiders, those on whom totalitarian systems must make war, can be deceived.

Totalitarian organization depends less upon levels of authority than upon levels of deception. Hannah Arendt described it as an onion compared to the pyramidal structure of authoritarian organization. Perhaps it would be easier to understand as an onion superimposed on a pyramid. The routine of social organization cannot be dispensed with: the workers must report to a first line supervisor, who must, in turn, report to a low-level manager, who must, in turn, report, and so on. Thus, on the basic level of accomplishment of tasks, allocation of manpower and resources, and evaluation of performance, a totalitarian system appears to be quite ordinary. Within that organization is another, a series of circles, the party. Party members may work at any level within the pyramid, but the party structure of circles of initiation to the secret goals of the organization enables a person at the lowest level on the pyramid to be the equal of someone on a much higher level in the party apparatus.

If these superimposed organizations were converted to the ordinary table of organization used in business, the chart would have one dotted line for each solid line, with each dotted line jumping over at least one level of authority in the solid line structure. In such an organization no one can have clear authority over anyone else until the lines and circles converge in the place occupied by the chief executive or leader. All others are caught between the onion and the pyramid, having to obey those above them and those below them, in fear of both, so disoriented that they literally cannot tell which end is up.

In the empty space between the onion and the pyramid the bureaucracy flourishes. Since the lines of authority are blurred, no one can have clear responsibility for any act, including the leader at his great remove from the quotidian workings of the organization. Arendt called it "the latest and perhaps most formidable form of . . . domination: bureaucracy or the rule of an intricate system of bureaus in which no men . . . can be held responsible, and which could be properly called rule by Nobody.

". . . Rule by Nobody is clearly the most tyrannical of all, since there is no one left who could even be asked to answer for what is being done.

"Bureaucracy is the form of government in which everybody is deprived of political freedom, of the power to act; for the rule by Nobody is not no-rule, and where all are equally powerless we have a tyranny without a tyrant."

In *The Castle,* Kafka's attempt to destroy bureaucracy by pointing up the absurdity of it, the hero can find no home among the people down below or among the people on the hill where the castle stands. The novel has suffered innumerable interpretations, from Mann's vision of the divine to Arendt's understanding of the hero as the Jew in the role of pariah. She does not credit Kafka with a description of totalitarianism, possibly because his view does not coincide with hers. Kafka's novel includes both a bureaucracy and a leader, an onion and a pyramid. Read for what it says rather than what it might mean, *The Castle* contains a clue to the ultimate ingenuity of totalitarian organization: a leader (either one person or an oligarchy) rules over a bureaucracy, making society answer to a despot in the person of Nobody, leaving the people utterly helpless and hopeless, without the possibility of appeal either through the layers of the onion or the heights of the pyramid.

Kafka's picture of the organization was borne out at the Nuremberg trials, where the defendants pleaded not guilty, with but a few exceptions. Indeed, many of them may not have believed themselves guilty, so deeply were they bound to the organization and so uncertain was the order of responsibility. There can be no doubt that they were criminals, but when a crime is committed according to the rules of Nobody everybody must be guilty. The deciding issue at Nuremberg was responsibility in the familiar pyramidal form. Had it been based on the nature of the consent of the participants, as well it might have, the number of those judged guilty and sentenced to death or imprisonment would have been unmanageable.

The issue not resolved at Nuremberg or since is how totalitarian systems arise, whether they must always have control of entire nations to be totalitarian or whether the tactics of totalitarianism can exist under other forms of government or in parts of societies or in combination with other forms of social organization. Given the inefficiency of its methods, the suffering it causes would seem too great a cost for anyone to accept; then what promise does totalitarianism hold that has enabled its adherents to dominate, at one time or another, the greatest part of Europe and Asia?

Of all the works on the subject Arendt's is both the broadest and the most penetrating, but even she was limited by the shadow of monsters and the insane horror of the death camps, which would have been her fate had she remained in Germany. If we, having the benefit of almost forty years of perspective, are to avoid totalitarianism in the future, we shall have to accept the most unsettling view of man's will: that every act leads to contingencies—morally neutral or even benevolent acts can result in totalitarian organizations. To think of Plato, Rousseau, Hegel, or Marx as enemies of man is absurd, but to deny that their ideas could or did contribute to the establishing of totalitarian rule is equally absurd.

Man is always the potential victim of his own mortality. He knows instinctively the advice Solon gave to Croesus: "Life is a chancy thing. Look to the end, no matter what it is you are considering. Often enough God gives a man a glimpse of happiness, and then utterly ruins him." He cannot be sure of happiness in his lifetime and he knows the limitations of that life: an immortal destiny, either in history or heaven, holds out hope for him; a certain destiny provides the antidote for a short and chancy life. He seeks answers in God, ideology, or technology, inventing those alternatives to the natural known world and then losing control of his life to his own inventions. The willingness of men to trade their freedom for the promise of order, security, and a comforting destiny is the legacy of mortality, given that freedom creates risks and that men are afraid of both death and life.

Men endure oppression out of necessity or out of hope. Necessity came up with man from his origin as an unthinking animal: nature constrains all creatures to behave in ways that enable them to survive; it works violently, compelling behavior by force. Toynbee has described the progress of man toward civilization as three stages in his relationship with nature: nature dominates man, man and nature live in equality, man dominates nature. In his early stages man endures oppression entirely out of necessity. As he becomes civilized, he begins to dominate nature, to believe that he can will perfection, a sure road to happiness; he creates a new necessity.

The power of totalitarian thinking is this belief in the ultimate perfection of the world, this resolution into certainty that will provide happiness for all forever. Obviously, the autonomy of individuals and even of political entities, whether cities or states, is inimical to certainty. Herein lies the opposition between Kantian thinking and all totalitarian ideas: Kant begins with man, totalitarianism begins with a concept greater than man, and even though that concept is his perfection, the use of man as a means robs him of his dignity. To raise man up to perfection by debasing him is a contradiction: totalitarian goals of perfection are logically impossible.

The theory of perfection has two names in the literature of totalitarianism: technology and messianism. Much has been written about both names, most often as if they were distinct and different routes, but in reality the names are synonymous: both technology and messianism will the transformation of nature into a higher, ultimate order in which contingency has been eliminated. A more descriptive name than totalitarianism might be technological messianism: messianism in that it promises deliverance from earthly woes, conflicts, and uncertainties; technological in that it is a rationalized order of men and things.

Hans Buchheim, following the lead of Hans Freyer, sees several dangers in technology: it proceeds from a world per-

spective and a belief that there are no limits to the "calculabil-
ity and controllability of the world as well as human nature";
"the theoretical objectification of man" can lead to the claim
of control; all technological systems are self-contained, man-
made, applicable as required; technology aims at the planning
of human nature, which cannot be planned; "every technical
advance forces on human society a part of the conformity of
mechanics." He cites as an example the shift from social science to social engineering, psychology into psychotechnology,
which we know as the "human relations movement" in organizational theory. In that it aims to produce an artificial society,
technology intrudes upon the political realm.

A similar view of technology is given by Jacques Ellul, who
says without qualification that technology "causes the state to
become totalitarian, to absorb the citizen's life completely."
Ellul does not exempt any state: "Even when the state is
resolutely liberal and democratic, it cannot do otherwise than
become totalitarian. It becomes so either directly or, as in the
United States, through intermediate persons."

Ordinary descriptions of totalitarianism, those connected
with war, torture, terror, ideology, and inefficiency, are to
Ellul errors in the understanding of the use of technology to
transform man into a thing. Technology, as he points out, simply cannot deal with individuals: it objectifies man into the abstract atom of the mass, after which its methods and statistics
become highly efficient. The process, according to Ellul, requires only that the state, directly or indirectly, gain control of
one thread of technology, for all technology, from propaganda
to nuclear physics, is intertwined, and the control of one
thread leads inevitably to the control of all.

The messianic aspect of totalitarianism has been connected
by Carl J. Friedrich to its genesis in Christian nations, particularly Protestant nations, with their theological certitude. J. L.
Talmon distinguishes religious from secular messianism by
their points of reference: the former begins with God, the lat-

ter with the reason and the will of man. The salient characteristic of both forms of messianism is their intent to transform
the world, the goal that permits them first to control the world.
The culmination of religious messianism comes in heaven on
earth, secular messianism aims toward some point in history
when all men will be free, equal, and happy. In both forms all
promises are to be found in the future, all arguments are to be
proved in the future. No rational argument can be made, as
Arendt noted, against a thought or an idea in the present when
the justification or proof is said to exist in some distant time
unknowable except to the initiates of the movement for whom
it is certain.

When is the future? When will totalitarianism be total?
Never. Totalitarianism is the will to be greater than all imagined gods, to control the world and the will of the world so
that man can live in order so perfect he is incapable of sin
or the thought of sin against the given happiness. It is, in concept, an abstraction, vague and limitless, naming nothing, as
unattainable as the definition of happiness imposed upon men
to destroy their dignity. In reality it is a continuous process, an
unending series of acts aimed at the destruction of autonomy.

It cannot ever be total because of the complexity of human
society, which is never stable because each birth adds another
biologically unique creature, capable of thought and destined
by nature to be free. For all the fear, suffering, abstraction,
atomization, massification, insinuation, delusion, deception,
debasement, constriction, constraint, and objectification it can
wreak on man, totalitarianism can never remove the possibility
that some tortured prisoner in some gray cell will be visited by
his ancient nurse, Philosophy, who will set him to thinking,
which is the beginning of autonomy, which is the root of dignity and the impetus to politics; and man in his political life is
unpredictable and therefore indomitable.

Yet, in all the long history of the speaking, social creature,
in all the thousands of tribes, cities, states, and nations, totali-

tarian forms have been the most common relations between men. It is as if man, elevated above all other creatures on earth by the capacity to think and speak, the only creature capable of exceeding the mechanical bounds of nature, wishes to leap backward to be again something less than human.

5

Goodness Surprised

If we can assume a totalitarian element in some forms of tribal organization, the literature of totalitarianism may be the oldest literature on earth, with a history of tens of thousands of years of evolution, begun in those dark times when man first sought to separate himself from animals through language and social organization. This long and complex literature can be divided into five distinct types:

Type 1: Tribal myths used to achieve full consent in the organization of the tribe and its rules of conduct. The relation of these myths to modern totalitarianism is highly questionable, however, since the necessities of nature and the necessities made by man have different functions, and the element of reciprocity, as described by Lévi-Strauss, in tribal organization is to a great extent absent in modern totalitarian systems.

Type 2: The disputed works of political philosophers whose ideas may have contributed to totalitarian systems but whose moral sense would be outraged by the systems in practice. Plato's *Republic* and Machiavelli's two major, apparently opposite, and certainly unclear works have generated endless debate over their effect and intent, as have the works of Rousseau, Hobbes, Hegel, and others. Marx and his followers cause the greatest difficulty among these, because it has become virtually impossible to extricate Marxist thinking from its perversions in practice.

Type 3: Works promoting totalitarianism or tactics leading to totalitarian systems. There are few of these of any importance other than Hitler's *Mein Kampf* and the various extensions of those ideas in the words of his followers.

Type 4: Anti-totalitarian works, both the theoretical works of Arendt, Buchheim, Ellul, Talmon, Friedrich, etc., and all the histories of Nazi Germany and Stalinist Russia which take the side of democracy and so seem to us objective. Some of the work of Simone Weil and Albert Camus should be included in this category, even though it deals with totalitarianism only tangentially.

Type 5: Antinomies comprise the largest and most rapidly growing type of totalitarian literature. These works, purportedly on behalf of man's freedom, happiness, efficiency, and physical well-being, are insidious, because by accident or design they promote oppression in a manner that cannot easily be recognized. They are the work of well-meaning men, from Taylor to Mayo to Ewing, and they may be found in one form or another in the library of almost any businessman or bureaucrat. They transcend economic systems, the practices advocated by these works become more widespread every day, and they seem to suffer no opposition but inertia. Since these contain the ideas that are generally looked upon as the best accommodations of man to the age of technology, their potential effect should not be underestimated: they will weigh heavily in determining the nature of work and society in the future.

Of the five types of totalitarian literature only two are important to work and social organization in America. Tribalism has nearly disappeared from a world geared to literacy and the accumulation of knowledge, and its return is unlikely if not impossible. The murderous and insane literature of the Nazis would meet with rather more skepticism now that the world has experienced its results, but there is always the chance that men in dire times will again accept the leadership of a madman in the hope that he could rescue them, which is not to argue that men have become more ethical, but to doubt the vulnerability of men to such unsubtle techniques. Finally, the works attacking totalitarianism are, with the exception of Ellul, rooted too much in the particulars of the past to make them wholly applicable to the present situation. Surely they have served to make men aware of the dangers of totalitarianism, and the history that supports their theories must not be forgotten; but the chief use of them can only be as analogues. Totalitarianism in our time does not have the odor of evil about it; the ovens of the death camps that sicken the soul are not required by modern oppressors, nor is there any need for jackboots and barbed wire. War has lost its value in a rich world and racism lingers in more virulent forms mainly among the fading generations who cannot escape their roots in less technological times.

Modern totalitarianism is not hysterical; it is too cool to hate, too controlled to risk war, too subtle to commit physical murder. Its methods seek efficiency, ever increasing domination, an end to politics and contingency. The purpose of totalitarian thinking now is to make the world into a clock: routine, useful, perfectly predictable; a machine in which each part has a place and a function and a master operator who sets it in motion and makes whatever adjustments are necessary to keep it going, with no end in mind but the turnings of the machinery in the prescribed orbit. Walter Kaufman has described one form of oppression as benevolent totalitarianism, a term that applies to the organization of work and life now forced upon many Americans. The proponents of this form of oppression have only the best of intentions toward man and society, much as Rousseau and Plato, who preceded them as victims of contingency, misunderstanding, and misuse.

Whether these disputed works are totalitarian or not depends on how they are read and by whom. Furthermore, if an ultimate indisputable theoretical conclusion were reached about any or all of them, it would serve less purpose than even the cursory restatements of the accusations against them that follow, for the light emanates from the disputes themselves, cautioning against grand schemes, certainty, the use of man, simplification, unlimited will, history as the future, chess master thinking, and unclear writing.

Plato

Karl Popper's roundabout advocacy of "piecemeal social engineering," *The Open Society*, makes the most widely known attack on Plato's political theory, concentrating on the utopian *Republic* and Plato's last and unfinished work, the *Laws*. Early on in his attack Popper wrote: "It seems that one has first to be disturbed by the similarity between the Platonic theory of justice and the theory and practice of modern totalitarianism before one can feel how urgent it is to interpret these matters."

He identifies five elements of Plato's philosophy and summarizes them as a program for totalitarianism:

(A) The strict division of the classes; i.e., the ruling class consisting of herdsmen and watch-dogs must be strictly separated from the human cattle.

(B) The identification of the fate of the state with that of the ruling class; the exclusive interest in this class, and in its unity; and subservient to this unity, the rigid rules for breeding and educating this class, and the strict supervision and collectivization of the interests of its members. From these principal elements, others can be derived, for instance, the following:

(C) The ruling class has a monopoly of things like military virtues and training, and of the right to carry arms and to receive education of any kind; but it is excluded from any participation in the economic activities, and especially from earning money.

(D) There must be a censorship of all intellectual activities of the ruling class, and a continual propaganda aiming at moulding and unifying their minds. All innovation in education, legislation, and religion must be prevented or suppressed.

(E) The state must be self-sufficient. It must aim at economic autarchy; for otherwise the rulers would either be dependent upon traders, or become traders themselves. The first of these alternatives would undermine their power, the second their unity and the stability of the state.

The philosophical core of Popper's case rests upon a line from the *Laws,* which he translates as "You are created for the sake of the whole, and not the whole for the sake of you." Popper stands alone in this translation, which he further perverts by claiming Plato used the Greek word *holon* to mean state. T. J. Saunders renders the same passage as "You forget that creation is not for your benefit: you exist for the sake of the universe." In context, the Saunders translation seems more appropriate, for Plato is speaking about metaphysics, the gods, and the soul, and not about politics; the line is best understood as part of Plato's continuing argument against man as the measure of all things.

The dangers of language are multiplied by translation and multiplied again when a writer, like Popper, is blinded by his desire to prove a point. Popper is even willing to cash in

Plato's appeals for wisdom, beauty, goodness, and justice as "propaganda," lies for the use of the philosopher/king. Of course, Plato read literally, as if the *Republic* were a news story, takes on different meanings, particularly if one then transports the literal reading into the twentieth century, making philosopher/kings of Hitler and Stalin and imagining fourth-century Athens as a technological society.

For Popper totalitarianism and tribalism are synonymous, and he quite rightly accuses Plato of dreaming in the *Laws* of returning to the golden age of Cronos. But the *Laws* and *Timaeus* and *Critias,* in which he also dreams of a golden age, are the works of an old and perhaps embittered man. These last three works were written some twenty to thirty years after the *Republic*. Plato's failures with the kings of Syracuse, where he had hoped to serve as advisor in the creation of an ideal state, must have played some part in the dull worldliness of the *Laws* and the nostalgic longings of *Timaeus* and *Critias*.

Did he wish to return to some form of perfectly stable, unchanging tribal society, as Popper suggests? It is quite likely. But Plato's vision of tribalism may have been far more sophisticated than that of Popper, who mistakenly compares it to totalitarianism. Plato's understanding seems to adumbrate that of Lévi-Strauss, who thinks of neolithic man as man in his natural state, unchanging, living in the circle of myth and tribal structure, man forever, rather than modern man, accumulating knowledge by virtue of his ability to write, breaking the circle of stability, moving forward in a straight line, doomed by entropy.

What was for Plato the modern age had less to recommend it than we sometimes imagine. He had lived through war, tyranny, treachery, and a democracy that (to paraphrase his allusion to Socrates in The Cave of the Shadows) laid its hands on the man who was trying to lead them up out of the darkness and set them free, and killed him. The harsh criticism of the political institutions of his own time implied by his utopian

state and his later praise of earlier tribalistic society may have
been justified. In our idealization of ancient Greece we tend to
forget that the civilization that produced Socrates also condemned him and caused Plato to flee Athens.

Taken literally, however, the *Republic* still lacks several of
the elements of totalitarianism. Plato advocates rigidly defined
classes, while totalitarianism seeks the breakdown of classes
into one mass of atomized men. Curiously, Plato even tells
how the class structure will destroy his ideal state in his description of timocracy. Secrecy, terror, crowding, murder,
atomization, propaganda (poets are banned because they tell
lies), moral disruption, lawlessness, and most importantly,
movement in the senses of futurism and imperialism, all vital
to the establishment of a totalitarian state, have no place in
Plato's ideal state. As a plan for totalitarian rule the *Republic*
fails by comparison to *Mein Kampf;* a man committed to the
rule of reason simply lacks the foundation in madness to will
the destruction of human dignity.

Plato's intent in producing a utopian state must have been
influenced by his own idealism as well as by the neolithic past:
an eternal form existed, he sought to find it, whether it existed
in the mind, the past, or the vision of the gods. He sought
some cultural authority in the golden age, a sense of limits as
opposed to the limitless nature of totalitarianism; "Courage,"
he wrote, "means preserving something." He lived in the dawn
of the modern age, at the beginning of science; and in the
midst of new political forms, the need to preserve something,
to hold to some limits must have seemed to him overwhelming.
In such circumstance appeals to unity, attempts to make the
citizens understand that they are part of society, with duties to
the state, may have had quite a different meaning from the
collectivist interpretation of some modern critics.

Defenses of Plato by exegesis, historical context, or psychohistory cannot absolve the *Republic* from its imposition of
a definition of happiness on the reader. By its very nature po-

litical philosophy generates arrogance in the philosopher: either he defines happiness or he runs the risk of being accused of not knowing what he is talking about. To escape the temptation to invent utopias, past or future, requires a Kantian faith in man and a Madisonian faith in the mechanics of compositions of autonomous persons and their organizations. Plato lacked both kinds of faith. His prescription for a clean canvas echoes in the atrocities of the Cambodian revolution. His philosopher/king and the *Führerprinzip* have much in common. His ideas on eugenics are not beyond comparison to those of Gobineau and Hitler. His ideal state and the total state share an undeniable resemblance.

In the course of his long attack on Plato, Karl Popper attempts to make a sale of his own philosophy of "piecemeal social engineering," which he compares to Plato's totalitarian "utopian social engineering." Popper claims a distinction in that his version of social engineering lacks an overall blueprint. Yet we read in Popper: "Speaking more generally, we can say that the engineer or the technologist approaches institutions rationally as means that serve certain ends, and that as a technologist he judges them wholly according to their appropriateness, efficiency, simplicity, etc." In his prescription for an "open society, for a rule of reason, for justice, freedom, equality, and for the control of international crime," one finds the elements of "technology, efficiency, simplicity, etc." that later writers have identified among the ingredients of totalitarianism.

"Not even to himself," Popper said of Plato, "did he fully admit that he was combating the freedom of thought for which Socrates had died; and by making Socrates his champion he persuaded all others that he was fighting for it. Plato thus became, unconsciously, the pioneer of the many propagandists who, often in good faith, developed the technique of appealing to moral, humanitarian sentiments for anti-humanitarian, immoral purposes." The recognition of antinomy cannot always prevent further antinomies, but the thoughtful dispute brought about by the recognition of antinomy in every attempt to impose a definition of happiness on man serves to despoil the plans of oppressors and to protect every man's autonomy.

Machiavelli

The great conflict between the advice to dictators in *The Prince* and the defense of republican freedoms in the lesser known *Discourses* has never been fully resolved. Attempts at integrating the two works have produced some astonishing knitting, not the least of which came from Machiavelli himself in his either/or statement, which advises republicans to get rid of nobles or princes to create a class of nobles. Due in part to the contrasting advice of his two major works Machiavelli has been credited with being the first political scientist, the first modern political thinker, Hitler's favorite advisor, the precursor of Lenin and Stalin, the basis of Madisonian democracy, the inventor of *Realpolitik* and the devil himself.

In defense of Machiavelli, Felix Gilbert has gone so far as to suggest that chapters 15–19 of *The Prince,* which advise against goodness, and for cruelty and deceit, were meant as satire. Antonio Gramsci made a Marxist/Leninist of Machiavelli. Hitler apparently put great stock in the advice of chapters 15–19. The identification of discord as a cause of freedom and strength in chapter 4 of Book I of the *Discourses* may have been Madison's bedside reading on the night before he wrote *Federalist 10*. One can find agreement in the works of Machiavelli for almost any political idea; the only real interpretive error is in oversimplification, as in Toland's biography of Hitler, which compares the Führer not once, but three times to the Florentine political thinker.

Certain aspects of Machiavelli's work are not subject to

wild swings of interpretation: He had a pre-Christian belief in the *vita activa;* he was a realist, a believer in doing what was possible. He had a powerful sense of nationhood and nationalism. His work was analytical, political science rather than political philosophy; he did not concern himself with the moral aspects of government. He cared more for the stability of the state than for its ends; expansion of the state rather than social justice within the state was his goal. Finally, there is a deep, almost bitter pessimism in much of his thinking; he seeks mainly to avoid the worst that may befall the state, from within or without, and his estimate of man leans toward the dark side. In Machiavelli's view the state may ultimately serve its constituents, but first and foremost the people must serve the state, even if one of them is a prince.

Seen in piecemeal fashion Machiavelli's works abound in totalitarian notions, beginning with the pre-eminence of the state and the intense nationalism that permeates his thinking. Autonomy for him concerns the state and the state only; man can be useful to the state only when he is properly governed. Growth and expansion are vital to his conception of an enduring state, modifying his notion of stability to encompass the dependence on movement associated with imperialism as a totalitarian trait. He endorses the use of religion as a unifying, controlling force, a justification of laws promulgated by either the prince or the republic; and he rails against the divisive influence of the Roman Church for its destruction of the kind of religious feeling that could aid the state. He opposes deceit as a general rule but endorses it as a tactic for the prince. The purges recommended for the establishment of a republic bear a strong resemblance to the purges executed under Stalin, Mao, Pol Pot, and to a lesser degree Hitler; while the establishment of a class of nobles in the creation of a principate compares with the onion metaphor of totalitarian organization. Finally, the violence underlying much of his advice for both internal and external affairs implies a view of man that does not respect his dignity, even as it applies to his right to life.

The lack of moral underpinnings in Machiavelli's work has often been pointed to as evidence of his fascist, totalitarian, tyrannical, or Mephistophelian philosophy, but one must invent a philosophy for Machiavelli—he has none. Machiavelli analyzes, works in the real world, does the possible; he has no grand view of man or history to propose to the world; he sees the future as the best that can be made of it; he offers no justification beyond practicality for his advice either to the prince or the republic. Were it not for his favoring of technological methods to regulate human behavior, Karl Popper's piecemeal social engineering would be perfectly Machiavellian: the solution of problems as they arise.

This practicality, amoral as it may be, separates Machiavelli from totalitarianism, because it roots his methods in the possible, which contrasts with the totalitarian preoccupation with the impossible, unattainable, perfectly controlled society of some future time. The destruction of human capability inherent in totalitarian oppression is utterly impractical, sheer waste, the weakening of the state, which Machiavelli would find intolerable; ideology for its own sake does not figure anywhere in his work.

His version of a republic, described in the *Discourses,* is at greater variance with totalitarian thinking than any practical political prescriptions but those centered around the writing of the U. S. Constitution. He proposed a raucous, disputatious society, made up of distinct classes that produce *virtù,* by which he meant—as no two translators will agree—a vigorous and manly sense of civism, brought about by conflict. How different from the silent, acquiescent masses of the totalitarian process!

In all, Machiavelli was a conservative. The prince was to occupy but a brief reign in his scheme of state; the role of preserving the state was to be left to the republican form of government, which was to be free, vital, populated by citizens who could depend on a system of jurisprudence learned from ancient Rome. If any authority beyond practicality can be found in his work, it is the authority of the foundations of civilization; human culture aims and limits his vision, unlike that of the totalitarian, who recognizes no authority but his own promise of the future. Machiavelli found his "true nourishment" in "the courts of the ancients." He was a civilized man, he opposed tyranny, he favored the rule of law, yet he lived in a time when his country was, as he wrote in the last, passionately nationalistic chapter of *The Prince,* ". . . enslaved . . . oppressed . . . scattered . . . without a head, without order, beaten, despoiled, lacerated, and overrun, and . . . suffered ruin of every kind." His own life was ruined by fortune, he suffered sudden and terrible reversals, exile, and loneliness. Bitterness gave him a cold eye and the dreamless character to invent political science, but it did not dissuade him from the idea that the most practical prescription for the building of a great and enduring state is freedom for its citizens.

Rousseau

> In me are united two almost irreconcilable characteristics . . . I have a passionate temperament, and lively and headstrong emotions. Yet my thoughts arise slowly and confusedly, and are never ready till too late. It is as if my heart and my brain did not belong to the same person.
>
> *Confessions*

Ascription of the origins of totalitarian philosophy to Rousseau has become a commonplace of modern liberal political philosophy. The great romantic's notion of a General Will greater than and beyond the will of all, his belief in the need for a Legislator to point out the General Will to the people, and his role in the totalitarian thinking of Babeuf and Robespierre have led many writers to the conclusion that this man, who believed there could be no morality without civil liberty, was the father of the process of destroying autonomy. Kant, on the other hand, credited Rousseau's writings with leading him to love man and man's freedom. Improbable as it may seem, both views find justification in Rousseau's works, for he was a political philosopher who wrote with the exciting ambiguity of a poet and an artist who applied his imagination to political philosophy, anthropology, psychology, and education.

Rousseau lived most of his life in argument and irritation. Even as a child he was excoriated by what he recalled as injustices. He changed religious affiliations several times, educated himself in music and literature, enjoyed the favors and protection of rich women, and acted the perfect cad to the poor woman with whom he had five children. He did not ever completely enjoy the confidence of governments or men. Misanthrope, cad, and troublemaker, he seems to have found a home in theory, imagination, and finally in confession. His attempt at systematic thinking, a new method of notation for music, was a failure, but his imaginative works, including his essays into political philosophy, have had the power to excite men to action. He provided the justification for the French Revolution, his words killed kings and rendered God powerless.

Out of Rousseau's imagination came the primacy of man. For the first time the collective noun had meaning. The General Will, that foggy notion, was not the will of a man or of men, but of man. It floated above the collective creature somewhere, in Platonic fashion, perfection awaiting discovery by the Legislator, a person or body of persons every bit as vague as the General Will. But that foggy notion changed forever man's view of himself: the General Will came from man, not from God; man became the mystery, man created man, the messiah was on earth in the form of the General Will, which is always right and always for the good of the people.

For all its infallibility the General Will may be thwarted on the way to paradise on earth. Without the Legislator, it may not be recognized; and even if the Legislator points out the General Will, it may still be challenged by the will of factions or of individuals. The course Rousseau sets requires the will of every man to be subsumed under the General Will: every man must be completely alienated, for he must have sold his will to the General Will in return for freedom and equality. That is the compact men must make with the General Will if they wish to live in peace and happiness.

How similar it is to a wedding with God! Rousseau is not a political thinker; *The Social Contract* is a religious work, a Koran for the totalitarian left! One need only substitute the word God for man or society to realize the religious nature of Rousseau's ideas. His vision is anti-political, a method for eliminating the risk of politics, for putting men in relation to a mystical will that is above them rather than in relation to each other in the flesh and sweat of the possible world.

His primitivism places man in an Eden without property or egoistic pride, a creature prior to individualism and conflict, in a golden age of simplicity and innocence. Property, individualism, the mistaking of what seems to be with what is, a world of deceit leads man to the middle of the eighteenth century, by which time only his complete alienation in the General Will as identified by the Legislator can resurrect a life as good and happy as in the golden age.

By the preceding familiar interpretation Rousseau can be made out to be the father of modern totalitarianism: the Legislator becomes the leader, the General Will becomes the will dictated by the proletariat, the primacy of man dictates

atheism, the alienation of men in the General Will becomes
the power of the state, and all individual thinking is punisha-
ble as a crime against the state. The messianic quality of totalitarianism in Rousseau simply cannot be denied. He was every
bit as frightening to James Madison as to a Prussian monarch,
and with good reason.

No man, not even Lenin or Mao, was a truer revolutionary
than Rousseau. It was instinctive in him, the conflagration of
his character; had he been able, he would have made revolutions in every area of human endeavor. The world did not suit
him as it was, which is not unusual, but it also did not suit him
in theory. His need to revolt came to him from both sources: *a
priori* and *a posteriori*. He found nothing in life or thought to
contradict his revolutionary impulses and ideas.

The failure of revolutions, beginning with the French Revolution, to make men free, combined with Rousseau's revolutionary heart, leads too easily to an understanding of him as
the provider of a philosophical prison for man. Psychohistory,
as used by Talmon, seals the case. The "paranoiac streak" Talmon finds in Rousseau enables the Israeli writer to compare
the author of *The Social Contract* to Robespierre, Saint-Just,
and Babeuf, and to find them all of a kind. Thus nonsense
proves misinterpretation. It is as if one were to study the Lincoln–Douglas debates according to the charm of the participants and find by virtue of his social grace that Douglas was
unalterably opposed to slavery. Rousseau must have been one
of the most intolerably nasty men in history, but that aspect of
his character led him also to an acute awareness of oppression
in every form. One has but to listen to the descriptions of his
early life in the *Confessions* to gain some understanding of
the emotional forces that set him against the great and small
enemies of man's freedom and dignity.

Of being falsely accused of breaking a comb when still a
child, he wrote: "Imagine a person timid and docile in ordinary life, but proud, fiery, and inflexible when roused, a child

who has always been controlled by the voice of reason . . . a creature without a thought of injustice, now for the first time suffering a most grave one at the hands of the people he loves best and most deeply respects. Imagine the revolution in his ideas, the violent change of his feelings. . . .

"The feeling was only a personal one in its origins, but it has since assumed such a consistency and has become so divorced from personal interests that my blood boils at the sight or the tale of any injustice, whoever may be the sufferer and wherever it may have taken place. . . ."

Later, apprenticed to an engraver whom he despised, he reacted to the demeaning world again: "I should have succeeded indeed, if brutality and unreasonable restraint on the part of my master had not disgusted me with my work. I stole the time that should have been his, to spend it in occupations of a similar nature that had for me the attractions of liberty."

In the *Confessions* Rousseau produced the psychohistory of Jean Jacques, describing the ground from which the lover of nature, freedom, and equality grew. Unlike Marx, who suffered poverty, but always lived the classless life of the intellectual, Rousseau knew something of work and something of the soured wealth of eighteenth-century Europe. He describes calumny and deceit in the *Confessions,* but in *Émile* he goes beyond mere description to attack the effects of wealth and greed, explaining that freedom consists in wanting what is possible, which is best attained by living a simple life close to nature.

The messianic aspect of totalitarianism, the need for endless expansion, the concern with the future are not to be found in the practicality of the *Confessions* or *Émile,* and in the latter he makes it quite clear that he has not abandoned the individual and his dignity to the collective: "Liberty is not to be found in any form of government, she is in the heart of the free man, he bears her with him everywhere." The great laws to Rousseau are the laws of nature, he is ever the author of the

Discourse on the Origins of Inequality, the loving anthropologist as political philosopher, the misanthrope who believes in the goodness of man, the romantic who raises reason to a place beside God. His belief in man knows no limits, he is ever surprised by the evil and unhappiness that have befallen a creature who is good by nature. The General Will is the will to the good, to the public weal, to liberty and equality. Property and the artificiality of a life ruled by property and grown beyond human proportion are the enemies that blind man to the General Will that emanates from the goodness of his nature. To make laws in consonance with the General Will and to live according to them enables man to be moral.

For all his love of nature he realizes that men live in society and he asks a social compact in which all men give themselves over completely to the good of each other, but he asks this in human rather than totalitarian fashion. In his argument with Montesquieu over the inclusion of country-dwellers in the polity and in his recurrent praise of nature and life close to nature, one feels the beginning of understanding of the effects of technology on man and his autonomous existence. Rousseau clearly prefers life under the necessity of nature to suffering under the necessity created by man and his technological will, adumbrating Heidegger's attack upon the limitless will of technology, "the will to will, to subject the whole world to its domination . . ."

In the General Will Rousseau seeks not domination and destructiveness, but autonomy. The General Will is the creation of man by his discovery of it, the General Will is the universal end toward which man strives; it is an end born of him, not thrust upon him; man finds his own happiness, for no will can be greater than the infallible General Will, which is man's own creation; he is autonomous, he has dignity. Kant's debt to Rousseau is clear.

Without the clarifying systematic genius of Kant, the philosophy of Rousseau is vulnerable to the use of totalitarian dreamers. In his work, as in his life, Rousseau could not defend himself. No one, not even Kant, said more passionately that man must exist as an end, yet Rousseau's words became the rationale for making man a means. His theory of a society of men consenting to unite in the search for the practice of their own autonomous will became a blueprint for the collectivization of man in the exercise of despotic power. His wish for a moral life under just laws became the rationale for lawlessness. The freedom of man to pursue the universal end, his own happiness, was perverted to mean a limitless freedom for the state to oppress its constituents. The distinct roles of the Legislator and the Administrator were united in the leader. The deceit of totalitarianism turned Rousseau's love for man in his own time and of his own nature into the tragedy of philosophy: ideas undone, their meaning changed into means toward inhuman ends.

Marx

When he was old and ill and famous, Karl Marx said of himself that he was not a Marxist. It was one of the few gleamings of wit in a life that produced a great shelf of ever more dour and turgid prose, and it was one of the few public signs of personal bitterness from a man who had lived most of his years in poverty, often in illness, and always as a pariah, an enemy of nations and a threat to power. He thought the world as if he were an omniscient chess master playing against inhumanity, beginning with a brilliant critique of his opponent, predicting the reply to each of his moves, making sacrifices, leaping, working always toward the certain future, excusing everything by the inevitable checkmate. But in his old age he saw the changing of the game: new technology, new politics, interpreters of his moves, commentators seeking to bowdlerize his vision before he had completed the expression of it. He made a joke. No one was dissuaded. Like Rousseau and Machiavelli, he provided a rationale for terror, a philosophical foundation for despots. Only the unforgiving mirror of his criticism remains unaltered.

In his attempt to bring what he called "the pre-history of human society" to a close he opened the way for inhuman society. Truly, nothing happened according to his predictions: history did not proceed along the inevitable course he envisioned; ideas did not arise from the material conditions, but conditions changed because of ideas, often because of his ideas; capitalism did not collapse with a moaning sigh, devoured by its own greed, left in poverty and overproduction; Marxism came not to Germany, but to Russia, not to an industrialized nation filled with proletarian revolutionaries, but to a backward nation, with a peasant class that vastly outnumbered the working class; and in that country socialism quickly gave way to despotism, the old classes were soon replaced by new classes, and the state has grown ever more powerful instead of withering away.

As a seer Marx was simply wrong. As the intellectual helmsman of human civilization through the completion of "pre-history" and beyond, he disappointed his own expectations of a good life for man: instead of peace and freedom, the result of the pattern he began has been murder and oppression. A failure of such proportion is composed of a great many parts, but none affected the fate of men quite so much as the "invisible hand" theory of history put forward by Marx. Unlike Machiavelli, his ideas had no pagan undercurrents; he was a religious thinker, a professed atheist whose mind worked in perfectly Christian patterns. In a very real way, the civil state has withered away in many areas of the world, as Marx predicted, but it has been replaced by a theocracy. The messiah has arrived in these theocracies, but neither in the form of the reason of the people as expressed in the General Will nor in the form of God's messenger; the messiah of Marxist states has come as bureaucracy, the form of oppression Hannah Arendt called "rule by Nobody."

Marx denied that his work was philosophy, which he compared to onanism; but he dealt with the concepts that are usually called philosophy, particularly the world view that predicts the inevitable road to communism. It is only when considering his work from the viewpoint of political philosophy that the oppressive qualities of a world view containing a series of inevitable acts leading to an inevitable conclusion become apparent. By eliminating other possible courses of action, Marx limits man and thus takes away his dignity, for creatures whose decisions are meaningless because their destiny has been determined can be neither free nor autonomous. A world without contingency reduces man to an actor in a tableau, a manikin, moved by predetermined forces, utterly without control over his life or destiny. Man serves as a means to achieve the destiny of the world.

From there the step to murder or enslavement comes easily. Marx himself accepts almost casually the destruction of the other classes by the proletariat; he gives them no role in the revolutionary society, which, on the way to the last convulsive struggle that produces communism, will be managed through the dictatorship of the proletariat. He admired Darwin as a brilliant materialist thinker, and may even have offered to dedicate the second volume of *Capital* to him. The cruelty inherent in Darwinian evolution was no more disturbing to Marx than to Spencer; he accepted the idea of the killing struggle as a part of the process of ascent; nothing could overshadow the process, for heaven was its end.

In his *Theses on Feuerbach,* Marx offered a key to the understanding of heaven as he prophesied it: "The human essence is no abstraction inherent in each single individual. In its reality it is the ensemble of the social relations." The differences between men will disappear in heaven, the collective of perfect happiness, where, Marx says, man will function in his social rather than political being, the political abstraction having been absorbed into social man.

Some interpreters of Marx, notably Lukacs, have taken a less certain view of future history, allowing contingency as a possibility, relieving man of the weight of oppression by pre-destination, returning some of his freedom to him to enjoy on the way to heaven. Perhaps these liberal interpreters of Marx have considered his heaven and found it wanting, for no less interesting place could be imagined than a heaven populated with citizens enjoying a perfectly peaceful, productive life, freed at last from religion, alienation, and the struggle between classes. But the freedom promised in a utopia such as Marx describes is not real, not when one is limited to the choice be-tween ambrosia and ambrosia. It is an apolitical heaven, for politics, which is the connection between men seeking to live with their differences, cannot be practiced in a society as solid and total as Parmenides' sphere; man cannot exist as a politi-cal creature when his notion of happiness has not only been defined, but predicted, for his city has become like a tree and he is no more than a leaf awaiting the change of the season and the coming of the winds.

The question must be asked: Does a creature without politi-cal life fit within our definition of man? Or has Marx envi-sioned the end of the dialectic in a great convulsion that pro-duces the final, unchangeable end of the species in a new species, one without need of freedom or dignity? And if that is so, is the end of man a higher or a lower creature? What is the nature of a creature without the will to autonomy?

As he noted before he died, the misfortune of Marx was the Marxists, followers and interpreters, seekers of utopia soon, men who neglected the early humanist writings of the less cer-tain, less scientific writer, whose inspiration came more from the world as it was than the world as it would be. The close connection to reality in the early work made young Marx a political man and a political thinker, engaged in the empathetic manner that faded from his later economic and prophetic efforts. The young Marx, although he suffered from the lack of experience in the world that excited him, could still imagine the smell of the factories and the longing of oppressed men to have a human life. He understood what the brutal first stages of industrialization wreaked upon the worker, how the rationalization of production reduced men to things. He had the truest understanding of any man in history of the dark side of capitalism, with its dehumanizing of the exploited and the exploiter in the pursuit of money.

Marx the critic of the use of man as a means fits poorly with the later Marx. The early writing has clarity and often a straightforwardness that is entirely absent from the tortuous economics of *Capital,* even though his early work criticizing Hegel may be the most difficult of all to follow, a fault that may be blamed as much on Hegel as Marx. It was the young Marx who developed the materialistic notion of man creating himself through his own labor, who found the direction of the *axis mundi* to be entirely wrong and righted it to reach from earth to heaven instead of down from heaven to earth. Montesquieu had said long before Marx that men were formed by institutions and even by the size of society, but the young Marx, having the world of the nineteenth century to observe, carried the idea on to show that the means of production formed men. In the *Economic and Philosophical Manuscripts* he isolated the moral flaw of capitalism:

> Political economy, the science of wealth, is . . . the science of renunciation, of privation and of saving, which actually succeeds in depriving man of fresh air and of physical activity. This science of a marvelous industry is at the same time the science of asceticism. Its true ideal is the ascetic but usurious miser and the ascetic but productive slave. Its moral ideal is the worker who takes a part of his wages to the sav-

ing bank. It has even found a servile art to embody this favorite idea, which has been produced in a sentimental manner on the stage. Thus, despite its worldly and pleasure-seeking appearance, it is a truly moral science, the most moral of all sciences. Its principal thesis is the renunciation of life and of human needs. The less you eat, drink, buy books, go to the theatre or to balls, or to the public house, and the less you think, love, theorize, sing, paint, fence, etc., the more you will be able to save and the greater will become your treasure which neither moth nor rust will corrupt—your capital. The less you are, the less you express your life, the more you have, the greater is your alienated life and the greater is the saving of your alienated being. Everything which the economist takes from you in the way of life and humanity, he restores to you in the form of money and wealth. And everything which you are unable to do, your money can do for you; it can eat, drink, go to the ball and to the theatre. It can acquire art, learning, historical treasures, political power; and it can travel. It can appropriate all these things for you, can purchase everything; it is the true opulence. But although it can do all this, it only desires to create itself and to buy itself, for everything else is subservient to it. When one owns the master, one also owns the servant, and one has no need of the master's servant. Thus all passions and activities must be submerged in avarice. The worker must have just what is necessary for him to want to live, and he must want to live only in order to have this.

So the liberal economists are damned in the most brilliant skirmish of a war that lasted all through Marx's life and in large part accounted for the inflexibility of his views of capitalism until the unfinished attempt to revise the second volume of *Capital*. Beyond the economic insight in that long paragraph is the revelation of the character of the writer, of his sense of the worth of a human being, even of a worker condemned to subsistence by the economists whose theories had justified the cruelties of the industrial revolution. At the core of the argument against the immorality and injustice of capitalism the alienation of man describes his loss of humanity. Alienation is the thesis, the result of man's labor under capitalism, the ruin of his life, the reason for revolution. The social relations among alienated men are imaginary, alienation divorces man from the product of his labor, it leads to the worship of inanimate objects, it makes man into a means, a thing.

Just as his analysis of economic history launched the systematic study of economics, his analysis of the role of alienation in the relations between men and other men and between men and labor and men and things led to modern sociology. In combination they produced an unfortunate vision of utopia as a seamless society, a prophetic method that limits freedom to acceptance of and compliance with the only and inevitable road to happiness. History has disproved much of the theory of history and the economic circumstances that determine it, although hardly anyone would deny the use of economics to understand the forces that determine human actions, and no serious challenge has been offered to Marx's attitude toward economic and social issues. But political questions about the central concept of his sociological views are raised by consideration of a world in which no one suffers alienation: what is a society of completely absorbed people? Is there no choice between absorption and alienation? Can alienation be beneficial to man?

Absorption

If Karl Marx were transported in time to Nazi Germany or Stalinist Russia, he would be the first to revolt against totalitarianism. Injustice in the use of man's labor angered him, the enslavement of man in a totalitarian system would have produced an even more violent response. The freedom he sought for man, however, was not unlike that of Rousseau's following of the General Will; utopian schemes are necessarily Platonic, defining man's freedom as realization of and adherence to an ideal, which may exist as a form above man or may emanate from man, but which seems never to be his conscious creation.

Utopia, the Greek word for nowhere, most often appears as a counter to a difficult or desperate situation; sometimes utopia serves as a goal—heaven, for example—but more often writers use descriptions of utopia to criticize institutions in their own time, as did Edward Bellamy in *Looking Backward* and Aldous Huxley in *Brave New World*. The use of utopian notions by earlier writers is not so generously revealed: Marx may have intended both functions for his utopian vision. But whether the critical function preceded the messianic function or the other way around, one can be certain that Marx proceeded from his own materialist method, believing that social conditions produced his thoughts.

If that is so, the Marxist criticism of Marx may perhaps be the best of all: he did not belong to the working class, material conditions did not produce his theories, and the flaws in his theory are a result of his life as an intellectual, separated from any class, outside history, an observer excluded from the material forces. His view of alienation, while useful in the criticism of the conditions of labor in the middle of the nineteenth century, lacked the subjective basis that might have led him to understand the uses men make of alienation in creating their autonomous existence. Marx learned to despise poverty from firsthand experience, but his understanding of the conditions of labor, according to his son-in-law, Paul Lafargue, came from the study of the Blue Books containing the reports of British factory inspectors. He bought them from "old paper dealers in Long Acre," who purchased them by the pound from Members of Parliament and other uninterested recipients of the reports. Marx lauds the competence and objectivity of the inspectors in the preface to *Capital,* and while the praise may well have been deserved, Karl Marx's experience of the conditions of labor was nonetheless thirdhand.

Alienation, like totalitarianism, is not an observable phenomenon in the victim; one cannot observe ten people seated on a bench and tell from their faces which of them is oppressed or alienated. There is rarely anything ostensible in the condition of the human spirit except in action or language. What the British inspectors saw were the miserable working conditions and destructive poverty of nineteenth-century factory life, and in their reports Marx found proof for his theories. The intellectual pitied the laborer, and out of pity he made alienation an evil, a situation that would not exist in utopia. It was Feuerbach who taught him about alienation in theory and the British factory inspectors who gave him lessons in the practice. He never felt the grasp of the company or the objectification of himself in the product of his labor. He did not know the fear of losing miserable employment. Neither did he know the close camaraderie of men against the boss, the company, and the weighing world. Karl Marx did not know how to dream himself separate from the movements of his hands; his own work occupied him body and mind, it devoured him; he could not imagine men working because they wanted something other than the product of their labor. In utopia there would be different work, human work: "From each according to his ability, to each according to his needs!" was his response to the notion of "fair distribution of the proceeds of labor" in the Gotha Program; that would be the end of money, alienation, and inhuman life.

He greatly admired Aristotle, as he said in *Capital,* but the unity of men who have no individual essence, only a social essence, was not what Aristotle meant to praise in his statement on unity in the *Politics:* "Is it not obvious that a state may at length attain such a degree of unity as to be no longer a state? —since the nature of a state is to be a plurality, and in tending to greater unity, from being a state, it becomes a family, and from being a family, an individual." Yet the idea of the withering away of the state in Marx is very like Aristotle's. He speaks on the one hand of individuality, and on the other of an "authentic common life."

Without this authentic common life and under the conditions of bourgeois society, Marx finds man alienated in five ways: He is alienated from the product of his labor because he does not own it, although he desires it. He is alienated from the activity because the work he does reflects the desire of the owner and not of the worker. He is alienated from his potential for freedom and creation because he spends so much of his life at his job, which robs him of his humanity; and since he must sell himself (labor as a commodity) in the job for which he will be paid, he becomes a specialist in whatever will pay him rather than in what he could possibly do with his individual talents. He is alienated from nature by the process of production using machinery in a capitalist system that assumes nature exists to be exploited. He is alienated from other men in a radical way because competition forces him to struggle against all other men to assure his own survival.

In a society without private property, Marx says, "My labor would be a free manifestation of life and an enjoyment of life. Under the presupposition of private property it is an externalization of life because I work in order to live and provide for myself the means of living. Working is not living."

What Marx does not say is who, in the utopian society without private property, will as part of his authentic common life work in the mines and the mills, in the forges and the factories. What man in his right mind will desire to descend into a coal mine? What man will desire to crawl across the bricks above the hellish furnaces of a steel mill?

Diderot raises similar questions and offers an equally impossible solution in the *Bougainville Supplement*. Orou, the Tahitien, tells his guest: "Do you not see that in your country, you have mixed up two different things? That which has neither feeling, thought, desire nor will, and which one can take, keep or exchange, without its suffering or complaining; and that which cannot be exchanged or acquired: which has liberty, will, desires: which can give itself and refuse itself for a single instant, or forever: which complains and suffers: which could not become a mere article of commerce without its character being forgotten and violence done to its nature? These precepts are contrary to the general law of existence."

The Tahitien's quarrel, like Marx's, is with alienation. In primitive societies man existed in common with nature, man and nature were equals, necessity ruled, production was equal to consumption. "If thou persuadest us to cross the narrow limit of necessity," the Tahitien asks, "when shall we stop working?" The question reveals the essence of modern civilization, which has achieved such velocity in the accumulation of knowledge and the conquest of nature that it can never stop working without collapsing. Plato, Diderot, and Marx have all come too late to the world to change the direction of civilization. Each of them offers vital criticism and visions of utopia past or future, each of them seeks an end to alienation in all of its forms, each of them seeks from a different viewpoint—philosophical, anthropological, socioeconomical—to return the world to a golden age of human life; none of them will settle for an accommodation with reality, none of them is concerned with the possible.

Leon Trotsky, giving advice to organizers of revolutionary movements, told them to look among members of fundamentalist religious sects. In so doing, he revealed several astonishingly clear perceptions of men and Marxism: the religious nature of Marxist revolution and the kinship between men who are preoccupied with goodness and its struggle with evil. For the Fundamentalist the problem of man is his alienation from God; for the philosophers of goodness the problem is man's alienation from himself, from the product of his labor, and from his fellow man. Machiavelli differed from Plato,

Rousseau, Diderot, and Marx in that he advised the Prince to consider men as if they were evil and he believed the stability of the state as a republic would come about through the vitality of men in constant opposition to each other. Machiavelli accepted alienation and wished to make the best of it; the religious thinkers have higher hopes.

Alienation, however, is basic to the definition of man. He is *Homo sapiens,* and to merit that name he must be sufficiently alienated from the world to have the sense of wonder that led the Greeks to philosophy. He is not, as Marx said in *The German Ideology,* different from animals because he produces; he is, as Marx said in the same work, human because of his consciousness: "Consciousness is at first, of course, merely consciousness concerning the immediate sensuous environment and conciousness of the limited connection with other persons and things outside the individual who is growing self-conscious. At the same time it is consciousness of nature, which first appears to men as a completely alien, all-powerful, and unassailable force, with which men's relations are purely animal and by which they are overawed like beasts; it is thus a purely animal consciousness of nature (natural religion)." He goes on to argue against his own recognition, calling the consciousness born of alienation from nature "sheep-like or tribal." Yet he says that consciousness of other men leads to language, which he calls "practical consciousness." Animals have no language, according to Marx, because they have no relationships. Neither can animals be alienated. The attempt to resolve the contradiction in *The German Ideology* between consciousness and production as the defining characteristic of man turns on a trick of language every bit as embarrassing as the notion of "pre-history."

To oppose alienation is the problem of a man who wishes an earthly paradise for man, as Marx did when he wrote: ". . . in communist society, where nobody has one exclusive sphere of activity but each can become accomplished in any branch he wishes, society regulates the general production and thus makes it possible for me to do one thing today and another tomorrow, to hunt in the morning, fish in the afternoon, rear cattle in the evening, criticize after dinner, just as I have a mind, without ever becoming hunter, fisherman, shepherd or critic." In that famous passage, Marx shows no less love for man than the greatest saints of the Church, he too finds heaven at the end of earthly suffering; the last convulsive struggle before communism is akin to the death that releases us to heaven.

If there are public toilets in communism, who will clean them? If there are books to criticize in communism, who will work in the paper mills and type shops and binderies? If there is meat in communism, who will work in the slaughterhouses? Who will find himself happily objectified in a public toilet or the stench of a paper mill or the blood rivers of the slaughterhouse? When men find their desires fulfilled by scrubbing away the stains left by the excreta of other men's bowels, we will have found hell on earth rather than heaven.

It is man's capacity to feel alienated that makes him human. Maggots and rats live happily in sewers, a thirsty dog drinks gladly from the water in a public toilet, an ant lives unconsciously through the routine of its life, the ox takes to the plow and the horse to the harness, man seeks more; he is capable of discontent, and as long as he is discontented he remains human, the seeker who finds his greatest solace in the search.

Alienation from nature gave wonder (*thaumazein*) to the Greeks, who began philosophy by stepping out of the world to examine it. Alienation from the conditions of slavery gave revolt to the Hebrews who crossed the Red Sea into freedom. Alienation also fired the revolt against Rome led by Spartacus. Alienation from the world led St. Paul to locate freedom in the mind. Alienation destroyed feudalism, led to labor unions as capitalism became intolerable to the workers, and has begun to lead men to the modification and perhaps the eventual destruction of capitalism. Alienation as part of man's consciousness always leads him toward freedom and improvement of the material conditions of his life.

Even neolithic societies, those very like the communism Marx describes or more accurately hints about coming after the period Lenin explains as "the whole of society [having] become a single office and a single factory . . ." are rich in alienation. Some anthropologists place the number of different, that is, mutually unintelligible, languages in pre-Columbian America at over 2,500. If we accept as given that people sprang from some central source or language group rather than popping up overnight like so many mushrooms, the sense of alienation from the tribe, its leaders, and its work patterns must have been so great in at least 2,500 instances that men moved to a new place and founded a new culture. There must be something imperfect in paradise.

The imperfection in paradise can only be man, his quickness to feel alienated and discontented, living in a world promising such infinite possibility that even the closed circle of the neolithic worldview could be broken open by discontent. What numbers of primitive men and women died in deserts and snows, oceans and mountains can never be known, but it can be assumed that they were substantial, perhaps in proportion even greater than those who died in later, modern wars of revolution and liberation. The nature of man, contrary to the views of such cranks and hucksters of chemical oppression as the current sociobiologists, is to be alienated from his own nature and from nature in general; he enjoys the inevitable discontent of consciousness, for he can compare his life to his infinite imagination. The idea devolves from Hegel: "The alienation on the part of spirit from its natural existence is . . . the individual's true and original nature, his very substance." Man's only home is in his consciousness, where he is not a stranger.

How strange the social world is, where all men are of equal

value and none are valued equally! The failure of reason cannot but produce an apotheosis of reason, as in Rousseau and Marx. How can man be human unless he is not himself, unless he is more than the animal that he was born? If man does not, as Hegel said, create himself by his own thought, he surely differentiates himself from other animals and other men, he creates his estrangement, which distinguishes society from the herd.

Unalienated, man belongs to the herd, each man like every other. In that situation his loneliness would be unbearable, for there would be no one in the world for him to know but multiples of himself. Without plurality, which comes only from estrangement, men would be mute beasts, like the imagined ancestors of *Homo sapiens* sold to the public by dime store anthropologists.

Erich Fromm and to some extent Simone Weil describe alienation as passivity, the role of the object, the receptor. The error in that description comes as a result of considering man's situation rather than man as primary. By their point of view they make man an object and say that the object suffers alienation. More accurately, one would say that because of a certain situation man *feels* alienated, he initiates alienation as his response to the situation; only when he is in an alienating situation and does not feel alienated is he passive. Is it possible for man to be estranged, oppressed, made into the herd creature, mass man, without feeling alienated? Of course; all through history men have suffered in silence, accepting their suffering, "adjusting" to it. That is what Rousseau meant when he said, "Slaves lose everything in their chains, even the desire of escaping from them: they love their servitude, as the comrades of Ulysses loved their brutish condition. If there are slaves by nature, it is because there have been slaves against nature. Force made the first slaves, and their cowardice perpetuated the condition." Perhaps not cowardice exactly, but passivity, the inability or fear that inhibits the feeling of alienation, that peculiarly human discontent.

Man feels alienated when his autonomy and thus his dignity has been affronted. But we have also come to understand, through Hegel, that alienation is at the root of his humanity. Can alienation be both the feeling of being human and the discontent of being less than human? We would do better to distinguish between the two feelings by using different words for them than by having to attach a definition to each use of the word. Hegel meant by alienation the separation of man from unconscious nature, the self-consciousness that has substance, estrangement from an undifferentiated universal unconscious. We can distinguish Hegelian alienation by calling it *wonder*.

For Hegel's sense of the alienation of property, the giving of a thing into another's possession, which for Marx becomes the alienation of the product of one's labor and therefore the alienation of oneself, we can use the word *loss*.

The joining in some form of social contract in which one surrenders or transfers his rights we may call *cession*.

Estrangement thus comes to mean loneliness, the feeling of not belonging.

Cession may be a way to overcome estrangement, for example, but in the extreme it destroys wonder, leaving man less than human.

Finally, *alienation* is the active feeling of discontent, a response to loss, estrangement, or cession in the extreme. There are two effective cures for alienation: extreme cession, the reduction of man to a passive state, as in totalitarian societies; or destruction of the sense of wonder, which leaves man incapable of alienation. In the process of destroying alienation, estrangement becomes a means for leading man to extreme cession, the state in which he no longer consciously suffers loss. The great delusion of extreme cession is happiness as defined by others, the carrot that is employed along with fear of estrangement and fear of physical suffering (hunger, poverty, etc.) to destroy man's autonomy.

In the total cession demanded by Rousseau, Marx, and Plato, man becomes a completely passive creature. He may, by ceding his alienation, achieve happiness, but only at the cost of his humanity. The philosophers who know man best perhaps love him less than do Marx or Rousseau, but they are willing to permit him to live in his blundering, human way. The republican views of Machiavelli and Madison expect small cessions to social and political order, but they encompass alienation as an active force, they demand discontent to feed man's vitality, they are satisfied with the pursuit of happiness as the only happiness possible for man. They are the pagans who believe the stability of nations is made by the political acts of autonomous men. For them there is no means but conflict in freedom and no end but man himself.

A Literature of Inadvertence

The decline of political philosophy occurred at the same time as the rise of technology. In the twentieth century the main currents of philosophy turned to ontology and analysis and the contemplation of man as a political creature was abandoned by most writers and teachers in favor of the apolitical viewpoints of psychology and sociology. The psychologist, unlike the political philosopher, laid claim to the methods of science: he constructed experiments, devised tests, used machines, and wrote down the data in the same fashion as his brethren in science who studied the interactions of chemicals or subatomic particles. His aim was to employ objective methods to gain a scientific understanding of human behavior; and by virtue of that objective knowledge he sought to help man find happiness, which many psychologists defined as making a good adjustment to one's circumstances.

Experimental situations involving human beings led to bizarre ideas: some psychologists determined that rats were suitable analogues for man; others chose synecdoche, believing that man could be represented by the movements of his eyes or the temperature of his skin at the fingertips; schools of chemical man and electrical man experimented with drugs and electric shock; and the experimenters in behavior went to the extremes represented by Stanley Milgram's study of obedience, in which men and women were ordered to torture another human being under laboratory conditions.

There were exceptions, of course, mainly in the psychoanalytic school. Some, like R. D. Laing, opposed the idea of adjustment to a society gone mad, arguing that wars, purges, nuclear weapons, and hunger amidst plenty were more certain signs of madness than the fantasies of those we generally institutionalize. Still others told their patients that adjustment to misery in their own lives was ridiculous, advising them to fight misery rather than learning to be content and comfortable with it.

The exceptions were few. Psychology and its sister pseudo-science, sociology, held that the world was a given and that man had simply to make the best of it. The fields produced revolutionaries in the direction of control rather than freedom, for most psychologists viewed man as the chemist viewed molecules and the botanist viewed wheat. Psychology is technology applied to man himself as if he were a thing to be dissected, changed, used; and no matter how humanistic their intentions, the psychologists could not overcome the politics of the distinction between the observer and the observed.

A good example of the danger of that distinction occurs in Studs Terkel's *Working*. Mr. Terkel is an old Left celebrity, a sort of media Wobbly, very much on the side of the poor and downtrodden of this earth, but his journey through various occupations in America turns up only one that is truly satisfying, interesting, meaningful—and Mr. Terkel has that job. For the rest of America, working is "a Monday through Friday sort of dying." In a military officer ordering the killing of soldiers or civilians of another race or culture that kind of response is the thesis of the Gook: those who are different from us are a lower form of life, less than human. In Mr. Terkel, a certifiably compassionate man, it serves to illustrate the tendency of the student of man to raise himself to the level of a god in the process of getting a good view of the situation.

Political philosophy treats man as the subject, psychology treats him as the object to be studied, and objectification demeans man. At its worst, psychology turns to statistics to create mass man in the computer, using the technique of polling, with its conflating questions that prohibit individual variation and put subtlety into oblivion. As a statistic, man has no political existence, because politics exist in real relations between men, which are not accounted for in statistics. Mass man, the product of the psychologist's statistics, is utterly without dignity or meaning; in America, for example, a sample of a thousand adults will most likely have a statistical error of plus or minus three percentage points when applied to the entire adult population, meaning that the death of any single adult in America, whether included in the sampling or not, has no effect. That is quite unlike the vote of one person in a democratic election, where each vote is counted and there is theoretically no statistical error: one vote could decide an election, but the sampling error inherent in statistics eliminates the meaning of any individual.*

Statistics perform violence on everyone in the nation by forcing the cession of their individual views into narrow channels and then committing mathematical murder on the au-

* For a more detailed discussion see this writer's "Market Democracy," *Harper's,* November 1978.

tonomous existence of the entire population. Man may defend himself against statisticians with laughter or he may learn enough about the gathering and interpretation of statistical information about human thoughts to defend himself with scorn. He may spare himself the ideas of clinical psychologists by avoiding their works in print and by choosing not to seek their help in solving his personal problems; only the industrial psychologist cannot be avoided, for industrial psychology has become as much a part of the job in America and all other industrialized nations as the payroll tax; and like the tax, industrial psychology is imposed upon the worker for the ultimate benefit of him.

The industrial psychologist truly believes that he is contributing to the welfare of both the owner and the worker. However, workers do not pay industrial psychologists to improve their lives; owners and managers use psychology to improve efficiency and return on investment. The economic incentive weighs heavily on the side of management even in the writing of books and articles, for workers are not likely to purchase books on management and motivation, and the universities that take joy in the publications of their faculty members are not likely to receive gifts from blue collar workers or middle managers. Business schools are for business; there are no labor schools. Thus the whole thrust of industrial psychology, organizational study, and management theory is aimed at using the worker for the good of the organization. Even his happiness is important to the industrial psychologist only insofar as it benefits the organization.

It would be unfair, however, to characterize the industrial psychologist or the management theorist or even the efficiency expert as a conscious enemy of the worker. These people have made major contributions to the improvement of productivity, which has led to a higher standard of living for many workers, and they have helped to some extent in the struggle for better working conditions. The oppressive effect of their suggestions on the worker up through middle management has been almost entirely inadvertent. No major theorist in the field would consider himself a proponent of totalitarian methods of management; yet that is exactly what they propose as the solution to problems of efficiency in modern business, and as the production worker gives way to the knowledge worker and the service worker, the use of totalitarian methods increases. The knowledge worker, who more or less manages himself, will become the most important target for the purveyors of methods of motivation, for he occupies the position of a middle manager in relation to the executive.

The first effort to move from authoritarian to totalitarian methods in managing labor was Frederick Taylor's scientific management. Taylor presented his system of the extreme rationalization of labor as a panacea, claiming that it would increase production through efficiency, raise wages, and bring about such harmony between labor and management that strikes would seldom, if ever, occur. Taylorism simply reduces men to atomized parts of a happy machine by lowering job content to a level at which man can perform without thought. The manager discovers everything about the job in Taylorism and then prescribes the most efficient way of performing each simple task. In 1918 Lenin gave the back of his hand to capitalist brutality and then advised the Soviet Union to study Taylor's principles of scientific management to improve the efficiency of workers.

It would seem curious for Lenin to praise Taylorism, which has often been cited by American unionists as the most demeaning system of work, but that is not the case at all: industrial psychology and Marxism are similar in that both have as a goal the elimination of the worker's feelings of alienation. Even before Taylor, the Frenchman Fayol was preaching esprit de corps, subordination of the individual interest to the general interest and harmony between manager and worker. But the extension of his methods of management to the general society horrified Fayol, who was, with good reason, unable to imagine the size and scope of the modern corporation or its existence as a society within a society.

Fayol and Taylor set a pattern for industrial psychology that has not been broken: they opposed the conflict of alienation as inefficient and inhuman and attempted to replace it with methods that would make the laborers a seamless extension of management, harmoniously interlocking in task and goal like the warp and woof of finely woven cloth. They did not use the terminology of Marxism, but as Lenin demonstrated by embracing Taylorism, the distinctions between socialist and capitalist executives in their relation to middle managers on through laborers have little meaning: a Marxist steel mill and a capitalist steel mill make identical demands on the coal shoveler of Taylor's famous example of scientific management. Karl Marx's interest in harnessing the productive forces of men differs not at all from that of Andrew Carnegie; the American industrialist merely lacked Marx's utopian vision.

Industrial psychologists, Marxists, and executives all want men to be happy in their work, and the happiness they define is the disappearance of the man into the group or organization or society. His feelings of alienation, the active opposition to cession of himself into the group, corporation, or state, are in all three views counterproductive: alienated men are political in that they are aware of their relations with other men, and politics makes men difficult to control because they see themselves as ends, putting the pursuit of their own happiness before the happiness that makes use of them. Political men, of course, can and do compromise their alienation by ceding part of their freedom to the group, but alienated men tend to drive hard bargains: they are no more likely to permit themselves to passively accept the dictates of the state or the corporation than the first men to discover their alienation from nature were willing to live under the dictates of nature. As the Greeks were led to science and philosophy by their alienation, modern workers are led to freedom and individual dignity.

The Human Relations movement, founded by Elton Mayo, whose analysis of the Hawthorne Electric experiments led him to a different understanding of how to manage workers, extended more deeply into the organization the effort to thwart the active feelings of alienation. Mayo became interested in group relations among the workers as well as the relations between individual workers and their supervisors. He sought ways to increase co-operation within the group, but at the same time he removed the management view of the worker from the individual to the group—the object became larger and more distant, cession at an earlier level was encouraged.

Nearly thirty years after Mayo's experiments began in the late 1920s, Chris Argyris wrote that "One of the basic assumptions of the approach is that the individual and the organization are not separable." For Argyris as for his predecessors, "Unfortunately, the formal organizational strategy hits some snags—the primary one being the individual human being." It is a sentence worth mulling, for it holds in its choice of language a key to the view of man held by the modern industrial psychologist. One cannot imagine Machiavelli, Madison, or Marx describing individual human beings as "snags." The loving attack by Marx on the alienation of man has been turned against man. Both Marx and Argyris would dispute the Machiavellian view of a republic made stable by conflict, but Marx is willing to cede the spirit of man only in a communist utopia while Argyris gives his "snags" over to the organization here and now.

Rensis Likert believes that "an organization will function best when its personnel function not as individuals but as members of highly effective work groups with high-performance goals." Frederick Herzberg has developed a "motivation-hygiene" theory, which has "personnel adjustment" as its goal. Eric Trist wishes to overcome alienation by combining the methods of sociological and technological studies of organizations. An astonishingly management-centered view of alienation has been presented by Richard Walton of the Harvard Business School. Writing in *Work in America,* a work produced by a task force under the auspices of the Department of Health, Education and Welfare, Walton defines alienation by its symptoms: "tardiness, absenteeism and turnover, and inattention on the job . . . pilferage, sabotage, deliberate waste, assaults, bomb threats, and other disruptions of work routines." He also considers it alienation when employees cooperate with "newsmen, congressional committees, regulatory agencies, and protest groups in exposing objectionable practices." Walton's concern, of course, centers on production and not on freedom; the politics of laboring do not exist for him.

The inability to understand the politics of laboring derives directly from the godlike view of man adopted by sociologists and psychologists. Even in the work of Robert Blauner, which takes a Marxist (with modifications) view, one may read the following:

> Still, studying the worker from the viewpoint of the intellectual observer with his own values and conceptions of freedom and self-realization, we must conclude that alienation remains a widespread phenomenon in the factory today. But we must also approach the problem from the perspective of the worker. . . . People with limited educations are most concerned with being free from restrictive and oppressive conditions. The absence of opportunities to develop inner potential, to express idiosyncratic abilities, and to assume responsibility and decision-making functions, may not be a source of serious discontent to most workers today. For this reason, empirical studies show that the majority of industrial workers are satisfied with their work and with their jobs.

A tradition begun by Marx continues in writing about work at all levels in business: the conclusions are based on thirdhand or at best secondhand information. The worker never speaks as subject, only as the object of interviewers or observers, whose work, in turn, becomes the object of further observers. The variety of people who earn a living by laboring in factories cannot ever become evident to the observers because there are no questions on the interview forms to elicit their individuality. A man who passed most of thirty years on an assembly line in Michigan by reciting long speeches from Shakespeare to himself would hardly fit into Blauner's picture of a factory worker, but such a man exists. Another assembly line worker has a passionate interest in Beethoven, and another has escaped from the stress and low wages of teaching in a high school to the highly paid routine of factory work, and yet another saves his money to travel to distant places. Vast numbers of factory workers have completed high school and attended college for a year or more. I have personally lost at chess to a railroad laborer and learned about underwater motion picture photography from a longshoreman. I have admired the paintings of assembly line workers and discussed gourmet cooking with sewing machine operators. A laborer in the sugar cane fields of Hawaii gave me lessons in ethnography, and a most lucid explanation of a certain period of Mexican history was delivered to me and several other surprised travelers by a migrant fruit picker returning to his home in Zamora.

It is not a romantic view of laboring people that contrasts with the cruel maxims of the sociologists; reality contradicts their generalizations. There are many dull-witted people working in fields and factories, but there are also many dull-witted people practicing medicine, teaching school, managing corporations, and working as sociologists. The assumption that a man and his labor are of the same intellectual or cultural level is founded in the arrogance of the observer. Despite the structural similarity of men and of the minds of men, both men and minds are infinitely variegated, and the Marxist notion that man creates himself through his labor simply does not prove out in reality. Neither can it be shown that labor creates man.

Man can only create himself, as Kant might have said, through his freedom; otherwise, he is created, an object, without dignity. Yet those who would aid him in his life and his productivity are often willing to sacrifice his autonomy, which is his essential well-being, on behalf of his physical or social well-being. Anthony Downs, in his work for the Rand Corporation, *Inside Bureaucracy*, makes this clear: "The word *freedom* has two very different meanings: power of choice, and absence of restraint. It is true that bureaus place far more restraints on the average man today than they did formerly. However, today's citizen also enjoys a much greater range in choice of possible behavior than his predecessors did. Moreover, the number of behavioral options open to him is growing every year through such changes as supersonic aircraft, new medicines, rising real income, increased foreign trade, better highways, longer vacations, higher retirement pensions, and a host of others."

The promise of Mr. Downs's work has been made by all totalitarian theorists: in return for the cession of one's autonomy one receives material benefits. He expresses a peculiarly bourgeois understanding of freedom, the very understanding that leads Hannah Arendt, for one, to attack the bourgeois for being the first and most willing accomplice of totalitarianism. Not one present-day sociologist or industrial psychologist suggests that man should merely sell his labor in a bargain with his employer, giving his loyalty insofar as he is paid for it. They have all adopted the Marxist view of labor in which that extremely limited bargain results in alienation, estrangement, normlessness, etc. None will accept that man could sell but little of himself in a straightforward bargain between buyer and seller, retain the greatest degree of freedom, and still perform his labor effectively.

Even those who claim to be defenders of civil rights, like David Ewing of the Harvard Business School, are, when dealing with business, seeking to meld men into seamless, efficient organizations. In his book *Freedom Inside the Organization,* Ewing says, "Rights also create devotion to the enterprise. They create the kind of spirit which leads a person to think, 'I am a small part of my company, but my company is a big part of me.'" The basic problem in Ewing's work is that he compares the company to a nation, using the original thirteen states of the Union as an example. From that beginning, he can comfortably cede the autonomy of the individual to a corporation that cannot be dismissed, for one lives in the corporation that Ewing imagines, having the kind of loyalties one might have to his own land, his own country. It leads to the kind of confusion that plagues Rousseau: man is to be free inside the society (the corporation), but the Legislator (executive) is to lead him to knowing the General Will (corporate policy), which is the best interest of man.

"No realist," writes Mr. Ewing, "will argue that companies, government bureaus, and other public agencies should be run democratically. There must be discipline. There must be control." Curiously, he recognizes that totalitarian methods are used in corporations, even quoting executives of Sears Roebuck and ITT to support his thesis; yet the purpose of his book is to extend the corporation more deeply into the employee, to achieve the kind of control that makes the more crude, ostensible coercions of totalitarianism unnecessary. His rationale for promoting identification of the worker with the organization is the same as that of Blauner, Argyris, Fayol, and others: ". . . To regard people and organizations as existing on opposite sides of a wall cannot be healthy."

The Ewing work makes obvious the inherent contradiction in the efforts of well-meaning sociologists and industrial psychologists, a contradiction that Freud recognized when he described "the principal phenomenon of group psychology" as "the individual's lack of freedom in a group." In the effort to prevent the activity of alienation by eliminating the sense of estrangement and disguising the feeling of loss, they endanger freedom by ceding more and more to the group. Blauner noted that "dissatisfaction is dignity," which is among the fruits of freedom. Gorky went further in his autobiography, saying, ". . . men are created by their resilience to their environment." The alienation felt by the novelist in tsarist Russia led him to overcoming his failure to be accepted at any university, his background as the child of a beggar, and his labor in bakeries and on the docks. Alienation in Gorky became revolt.† Ewing and his school do not want revolt. Cession is what they are after, the kind of utter cession advised by John Cowan in *The Self-Reliant Manager:* "The myth that the company has no right to your soul was invented by those lazy employees who hope to put in only seven hours a day and be successful as well. The company certainly can't demand that you give your soul, but it will reward those who do far more than it will reward those who do not."

Men like Cowan, Ewing, Argyris, and Herzberg understand very well Spinoza's maxim: "If men's minds were as easily controlled as their tongues, every king would sit safely on his throne. . . ." The role in which they are cast is that of defender of the king. They minister to the minds of workers who report to the executive, devising methods to make the seat of power safe from the alienated acts of individuals who use their freedom.

The method itself requires the sabotaging of the distinction between work and labor, although the putative mission of industrial psychology is to convert labor into work, to make the repetitions of labor into the satisfactions of work, to convert

† Gorky's capitulation to the state in the declining years of his life is one of the tragedies of men wrought by weariness and fear. Young men have always made the best soldiers and the most dedicated radicals; they come naturally by their courage. When an old man, like Socrates, acts according to his considered principles, the triumph belongs not to nature but to man.

the atomistic feelings of the laborer into the wholeness of the worker, to make emptiness into fulfillment, to change the loneliness of the laborer into the solitude of the worker, to make the product of labor equal in comprehensibility and permanence to the product of work. But the task is impossible. Labor is not work. The literature of inadvertence advises in reality nothing more than a grand deceit: to dress labor in the costume of work. The increases in productivity ascribed to industrial psychology are more properly ascribed to improvements in technology. With the recent slowing of those improvements, productivity has ceased to increase. For all that it takes from men's dignity as autonomous creatures, industrial psychology gives very little in return. Neither can industrial psychology be credited with much of the change to more tolerable working conditions in offices and factories; those changes came about mainly because of the union movement. The inadvertent literature of totalitarianism produces a definition of happiness useful to the accomplishment of executive goals and devises means for imposing that definition on employees. It is an instrument of power instead of the way to freedom it wishes to be.

6

Aliens

Workers have no human history. They are silent, invisible, like the things of the earth and the blind events generated by great forces. A collective of workers has power, but no single worker, blue collar, white collar, or middle manager, has a human existence beyond the sound of his voice or the stench of his sweat. The literature of workers is as fraudulent as objectivity and as deceptive as a liar's inductions. Labor, the engine of society, is hidden under a smooth and shiny surface, like the engine of an automobile.

All that the world knows of workers and their lives at work comes from the observations of passersby. Marx knew nothing of factory work, Simone Weil spent six months in a factory, Harvey Swados took his notebook with him to his job *On the Line,* Alan Harrington passed through *Life in the Crystal Palace,* Studs Terkel learned about *Working* with a tape recorder, William Gaddis has permitted form to eliminate the content of what he knows. In movies and novels, work appears as a backdrop for the personal and emotional actions of the story, work is never the story. Yet work is the center of most lives, the home of most men and many women.

The failure of work to have made a human history for the

worker lies in the conflict between the kinds of work required
to make histories and the kind required to mine coal or build
bridges or balance accounts or manage small groups of people: art is the work of artists, and the artist who labors in other
fields merely pretends; and so it is with journalists and psychologists and sociologists and philosophers; a man with two labors is an amateur at one of them.

Records reveal tons of coal mined, numbers of automobiles
assembled, hours worked, wages paid, accidents suffered, promotions, dismissals, retirements, deaths, but not the human
history. Thoughts remain secret. The aches and pleasures of
the laboring man's life die with him. In the popular culture—
television, cheap novels, newspaper stories—he is a dunce and
a victim, racist, narrow, venal, angry, acquisitive, and utterly
defeated. In the sophisticated literature—academic research,
documentary films, and writings—he is a dunce and a victim,
racist, narrow, venal, angry, etc. The lack of distinction results
from the similarity of viewpoint: a silent man seen from a
great distance seems the same no matter who views him; there
is simply not enough information for the more subtle mind to
engage the subject.

Or is that view of the observer too charitable? Workers may
provide the comforts of status to those who belong to the class
of observers only if workers are unhappy, stupefied by their labors, unable to look to the future with hope. If the labor of a
union member in the steel industry were not unbearable, how
could the schoolteacher, who earns considerably less money,
justify his life in the classroom? The exploitation of labor by
pity has interesting economic consequences. Pity of blue collar
workers is the primary means of holding down the wages of
white collar workers: they are compensated with prestige for
what they do not receive in their paychecks. Similarly, pity for
blue collar workers serves to keep white collar workers from
forming or joining unions.

The lowest-paid white collar workers, of course, are the

most in need of prestige and therefore the least willing to form unions. At a meeting of non-union white collar workers in San Francisco in the late 1960s, the most successful and highest-paid people in a specialized field sought to form a union, mainly to protect their colleagues who were less well paid and less secure in their jobs. Before the issue could be called to a vote, the lowest-paid members of the group angrily walked out.

An executive of a New York publishing house with an immaculately left-wing list often entertains dinner companions with discussions of the sufferings of assembly line workers. Clerks and editorial assistants in his publishing house are paid less than half as much as assembly line workers, get few fringe benefits, and have no job security. One young woman in that publishing house was invited to bed by her male supervisor; when she rejected the invitation, it was made clear to her that she would have to leave the company.

Foremen in assembly plants also proposition the women they supervise, but the foreman who attempts to dismiss a woman who has rejected him risks shutting down a plant or even an entire industry, if the woman belongs to a strong union. By contrast, the woman at the publishing house first attempted to transfer to another department, and failing in that, perhaps for lack of a good recommendation from her supervisor, quietly resigned.

Pity for the blue collar worker demands revulsion at the thought of his work and the assumption that he would prefer to do the work of the observer; in other words, the assumption that all men are the same and given the same opportunity would choose to do the same kind of work. Happiness, as always, belongs to those who define it, and happiness has never been defined by men with blunted fingernails and grease-stained hands.

Reality differs somewhat from the economically efficient myths of laboring. Two psychiatrists and a psychologist from Rutgers University Medical School, writing in the *Archives of*

General Psychiatry in 1974, were surprised to find no abnormal incidence of mental illness among workers in a Baltimore automobile assembly plant. They were more surprised to find that 95 per cent of the workers were satisfied with their jobs (confirming similar data gathered by the University of Michigan Survey Research Center) and 71 per cent "reported no part of their work as tiring or upsetting." The researchers were able to admit that their surprise resulted from the bias they brought to the project. Furthermore, they found that some of the assembly line workers thought the work of sociology "more boring, more alienating, more fraught with anomie, than [their] own existence."

Mental illness was lower in proportion to the population among the blue collar workers studied in the Baltimore plant than in the midtown Manhattanites studied by Srole. The incidence of breakdowns, according to the authors, was the same among the assembly line workers as among fishermen in Nova Scotia and workers in rural North Carolina. Their paper expresses disagreement with Fromm and Marx, not for political reasons, but over the difference between theory developed in the nineteenth century and the reality of the last third of the twentieth century.

At the base of the failure of Marxist thinking to apply to modern blue collar workers one must suspect the development of the union movement and the change it wrought in the meaning of alienation. A survey of 1,515 workers by the University of Michigan Institute of Social Research lends inductive credence to the foregoing deduction: 71 per cent of the blue collar workers studied in 1977 said they were satisfied with their own union; 66 per cent mentioned only such positive goals for union efforts as improving job security or economic benefits.

In a less structured fashion, I have talked with more than a hundred factory workers in the past four years, some of them at length, some for only a few minutes, and I have found them

interesting, discontented, and dignified. They are united in
their dissimilarity: every man or woman I talked with defines
himself or herself by life outside the factory. Many are deeply
involved with their children, and they speak proudly of college
students, clergymen, athletes, engineers, sons who have moved
into the management of the very factories in which their fathers labor on the assembly line. Factory workers may devote
themselves to fishing or classical music, the study of Shakespeare or softball, some go home from their factory jobs to run
small family farms, others save their money to spend it on vacations in Europe or Florida, many have been able to buy a
second home beside a lake or in a wooded area. The exception
would be the man or woman who goes from a grim job to a
grim little house and does nothing but drink beer and watch
television. Unionized blue collar workers belong to the middle
class, and they have middle-class values: it is not uncommon
to hear an electrical worker complain that cars cost too much
because auto workers are overpaid.

One need only glance at the modern union member's work
schedule to understand why he devotes so much of his energy
to life outside the job: four fifths of his life takes place off the
job. Spread across a full 365-day year the factory worker with
a strong union spends less than five hours a day on the job. He
is a man very like the creature dreamed of in Marx's *German
Ideology:* he does one thing today and another tomorrow, he
hunts in the morning, fishes in the afternoon, rears cattle in the
evening, and criticizes after dinner; he is human and free, paying but one fifth of his life to enjoy the rest of his days, and
doing so for only twenty-five or thirty years until he retires. A
man who lives seventy-five years, spending but one third of
those years in factory work, retiring on a decent sum, pays but
one fifteenth of his life to his employer. That amounts to an
average of one hour and thirty-six minutes a day over the
course of his life or two and one half hours a day over the

course of his possible working years. He devotes himself to his leisure by necessity: it is the major portion of his life.

But what happens during those brief hours of work also affects men's lives. No one can deny that much blue collar work is hard, repetitive, boring, frequently unhealthful, and sometimes dangerous. Even so, the psychological battering of work on the assembly line cannot compare to the totalitarian methods used with white collar and middle management workers. I have asked at least a hundred factory workers in dozens of different unionized plants, "Who are you afraid of around here? Who do you have to watch out for?" And each of them has given the same answer, almost to the word: "You don't have to be afraid of anybody, if you do your work." And many have gone on to say that it wasn't necessary to be afraid of anybody in that plant whether one did his work or not. The question about fear always comes as a surprise; it isn't part of the consciousness of the modern union member. He worries more about the national economy and the sales of the products he makes. He complains about inflation, taxes, government spending, the effect of government regulation on the products he makes, and then he talks about his job-related problems. He doesn't like management and he takes his union for granted. Alienation has made him rich, alienation has made him free; he cherishes and nourishes his discontent.

Although it is not the purpose of this book to essay the situation of blue collar workers, it may be of use to consider the lot of the blue collar worker in a brief way so as to illuminate by contrast the life of white collar and middle management workers. Historically, the blue collar worker has been considered the victim of economic society, dehumanized, exploited, enslaved, and since the industrial revolution a powerless appendage of a machine. The question to consider here, knowing that blue collar workers in union shops are well paid and no more subject to mental illness than the general population, is whether the blue collar worker is subject to the tactics of totalitarianism or whether his work, his union, and his alienation protect him.

Twenty-five aspects of blue collar work in a union shop are outlined below. They do not include health hazards, boredom, or the lack of social status, which we have seen have other economic uses. The only criterion used in assembling the following list was whether or not these aspects of life in a unionized factory were relevant to the politics of working.

1. When Simone Weil was only twenty-five years old, she wrote of the life she had seen and known, however briefly, in four months at the Alsthom electrical works and a little more than two months at the Renault automobile plant. No writing before or since has been more loving of man, more appreciative of the value of work itself, or more touching in its wish to rescue man from his bondage to the machine and his sense of helplessness before the power of the bosses. In the later works of her brief life, Weil considered the stability of balance as an answer to the problems of power, rejecting that notion as a "chimera." Yet it is just such a balance—the dream of Machiavelli, Balzac, and Madison—between the company and the union that has alleviated the blue collar worker's sense of helplessness on the job. Away from his place of work he may feel helpless to prevent war, stop inflation, control his own government or even his own children, but in the factory he deals with the company as an equal, because he negotiates as part of a union. In isolated confrontation with a foreman or supervisor, the balance of power may actually be on the side of the union worker.

2. Journalists and academicians who spend a few days or months on an assembly line cite the lack of communication between workers as one of the dehumanizing elements of factory work. They are more likely to be reporting their own loneliness on the job, for elitism is not tolerated on the line, and men who speak and dress and act in the manner of another class are considered interlopers. In reality, the line is not critical in its judgments of people, nor is it demanding: one may be gregarious or silent, a busybody or a loner; the line tolerates great variation in styles of behavior. It is a place where secrets have no use and no place, for the leveling of unionism and of the line itself relieve men of the need to compete; if the workers on the line struggle, they struggle together against the boss, the working conditions, or the work itself.

3. Workers in factories have no sense of estrangement from the product of their work; they do, in fact, have a simple but clear conception of the product that eventually comes from their labors. Their experience with the product or some part of it is direct, involving, "hands on" experience.

4. Blue collar workers belong to the class of blue collar workers, which is not defined as much by economics as by the type of work and the place in which it is done. The astonishing rise in wages brought about by collective bargaining has moved most blue collar workers into the middle class. While blue collar workers still retain many of the cultural values of the old working class, they have also taken on much of the life coloration of the middle class. Only blue collar workers in some service industries, agriculture, and a few non-union plants retain the complete mentality of the working class. In strict economic terms, auto workers, steelworkers, teamsters, rubber workers, electrical workers, communications workers, and members of many other unions belong to a new bourgeoisie, one whose property is the pension fund and the supplementary unemployment benefit. This new bourgeoisie differs from the shopkeeper class in that it achieves its wealth through union rather than through atomization and competition. That this new subgroup within the middle class has not been recognized as such by journalists and academicians is a tribute to the need of the middle class to define itself by re-

stricting upward mobility and to the ability of the society to
maintain the white collar middle class at a low standard of living by supplementing its wages with status.

5. Whether one accepts the Marxist concept of class struggle or accepts the more overtly tautological definition of a
class as a subset within a society struggling to achieve something, if only its own identity, blue collar workers are a class
united by their struggle. Moreover, they are united in the most
powerful way: they have had some success. Whether entrance
into the middle class and the adoption of many bourgeois
values will eventually destroy the class unity of blue collar
workers is difficult to predict. There is no precedent for Western industrial society, with its great gap between the bourgeoisie and the lumpen proletariat. Blue collar workers may
very well choose to remain a class within a class or they may
blend into the great middle class. The latter seems an unlikely
prospect for the near future, since the other members of the
middle class will continue to define blue collar workers as a
class by according them low social status.

6. Wage agreements made through collective bargaining
contribute to the class unity of blue collar workers. The
knowledge that all men on an assembly line who do similar
work earn the same wage eliminates the sense of work as competition, uniting men in far-reaching ways. Not only do they
avoid the atomizing effect of secrecy, they live in similar fashion, enjoying similar opportunities for recreation, buying of
goods and services, and education of their children. One man
may choose to spend his money on beer and motorcycles while
another uses his wages to send his children to Yale, for unity
in an economic class does not make men into robots or dupli-
cates; the economic similarity merely gives them the same
range of options within which to express their individuality.

7. Class distinctions in factories have begun to disappear.

The foreman, who once came from the middle class, now comes up from the working class or the blue collar subgroup of the middle class. As the first line supervisor and the person most likely to affect the lives of blue collar workers, the foreman sets the tone of work and class within the factory, and he no longer sets that tone from a distance. The foreman in many cases is now too much a blue collar man to enjoy supervision without ambivalence; his sympathies are divided between management and workers. He may be a better supervisor in many respects, but he is very much less the taskmaster than the organizer of work, he is taught to seek co-operation from the men he supervises, he does not seek obedience. The most severe pressures of work have been lifted from the backs of the blue collar workers and placed squarely on their ambivalent first line supervisors. Even second and third line supervisors in some factories have begun to blur the class lines, asking workers to call them by their given names, seeking co-operation rather than dominance, knowing that fear can not motivate men who feel that power has shifted far enough in their direction to achieve a balance between them and management.

8. The blue collar worker in a union shop knows exactly what rules he must live by while on the job. The rules are set in negotiation between the union and management. Workers use the negotiating power of the shop steward and the threat of a walkout to make certain that work rules are not changed capriciously.

9. Company towns have disappeared. Workers no longer need fear that they will find pink slips in their pay envelopes telling them they have been fired for failing to buy enough goods from the company store. Loyalty to the company, either through the purchase of products or through intellectual allegiance, is still desired, but can no longer be enforced. Zenith or GE workers may buy RCA or Sony television sets, and

workers at American Motors may park Volkswagen buses or
Ford pickups in the company parking lot. The Republican
managers of corporations fully expect their blue collar employees to vote for Democrats. The only loyalty demanded of
the blue collar employee is to the quality of the product or
service, the thing produced. Loyalty to an intellectual construct—the corporation or its political and social views—is neither demanded nor expected.

10. Workers need no longer suffer their grievances in silence in the plant or in their cups at home and in the local tav-
ern. All plants have institutionalized grievance procedures,
and many of them have developed some kind of arbitration
procedure. The blue collar worker is juridical man, and the
union is the instrument that gives him legal existence in his
daily life. He is not a thing on the line to be used by his employer as he will; the blue collar worker has the sense of being
a person, because he has rights guaranteed by a contract in
which he and the employer are equal signatories, a contract
that neither he nor the employer may violate without suffering
the penalties agreed upon in a negotiation where both worker
and employer were represented.

11. Since the blue collar worker belongs to a distinct class,
even though it is a class within a class, he is separated from the
leader of the corporation by class loyalty and unity. He accepts no responsibility for the errors of the leader; rather, he
points out the errors of the leader as part of his effort to maintain the balance of power between himself and his employer.
On the other hand, he does his best to attribute responsibility
for his own errors—poor quality in products, failures of service, even errors of judgment—to the leader. The worker uses
his negotiated contract with the leader to protect himself
against retribution from the target of his attacks.

12. Although the leader makes a regular effort to win the
union over to his side in matters of politics, the blue collar

worker's politics differ from those of management. In fact, the opposition is institutionalized. Management and labor do occasionally co-operate in lobbying efforts to protect an industry from economic difficulties that are perceived to be contrary to the best interests of both workers and management; but such efforts come about under conditions that resemble a formal truce rather than permanent rapprochement.

13. Obviously, the unionized blue collar worker has not been atomized, for he belongs to a union; but neither has he been collectivized. Men do not disappear inside a union. Democratic procedures inside most unions are flawed or nonexistent, many workers complain of cliques dominating locals, excluding other workers from power in the union, others openly disagree with union tactics, and there are some who pay their dues grudgingly and have no other contact with union business. Yet it is the very failure of the union to dominate that keeps its members from disappearing into the collective. A union is a loose organization, with little but the economics of working to hold it together; it is neither a social nor a political movement at its core, but has some political and social meaning in the lives of its workers because of economic needs. Thus the union does not overcome its members; it survives always under the threat of disagreement among its membership, and the union leader who forgets that his membership is many rather than one risks the loss of his job.

A clear example of the difference between unions and corporations takes place after every agreement reached through collective bargaining: management has the power to make an offer without consultation with either stockholders or management employees, but the union leaders must ask for ratification from the workers. In a collective, where men had ceded themselves to the union, ratification would be automatic, but the history of ratification proceedings in the United States demonstrates that union members have ceded very little of themselves: wildcat strikes by dissatisfied union members are common following collective bargaining agreements, and more than a few such agreements have been voted down.

14. Blue collar workers, particularly those who work in teams or on assembly lines, do not suffer loneliness on the job. An assembly line is less an organization of men attached to machines than a co-operative task made up of men operating machines or using tools. Each person on an assembly line must depend on the work of the person who precedes him in the progress of the line. It is not unusual to see people on an assembly line helping each other, nor is it unusual for a man who does shoddy work to hear complaints from men further down the line.

15. Most blue collar workers, particularly those in factories and on assembly lines, suffer from boredom on the job. But curiously enough, when assembly line workers are offered the opportunity to do varied jobs or to have the content of their highly rationalized tasks increased, they reject the opportunity. No one really understands why workers often prefer repetitive jobs, but one reason may be the freedom that accompanies so-called mindless work. The intellectual who enjoys puttering in the garden or painting his house may experience some of the freedom known to the assembly line worker: it is not at all the Greek notion of freedom to act, but a very Christian kind of freedom of thought, a freedom entirely within the mind. The assembly line worker daydreams as he performs his task. He is hardly Boethius being consoled by Philosophy in his prison cell, but he does exist in a kind of nirvana, his mind works, mulling over his problems, enjoying sexual fantasies, considering his substantial leisure. These flights of freedom are interrupted frequently, but not by fears or anxieties concerned with his work; the communal life of the assembly line draws him back to the fetters of reality. A factory is not made up of sullen robots, but of people who know each other very well, much like soldiers who are thrown together in intimate connection through circumstance. Even in places where the noise level would seem to make conversation impossible, such as forges or stamping plants, workers can be seen leaning close to each other, shouting conversations, often of a quite personal nature.

Harvey Swados, perhaps the most severe critic of factory work, inadvertently documented the sense of community and camaraderie of assembly line workers in *On the Line,* his affecting, if somewhat melodramatic, description of life in a Ford Motor Company plant. After a few months in the plant, Swados was able to write of the lives and feelings of his fellow workers. He described their involvement with each other, their opposition to the company, their very human existence in the course of performing the work of robots: Only someone like Swados, who had worked on an assembly line, however briefly, could know enough about the work to tell of his accidental discovery of the ability of men to remain normal social creatures while performing demanding, physically taxing, extremely repetitive work. His book stands in sharp contrast to the pronouncements of passersby, like Studs Terkel, or those who base their theories on the secondhand information gathered by passersby, a class that includes practically all industrial psychologists and all the gatherers and analyzers of quantitative research.

16. Young men drift, not knowing either their mortality or the duration of their productive years. They are foolhardy and romantic, believers in their bodies and their dreams, able to read the clock but not the calendar. In middle age, men become accountants and morticians; they substitute the dogged courage of fathers for the bravado of children. In recognition of the vulnerability of their mortal members, unions now offer to trade wages for pensions, safety for stability and the seniority system. The economics of tomorrow have become as important as the economics of today; the elimination of fear has replaced the elimination of hunger. Plants still close, businesses still fail, but the blue collar worker in a union plant in a stable industry now has less reason to fear long and destructive unemployment or penurious old age than at any time since the beginning of capitalism.

17. Class loyalty does not survive in general, as an intellectual construct; it must have a specific, active connection with the individual, and the loyalty must have time to reach into the various and changing aspects of the individual's life. For the unionized blue collar worker stability of employment provides the duration of membership in his class that nourishes loyalty. Unlike the middle class, which is based on mobility or the hope of mobility, the blue collar worker's stability leads him away from the temptation to betray his class; he succeeds as his class succeeds, he has a reason for belonging, he has a home.

18. Factories may close and workers may lose their jobs, although that is not common in large, stable industries, but within the factory and within the company, the blue collar worker who belongs to a strong union cannot be moved from place to place without his consent. He may choose to move to another job within the plant, he may even apply for another job or another place within the plant; in some instances, he may transfer to another plant; but he cannot be moved arbitrarily, he has control over that part of his life.

19. There now exists a great body of mainly nonsensical work describing how to achieve internal motivation of blue collar workers. The authors of these books, articles, monographs, and speeches study factory workers from a heavenly academic distance, then prescribe the methods management must use to motivate them to achieve greater productivity. Along the way a jargon has been invented, and it must be em-

bellished by each succeeding industrial psychologist who wishes to earn large consulting fees.

The basic problem with most attempts to motivate blue collar workers is that the motivation experts confuse union workers with white collar and management workers. The only internal motivation of unionized workers that can be accomplished comes from teaching them to accept the definition of happiness generalized in the society. Beyond that, the motivation of the blue collar worker is limited to external factors: wages, benefits, working conditions, job security, etc. To amend the psyche of the union member is virtually impossible, unless the union betrays him or he betrays the union by wanting to move out of his class. The willingness to acquiesce that characterizes the bourgeois does not yet exist in unionized blue collar workers.

The strike, the main weapon of blue collar workers, is unavailable to the bourgeoisie, because of who they are, not because of their numbers or the organization of their work.

20. The contract between the union and management spells out a rational, easily comprehensible system of work rules and rewards. Scanlon plans, in which workers share in the profits earned by their efforts, are slightly more complex, but the workers share in the rewards according to a prearranged schedule. The worker knows precisely what behavior on his part will produce precisely how much reward. He lives in an unexciting but rational world of work.

21. Expansion has no immediate meaning for the blue collar worker. He may have the opportunity to work some hours of overtime, if the product he produces sells very well, but overtime for many blue collar workers is now on a voluntary basis. Such business tactics as multinational manufacturing, "Sunbelt Strategy," mergers and acquisitions, or diversification have less and less effect on individual plants and workers as unions learn to defend their members from the threats to wages and stability arising from new business situations.

22. Peter Drucker's chimerical pension fund socialism could lead to partial control of the means of production by workers, although it is unlikely. Were the unions to gain important representation on boards of directors, the alienating adversary relationship between companies and unions would begin to change, and workers would be managed, in part, by the people they elected to represent their interests against management. In that circumstance, the value of the union to the worker would be lessened and eventually destroyed.

Many companies now seek to sell stock to blue collar employees, hoping to involve the workers more deeply in the fortunes of the company. In their present state, these employee stock plans do seem to have some effect, for workers want their stock to do well and earn money for them; but the amount of stock owned by the employees of most companies is so small that it has no effect upon the relationship between workers and management. It is ownership without power, the same illusion of ownership that attends any purchase of stock in a large company.

23. Much of the loss thought to be connected with blue collar work is imaginary. The worker enjoys alienation from the company, but his connection with the product is intimate and meaningful. The assembler of the components of a television receiver sees and feels the product of his labor. At the end of the line the receiver will display a picture. The steelworker may see his product in a bridge or as the door of a refrigerator. An auto worker can buy and drive the product he builds. The blue collar worker need not ponder the meaning of his labor, striving to connect pieces of paper covered with numbers to the power of a locomotive or the flavor of a can of soup; he can hold his work in his hand, touch, see, use what he has made; the meaning of his work is clear.

24. There is an ugly moment in Hannah Arendt's work on the life of action, *The Human Condition.* In that moment, she expresses a common criticism of Marx's theory of the emancipation of the *animal laborans,* arguing that in his leisure time he will merely consume, "and the more time left to him, the greedier and more craving his appetites." The view belongs to German intellectuals (one can find the same view, for example, in Walter Kaufman), who are rarely able to overcome their contempt for ordinary men. Kant said that he owed his admiration for the common man to the works of Rousseau; Marx's faith in the potentialities of ordinary men, however, remains the greatest exception to the Germanic connection to the Greek view of ordinary men.

Whether the blue collar worker should be categorized as *animal laborans* or *homo faber* raises the question of the use of the product of his labor. If the blue collar worker builds cathedrals or makes tools, he may fall under the strict definition of *homo faber;* if he produces electricity or dog food, he may be considered *animal laborans;* all service workers are laborers, for their labor is immediately consumed; but most blue collar workers fall into a gray area between man the laborer and man the maker, for the completion of their tasks is ostensible in the existing product, yet they repeat the work during all the days of their employment. Most blue collar workers live somewhere at the intersection of the biological cycle of necessity and the consumable labor required to satisfy necessity and the remaking of the world by the product of his work that gives stability and authority to man the maker.

25. When Ludwig Wittgenstein decided he would never again wear a necktie, he removed a symbol of the oppression of social convention from his life. Appearances are, after all, the world. Blue collar workers do not free themselves with the same heightened consciousness as philosophers, but they nonetheless resist symbolic oppression. One need only visit an assembly line and observe the styles of dress, speech, and action of the workers to realize the symbolic freedom they enjoy. Furthermore, blue collar workers live where they please, socialize with whomever they please and generally enjoy complete freedom outside the relatively few hours they spend at their jobs. When Henry Ford attempted to restrict the freedom of the men who worked in his company after they left the plants at the end of the workday, he succeeded less in dominating his employees than in creating resentments that contributed to the formation of the United Auto Workers. The nature of blue collar work leads men to demand autonomy. Marx was not entirely wrong in his belief that the working class would lead the revolution, although it was not until recently that Marcuse was able to explain in Marxist terms how much the owners of the means of production were willing to give up to the workers to maintain some semblance of ownership and to keep to themselves the power of capital. The revolution has been slow, but ongoing; the life that Marx said in *The German Ideology* would exist for the worker in communism is beginning to be real for many blue collar workers. Leisure exists, and the blue collar worker enjoys his leisure without real or symbolic constraints.

The blue collar worker grasped his alienation and allowed it to teach him autonomy and politics. Yet the society in which he lives, defined as civilization by the issue of the blue collar worker's hands, accords him neither gratitude nor respect. Those who define happiness think of him as an animal, endlessly laboring to fend off necessity. And in the deprecation of labor there is a meeting of the intellectual conservatism of a writer like Hannah Arendt and the political radicalism of Karl Marx, who would value the cowherd, the fisherman, the critic, virtually anyone, over the worker who made the bricks of the house in which he lived, the books from which he learned, and the paper on which he wrote. It is well to remember that Marx loved the working class, but not *qua* workers; he loved the workers for what they might be; he wished not only to make their lives better, but to make them better; he loved man, not men as they were.

Paul Valery said, "All political systems imply (and are generally not aware that they do imply) a certain conception of man, and even an opinion about the destiny of the species, an entire metaphysics which embraces the crudest sensuality and the most daring mysticism." Only one political system (republican democracy) values man; all other political systems that we know value only the perfectability of man. The dream of godliness haunts us, we are such imperfect images, waiting for heaven or heaven on earth. Perfect creatures do not sweat at their labors or touch nature with blunt, work-stained hands, so say Plato, Paul, and Marx.

No matter how much money a blue collar worker earns, he is considered poor; no matter how much he enjoys his work, he is thought to be suffering. In that way, white collar wages are kept low and blue collar workers suffer the indignity of low status, an indignity that has been the lot of working men since classical Greece. George Strauss, writing in *Work and the Quality of Life,* suggests that low status may be one of the most important causes of mental disturbance among blue collar workers. He interprets the data gathered by a University of Michigan Survey Research Center study done in 1971 to show that blue collar workers suffer no more job dissatisfaction than anyone else. A study done by the Survey Research Center two years earlier showed people in high-status jobs suffering more from job-related tensions. In study after study, more middle-class people report dissatisfaction with their jobs than do working-class people. But always there is the arrogant answer to these facts of the worker's life, as in Daniel Bell's analysis: "Workers, whose grievances were once the driving energy for social change, are more satisfied with the society than the intellectuals. The workers have not achieved utopia but their expectations were less than those of the intellectuals and their gains correspondingly larger."

Bell is, of course, wrong. Workers are not at all satisfied with the society. But their dissatisfaction is different from that of other classes: it is alienation, but not loss, or cession, or estrangement. The worker's alienation, as some psychologists are now discovering, is a healthy sign—dissatisfaction is dignity, as one psychologist has said, referring to auto workers.

The blue collar worker through his union has risen from *animal laborans* to his human destiny as *zoon politikon*. He is neither alone nor absorbed, he has joined with other men to gain enough power over his own life to force himself into the elite world of juridical men, and he enters that world as a partner in the making of the laws by which he lives. In the union, the society of blue collar workers, there is no end but man. As much as any man in society, and more than most, the union member has achieved autonomy. He is not rich, but neither does he suffer the corruption of idleness. He has not yet learned to define happiness for himself, not entirely, not with complete autonomy, but he has thrown off many of the fears that make men prey to the details of happiness defined by others. He cedes a portion of himself to the company to earn his living, but no man, not even a king, can enjoy society without some cession. In his alienation, the blue collar worker is aware of every moment, every movement he cedes to company, union, and society. He gives grudgingly, counting his losses, resenting every instance of estrangement. He is a political man; and no matter how weak or corrupt his union, it is his vital connection to other men, to the life of action, to the priceless dignity of an alien in a society organized to destroy autonomy.

7

Wolves

In the *Iliad,* Zeus sends a message to Poseidon, instructing the messenger to advise the sea-god,

> "But if he disobeys or disregards me,
> let him remember: for all his might,
> he does not have it in him to oppose me.
> I am more powerful by far than he,
> and senior to him. He has forgotten this,
> claiming equality with me. All others
> shrink from that."

When Poseidon hears the message, he gives an angry reply to Iris, the messenger, who asks if he truly wants his angry words to be carried back to Zeus. Poseidon retreats from his anger. He neither disobeys nor disregards Zeus.

The political organization of the Homeric universe bears a very close resemblance to modern totalitarianism. There are the masses of mortals, the front organization of mortals to whom the gods appear, and the gods themselves organized in layers rather than in a clear authoritarian pyramid. In place of technology the gods have magic.

Secrets, mistaken identities, betrayals, and capricious actions by gods and men abound. Alienation is unimaginable when the gods touch men's lives. Retribution replaces justice among men, whose tragedy it is never to be able to overcome fate; juridical man is an illusion. But this despotism of the gods is not limited to the lives of mortals. Poseidon, the great Earthshaker, born of Kronos, like Zeus and the god of the underworld, manager of a third of the universe, gives way to the Leader. There is no way to win a contest with the Leader except through guile. In a line, Homer clarifies the middle as all those between mortals and the Leader: ". . . for all his might, he does not have it in him to oppose me." The reader, knowing the status of Poseidon, understands the position of the sea-god: he is without the possibility of appeal, like the middle manager of modern business for whom no one can intercede. Poseidon, a part of the totalitarian system of the Homeric universe, himself a god, son of a Titan, stands naked before the power of the system.

With the objectivity of more than 2,500 years of distance and the clarifying filter of art to aid us, we have little difficulty in understanding the problems of the gods and heroes of Greece. Similarly, we can recognize the totalitarian systems of Nazi Germany and Russia under Stalin, for we have sufficient distance from them to see the symptoms of totalitarianism. But to apprehend totalitarianism in one's own time is more difficult: subjectivity and alienation are required, and one must also have a pattern to lay over a portrait of a society to see if it fits the definition of totalitarianism. Hannah Arendt, Hans Buchheim, and others have provided the pattern. In the following pages are forty portraits of modern business, each accompanied by a brief explanation of how the portrait fits the pattern of totalitarianism.

The reader will find neither the art of Homer nor the certainty of studies of Stalinism or Nazism in these pages. Modern totalitarianism in America works in subtle ways. It is effected from without, but it takes place within each man, almost always in silence. It has no flag but the company logotype, and no weapons but paychecks, promotions, and the promise of happiness. No total system is described, for none is possible: one of the characteristics of totalitarianism is that it can never be completed. The traits of totalitarianism affect men one at a time. When most men are affected by most of the traits of totalitarianism, we say that a society has become totalitarian and so describe it in our history books. To those who are affected by the traits of totalitarianism the judgment of historians matters not at all.

The people in the exemplary tales that follow are neither historians nor political philosophers. If one suggested to them or to their leaders that they are part of an increasingly totalitarian system, they would be astonished and angered, for it is no part of their intention either to make or to suffer totalitarianism. Therein lies the danger of an insidious enemy.

THE FRIENDSHIP OF UTILITY

He claims it as a merit for himself and his Church that at last they have vanquished freedom and have done so to make men happy.

> The Grand Inquisitor
> Fyodor Dostoevski

The former director of the section telephones less frequently. Sometimes the messages he leaves are not answered the same day. He remembers the yellow message slips, his frequent consciousness of their anonymity: they did not carry the name of the firm, they were unlike every other piece of paper he touched in the course of a day.

When his telephone calls are answered, he speaks in the voice he used before he left the company. The earnestness with which he shared secrets lacks content now. Once they had been the secrets of loyalty, and then the secrets of dissent, and finally, only the slow, deeply sounded words, the voice that could shout moderated to a rumble by intimacy.

He is a short, thick man, who gives the impression of vegetarian species: heavy bones, slow to anger, parental, capable of rages that cannot be terminated except in exhaustion. The most delicate things attract him, as if he were distressed by his very thickness and wished his life to be counterpoint or even denial.

Some people in the company had called him saintly, knowing that he was honorable in all things. Others had feared his devotion to his own conceptions of perfection, and the long hours, the tedious thinking and rethinking, working and reworking that accompanied his devotion. And others had thought him stubborn, inflexible, recalcitrant, like a herbivore.

He was demoted. A good worker, the management said, but not a manager. The demotion had not come as a surprise to him. Long before the announcement, the content of the shared secrets had changed. His friend advised him to accept the demotion. Honor caused him to resign.

His friend was thin and quick, streamlined, stylish. He puffed at cigarettes, he laughed at other men's failings, he drank gin. Secretly, he scoffed at the former director's devotion and pitied him for his loyalty. The friend was grateful to the former director for his generosity and for the confidence he expressed in his abilities; he enjoyed praise. However, he was certain of his own ability to perform better in the director's job.

On several occasions the director had said, "You could do this job better than I can." The friend had always given the same answer: "I don't have enough experience. And to be honest about it, I don't care enough about the company."

After the former director resigned, his friend was promoted to director of the section. He proved to be more capable. The section grew, sub-directors were appointed. The new director is careful never to speak ill of his predecessor. He intimates that the company made an error in demoting the former director. The management does not speak of the former director, so his replacement does not have to lie. He remembers how well the former director spoke of him when he was in the company of the executive vice-president.

In the course of the telephone conversation they speak of each other's children. They have difficulty remembering the names of each other's wives. The former director says the name of his wife to spare the friend any embarrassment.

The former director speaks of the problems of his new job, leading into implied criticism of the company where his friend is now the director of the section. The friend listens without answering. He remembers the former director's house: the workshop in the garage, the long dining room table, the silences of awkwardness that ended in bursts of laughter, the steak tartare that was too warm, the Christmas parties, the former director's children in their pajamas passing trays of tiny sandwiches and bowls of potato chips, the beautifully wrapped presents. He remembers liking the former director's wife, approving of her neurotic delicacy and her distaste for business.

The friend answers that the company has changed, improved, become more generous, more successful. He makes a joke of his loyalty.

They no longer have mutual enemies. They are unable to find a mutually convenient date for lunch.

The former director promises to call again.

Friendship belongs to the world of action. It is a political act, and true friendship is the province of autonomous men. That friendship and despotism are mutually exclusive comes from man's earliest understanding of politics. Plato wrote, "Throughout life, the despotic character has not a friend in the world; he is sometimes master, sometimes slave, but never knows true friendship or freedom. There is no faithfulness in him. . . ."

Aristotle, in the *Nicomachean Ethics,* said, "Each of the constitutions [monarchy, aristocracy, timocracy] may be seen to involve friendship just in so far as it involves justice." There follows an extraordinary perception of the politics of friendship:

> . . . in tyranny there is little or no friendship. For where there is nothing common to ruler and ruled, there is not friendship either, since there is not justice; e.g., between craftsman and tool, soul and body, master and slave; the latter in each case is benefited by that which uses it, but there is no friendship nor justice towards lifeless things. But neither is there friendship towards a horse or an ox, nor to a slave *qua* slave. For there is nothing common to the two parties; the slave is a living tool and the tool a lifeless slave. *Qua* slave then, one cannot be friends with him. But *qua* man one can; for there seems to be some justice between any man and any other who can share in a system of law or be a party to an agreement; therefore there can also be friendship with him in so far as he is a man. Therefore while in tyrannies friendship and justice hardly exist, in democracies they exist more fully; for where the citizens are equal they have much in common.

The "friendship of utility," he says, must always involve at least one bad man, because "he loves not the other person, he loves profit, he seeks advantage." It is, according to Aristotle, a friendship "full of complaints; for as they use each other for their own interests they always want to get the better of the bargain, and think they have got less than they should, and blame their partners. . . ."

In a friendship of utility men are not truly friends at all, but users of each other; the relation of man to man is a simulacrum of the relation between man and tool. No other form of friendship exists in totalitarian societies, for men whose friendship exceeds mere utility must know that they have value in themselves, that they are ends in themselves. Aristotle's perception and Kant's distinction between man as a means and man as an end have much in common, for both realize that man cannot be unique, dignified, and autonomous when he is used. Neither can man used be political man, for in that role the world acts upon him and he cannot act upon the world; he cannot be the beginning of anything, which is the mark of the slave.

Without true friendship, men live in loneliness, atomized, vulnerable to becoming mass man, who acts according to direction, but cannot initiate action. Such men seem useful to business, for they are not troublesome, their behavior may be plotted, like that of machines or metals. However, neither are they likely to initiate change or to resist improper instructions. A corporation or a state that reduces men to tools designs its own downfall by eliminating the possibility of new beginnings. In its drive for efficient expansion, the government or business creates a killing stasis: the elimination of the most fundamental political relationship—true friendship—opens the way for competitive businesses or governments to become a society of tools.

The methods by which men are led to the friendship of utility are many—competition, isolation, etc.—but none exerts a greater influence than a definition of happiness that does not include the enjoyment of the most basic political relations between men. Nowhere in the literature of management is friendship considered, for management is a method of using men, as the word once meant the using of horses. A properly managed horse will follow directions perfectly, initiating nothing. When the same view is applied to man, it achieves the same result: creatures in their stalls, with no concern for each other, awaiting the bidding of the master, docile, domesticated, alone, and happy.

THE MAZE

> At a distance behind him come his gloomy assistants and slaves and the "holy guard."
>
> The Grand Inquisitor

For eighty years the company had been managed by gentlemen. They had lunch at the best clubs, sailed their own boats to Tahiti in summer and hunted in Kenya in winter. All their wives were thin, schooled in New England, and devoted to charities. It was not surprising in such a company for the vice-president of marketing to be honorable and well spoken, kind to his subordinates, and mildly paternalistic toward his customers. Like the rest of the executives, he was a handsome man, athletic for his age, more curious than disapproving about the younger generation, interested in his church and loyal to his alma mater, where five generations of his family had been educated. He read Greek for a hobby, and he was fond of saying that Aristophanes and cigars were his only vices.

He was shocked when the family that owned the majority of the stock of the company chose an aggressive moneyman to be the new chairman and a former career military officer to be president and chief operating officer. His discomfort with the new top management was soon eased, however: the new president said he did not believe that war and business were analogous and so would not interfere in the marketing operation; but more comforting was the revelation that both the new chairman and the vice-president of marketing had not only attended Harvard College but had lived in the same house—the chairman before the war and the vice-president after the war.

Despite the president's deference, an attitude that sometimes bordered on awe, the vice-president could not accustom himself to life under his new superior. He was dismayed to learn that a former military officer had not read Caesar. The laconic style of the new president made him uncomfortable. He was averse, on grounds of taste, to men in middle age who wore their hair in the crew cut style. Very thin men, like the new president, made him nervous; he quoted Shakespeare on the subject. Furthermore, he considered war cruel and useless; he made no secret of his opposition to the growing American involvement in Vietnam; and although he had not discussed the subject with the new president, he assumed that a military man would approve of any war anywhere at any time.

As he said to his wife and to his friends outside the company, the new chairman was more his kind of man; a bit incautious perhaps, but well prepared. He cited the chairman's deftness in dealing with the press and he never failed to mention the sudden rise in the price of the company's stock. "It's highly irregular of me to mention this," he told his friends, "but I wonder whether a stock that's being traded so actively might not soon be listed on the New York Exchange." He did not reveal the chairman's plans for a major acquisition to be accomplished by selling stock held in the company's treasury as soon as it reached a price high enough to provide the necessary cash. While he regarded all conglomerates as swindles, he was unable to quell the excitement that rose in him at the thought of sudden growth.

Without warning, the stock market declined. It was considered inadvisable to sell stock at the time. Plans for the acquisition were abandoned. The vice-president was not unhappy. He was more concerned with the growing war in Southeast Asia. His son would be graduating from Harvard in a year and a half. They had talked about the boy registering as a conscientious objector and about going to Sweden or Canada. The son said he was not a coward. The father said there were many kinds of courage.

Since the company had controlled more than three fourths of its market from the first year of operation, the title of vice-president of marketing was something of a misnomer; in actuality the salesmen acted more as consultants and expediters than salesmen, and the vice-president was more valuable for his social graces than for his genius as a marketer. After the plans for expansion were abandoned, however, the president began to ask questions about the remaining fourth of the market.

At first, the questions were nothing more than that; the president seemed to be learning his job. Then they became more insistent. The president and the vice-president argued over a large price increase. "We'll lose volume," the vice-president said. The president demanded greater volume in spite of the price increase. He spoke of productivity, he said he had seen men loafing, machinery idle. "Fixed costs wait for no man," he told his vice-president. "Your salesmen aren't motivated. They lack esprit de corps."

"This is not war," the vice-president replied.

The president quoted Clausewitz. They argued. Every day there was a new criticism, a new argument. The president visited customers and reported that they were not properly serviced. He rejected reports because the paper was smudged. He accused the vice-president of having an affair with his secretary. "I can tell by the sloppiness you accept from her," he said. "It's a sure sign."

Sales declined at Christmas. "There has been a valley in December every year for the past eighty years," the vice-president explained.

"Unacceptable."

"I can neither change history nor the structure of our business," the vice-president said.

"I'm planning to name an executive vice-president for sales, marketing, customer service, and new product development. You'll report to him."

The vice-president said nothing. He looked at the president's hands. They were as delicate as a woman's hands. He thought they might be the hands of a New England woman. The fingernails were buffed, the cuticles were perfectly manicured. Each fingernail had its white quarter moon. "I'll have my resignation on your desk in the morning."

The president opened a folder on his desk. "Is there anything else?" he asked. He began to read.

At his farewell party the vice-president drank too much. He had not been able to find another job, his son had drawn a single-digit number in the draft lottery, the war was on his mind almost constantly: he read the names of the dead and wounded in the local newspaper, his job offers came only from companies that served the war, he had been to a peace rally, perhaps the only vice-president of marketing in attendance.

During the party he spoke of the president of the company, raising a toast to "the incompetent son of a bitch, the martinet." Before the party ended he cut his hand on a broken glass and wept openly at the sight of his blood, saying that he saw in it the danger that awaited his son. One of the salesmen drove him home, using the opportunity to question him about aspects of the company that had been kept secret.

The vice-president looked for a new job without success until he agreed to manage the sale of products to the military. Eventually, he even visited Vietnam. The chairman of his former company resigned to avoid a scandal and the new chairman's first act was to fire the president. Several years after the end of the Vietnam War the vice-president saw the general counsel of the company at Washington National Airport. They chatted briefly and arranged to meet that evening for cocktails.

During the first drink they inquired of each other's families and current jobs. After the second drink was served, the general counsel said, "I haven't seen you since your farewell party, if party is the right word. You know, you attacked the wrong man. It wasn't the president who was out to get you. He was just carrying out orders. In fact, he was quite an admirer of yours. The boss was the one who had it in for you."

"Why didn't you tell me?"

"I thought you knew," the general counsel said. "Everyone else knew."

———◄─◆─►———

Totalitarian organizations may be apparently structured in the classic pyramidal hierarchy, but they are more truly structured as Hannah Arendt described them: in layers, like onions. Within an authoritarian pyramid, a man may locate himself and his future, he may defend himself and even appeal his case in the fashion of juridical man; but when there is either an onion structure or a structure overlaid upon a structure, the employee, like the citizen in a totalitarian state, is helpless: power rests in the center of an impenetrable maze, radiating down corridors that seem to have neither beginnings nor ends. A man living in such a structure can never be certain that he has made a correct move; he must always assume that he is in error.

A man who heeds the lesson of the maze will learn that his choices are constant fear or complete obedience. His only hope is to follow every clue offered by the keeper of the maze, for everywhere along the bewildering corridors are devastating pitfalls. Even so, he cannot be certain of survival, for one of the rules of totalitarianism is caprice, destruction without reason. No man in a totalitarian situation may enjoy even the security of an obedient servant.

The result of this is that men lose their humanity inside a totalitarian structure, they become things, hostages to what seems to them to be a universal caprice, a caprice without end. Morality loses its meaning, political life declines because one cannot do politics with ghosts, one obeys, one ceases to exist as a man for fear that any human act, any beginning, may result in punishment; fear crowds the mind, and finally all hope is placed in the organization; law, logic, and dignity have been vanquished, nothing matters but mere survival.

One option available to a man who exists in a maze, unable to defend himself against the keeper of the maze and his caprice, would seem to be a corresponding capriciousness; but totalitarianism, as further examples will demonstrate, crowds out the possibility of the oppressed enjoying caprice, which is a kind of perverse autonomy. Totalitarianism occupies its victims, making them incapable of rebellion; decisions are made from without.

The leader, whose work it is to define happiness as well as to operate the structures, avoids confrontation with members of the organization, preserving his identification with perfection, the impossible total goal of the organization. If the leader were to do his work directly, the walls of the maze would fall and the victim would stand face to face with his accuser; he would then exist as a lawful being, a creature whole unto himself, capable of self-defense, juridical man, a human being capable of rebellion. The maze functions not only to confuse men with anxiety, but to isolate them from the source of their oppression, which is both the leader and the organization he manages. Without knowledge of their oppressors, men cannot rebel; they float, unable to find anything against which to rebel, incapable of understanding that they are oppressed by the very organization that keeps them afloat.

PROTEUS

> Tomorrow I shall condemn Thee and
> burn Thee at the stake as the worst of
> heretics. And the very people who have
> today kissed Thy feet, tomorrow at the
> faintest sign from me will wish to heap
> up the embers of Thy fire.
>
> The Grand Inquisitor

Card tables had been set up in the bar after dinner. There were two poker games and a gin rummy tournament in progress when the manager of the Dayton, Ohio, plant came in from a walk along the beach. The heavy evening air of Florida did not please him. He did not like the way it touched his skin, immediately intimate, like a fast woman. He thought of the snow in Ohio, the low relative humidity, the rapid condensation of his breath in winter. It irked him that he had begun to consider everything in life from an engineer's point of view, that the language of science was becoming his boundary. He remembered how pleased he had been when the Soviet cosmonaut said, "I'm an eagle."

The plant manager did not like to play cards. The game always turned into a chore for him, remembering cards, calculating odds, wishing for a slide rule and a pad of paper. He went to the bar and ordered beer. "Any kind," he said. Although he wanted some exotic brand to symbolize his sophistication, he could not recall any names but Miller, Schlitz, and Bud.

He was joined at the bar by the executive vice-president, who approached him with a flow of words about his daughter, his only daughter, who had that morning given birth to her first child and his first grandchild. "I'd rather talk to my baby on the phone than sit here in all this damned cigar smoke and beer stink. Hell, I don't care for cards anyway."

"I was walking on the beach," the plant manager said.

"The beaches are better further north, in Georgia, off the coast of Georgia. The beaches in Florida are too perfect, too artificial. There's something dishonest about a beach that's swept clean every morning."

They walked out into the garden adjacent to the bar. Thick palm leaves and tropical flowers encroached upon the walking space. The plant manager tried to think of the names of the flowers. It was nothing like Ohio. He searched for something to say to the executive vice-president. The company had been engaged in a battle over standards with one of the federal agencies that regulated their business. It had become more important to management than any other aspect of the operation. The plant manager asked how the fight was proceeding.

"We'll be ready to make our move soon," the executive vice-president answered. "I think the strategy will work. You and the other people in the field have done a good job. Damn good."

"God knows, we've tried. I've talked to so many PTA and civic meetings about the cost of regulation. . . ." He couldn't finish the comparative. Southerners always knew how to do it, they always had a funny comparative ready. He connected their humor with their success in the company.

"I think the feds are right: we should have shielded those cables twenty years ago," the executive vice-president said.

"Well, I thought so too, just based on the voltage and the heat generated by the resistance in the upper circuitry, but I was sure the people in central engineering knew what they were talking about. Those tests they ran on the conduction characteristics . . ."

"We made a judgment. The Washington office says there's an energy efficiency standard coming. We think we can trade the shielding standard for the energy standard. The shielding will cost us four cents a unit. It'll be five years before we can redesign for an energy efficiency standard."

"I talked to a lot of people. I asked them to write letters. I was quoted in the newspapers."

"Exactly." The executive vice-president put his arm around the plant manager's shoulders. "Without your effort the strategy wouldn't have stood a chance. We'd have nothing to trade."

"Now we'll fight the energy standard?"

"It would put us out of business, damn near. I figure an added cost to the consumer of more than double the price of the oil it would save, and that's at the rate we project for five years out, not including the windfall tax but factoring in about 10 per cent synthetics. You consider the demand elasticity in our high end lines and the added cost could put upwards of thirty-five hundred people on permanent layoff. You add in the multiplier effect, figure it industry-wide and you've got fifty thousand people out of work, a hundred thousand kids on welfare. It's just plain goddamn irresponsible. You get the drift?"

The plant manager lowered himself onto one of the beach chairs in the corner of the garden under the largest palm tree. It was slightly damp. The nights were cooler, he thought, just as the brochure said. He thought too that he must be getting older: it was difficult to balance the beer in the glass as he squatted and settled back in the chair. The fluids in his left knee popped. His hand trembled. The beer reached the edge of the glass. Some foam spilled. He wished he could concentrate on himself to decipher his feelings, but he had to answer the executive vice-president, he had to say something. Had he been a fool? A good soldier? A pawn? Or was he merely naïve? He knew formulas, methods, no engineering problem could defeat him. He had written a paper on fluid mechanics. Productivity in his plant was above the company average. He had raised the quality index from twenty-second to third.

"I'm just an engineer," he said.

"And a damn fine one."

The protean quality of policy in totalitarian organizations has been documented at great length. Perhaps the most well-known example is the sudden shift in Soviet policy to "socialism in one country," and its use in Stalin's attacks on Trotsky. Deutscher, in his biography of Stalin, describes another: "They [Gomulka, Rajk, etc.] had identified themselves with the 'rightist,' 'moderate,' and nationalist policy which they had in previous years pursued with Stalin's encouragement; and they clung to it even after Stalin had changed the line. This was their undoing. They were accused of collusion with Titoism, branded as wreckers and spies, imprisoned, subjected to blackmail and torture, and made to confess their sins, as the defendants in the Great Moscow Trial had confessed theirs."

In John Toland's biography of Hitler, the leader of the Berlin SA complains that Hitler changes his mind every few months, giving new orders, and that it is impossible to operate under such conditions. Arendt describes "the eternally shifting party line" of a totalitarian organization, and in her book *The*

Human Condition she analyzes the effect of a protean world: "Without being bound to the fulfillment of promises, we would never be able to keep our identities. . . ."

If the sudden shifts in policy on the part of governments or corporations were the result of discovered errors or new situations, their effect would be harmless, for the managers would say, without great discomfort, that the situation had changed or even that they had been in error, and the employees would be asked, in a most human way, to forgive the managers or to understand the new situation. Policy changes in states and corporations, however, are more often the result of carefully worked out strategies, or more properly, deceits. Apologies cannot be made without revealing the deceitful intent, nor can changed situations be blamed when the situation has not changed. The employee must accept each succeeding policy without question, for his question will elicit no answer but an accusation of disloyalty.

The understanding of deceit as an act of violence against the deceived has long been known. Most recently, Sissela Bok spoke of it in her work *Lying:* "Deceit and violence—these are the two forms of deliberate assault on human beings. Both can coerce people into acting against their will. Most harm that can befall victims through violence can come to them also through deceit."

While the injury of deceit can be so crude as to cause a person to lose a loved one or even to commit suicide, as in *Othello,* the kind of deceit practiced in totalitarian organizations affects men in a different way, because it requires their participation. The object of totalitarian deceit is to make the deceived a deceiver. Nietzsche recognized the process: "Of necessity," he wrote, "the party man becomes a liar."

By his participation in the deceit, the employee, however unwillingly at first, gives over his moral being to the organization. After the first deceit, he can never again know whether the policy he follows and espouses is a true course. He must assume that he too is a deceiver to protect himself from being deceived. Whatever changes in policy follow the first shift mean but little to him. He has abandoned his moral self, he has chosen not to exist as an autonomous person; his will to survive physically in the comfort of the corporate definition of the path to happiness has triumphed, he belongs to the organization. The natural world, in which truth can exist, the real world, no longer matters to him, he accepts as true the deceits of the organization, he lives within a manufactured world and behaves according to the situations within that world. If he loses contact with the world as constructed by the organization as a result of the natural alienation of human intelligence, his ability to make his way in the manufactured world will be severely impaired and he will have little or no chance of survival. The either/or proposition of the totalitarian organization leaves no room for aliens.

LONELINESS

And such is his power, so completely are the people cowed into submission and trembling obedience to him, that the crowd immediately makes way for the guards. . . .

The Grand Inquisitor

Late again, sure I'm late again. I'm late every goddamned night. I wish it was a girl friend. I wouldn't even care if she was ugly. She could have VD for all I care. I would

rather have a good dose of clap than what I'm getting from
sales analysis. That's a dose. I shouldn't have hired the man, I
knew it. So why the hell did personnel send him up if his record was so spotty? I needed a man, but not him. I needed him
like a third ass. But I wouldn't be any better off without him.
To sit there myself with the tapes from two hundred and forty-
six stores and eighty-one weather reports and drive myself
crazy trying to estimate sales for the man is more than one
human being is able to do when he has the rest of the sales to
handle. There's too much cash to handle, two hundred and
forty-six transfers a day. And the checks, how many bad
checks can our stupid managers accept? They're making me
the king of the overdraft. You can't pay for merchandise with
a handful of overdrafts. The man is right. I'm sorry. The national morality is declining, going to hell in a handbasket. We
should take more credit cards. The whole world should work
on credit cards. But 6 per cent. The goddamned banks are
eating us up: 6 per cent off credit cards, and the prime rate is
set by John Dillinger. They're getting us coming and going.
What the Hell are they doing with all the money? On the other
hand, what do we lose if we wait another two days before we
transfer money? The checks would clear, we'd worry about the
weather from yesterday instead of tomorrow. But the man
wants estimates, cash flow. He hates to pay that interest. He'd
rather pick up a few dollars on the float, beating the banks.
Who wouldn't? Does he think I don't know? That I don't
care? What can I do with a sales analyst who's off by 300
per cent? This man I hired is a fool, he doesn't seem to
know that sales drop in a blizzard . . . in a damned blizzard he predicts a 40 per cent increase over the previous
Saturday, when we had a sale . . . with him predicting, the
man expects a float of close to half a million and we come up a
hundred under, and he has to go to the banks. Doesn't he
know I hired a fool, a fool sent to me by personnel? A man
could score a thousand instead of ninety-two on their god-

damned tests, and if he has no common sense . . . Even the girls in the office know. I see it in their faces. I should have promoted one of them. Sure, I should have. The man would kill me every time she stayed out because she had the rag on. What can I do with a goddamned nineteenth-century male chauvinist pig boss? I'll call up the EEOC and then jump out the window when he finds out. God, it's almost ten o'clock. I think this train actually delivers milk. If I'd eaten at the office, at least she could have gone out to a movie or over to her girl friend's house. We need baby-sitter bills. I'll tell the IRS it's a business expense, because the old fart's a male chauvinist pig and I don't dare tell the girls in the office that I hired a jerk instead of giving one of them a shot at the job. "Staying late again?" "Just checking over some figures for the boss." As if they didn't know! They hold joke sessions in the toilet to talk about the asshole I hired. At least, at the very least, they could offer to give me a hand. Not them. *The Sinking of the Titanic* was the only movie they ever enjoyed. And him! If he was a human being, just a human being, not a gentleman, not a friend . . . Bean counters! Would I be any different? You could talk to me. Not about the interest, not about 14 per cent. I wouldn't accept the 14 per cent any faster than he does. But if you made a mistake, if you needed more budget to hire a man who could do the job, if you were up the creek . . . And personnel comes up with nothing. Was he the last man on earth? I see him there, picking his nose and guessing the stores will be mobbed in a snowstorm. "No shoppers in bad weather, buyers!" I could kill the bastard. Picking his nose. Jesus, there are dirty smudges on the sales slips where he gets snot on them! I would tell him, but a man'll quit on you if you attack his personal habits. When he goes, he'll go without notice. Clean out your desk. Pick up your two weeks from personnel. The new man will come in and I'll go home on time. Early. I'll catch the four fifty-two. Who rides the four fifty-two? What lucky bastards? God, I'm tired. God, why don't

you do something for me? Help me out. Talk to me. Don't
help me out. Just listen to me. You know what I mean? Like a
therapist. You don't even have to answer. Let me talk, and I'll
solve my own problems. I'm all bottled up, and I don't even
have time to go out to lunch. It's no goddamn fun. It's no goddamn fun at all. Whoever said it was goddamn fun? In seventeen years I'll be retired. By then that son of a bitch will know
you don't set sales records in a blizzard.

———————◄—◆—►———————

Loneliness, which has nothing at all to do with solitude, is the
antithesis of politics. Men live in society. Arendt noted that
the Latin synonym for "to live" is *inter hominis esse* (to be
among men). She noted too that Cato said he was never less
lonely than when he was by himself, for then he could think,
which put him among all men. The loneliness that destroys
men by atomizing them comes when they are among the familiar faces of strangers. Then they cannot be human, they cannot live: they do not have the opportunity of solitude and they
cannot speak anything but the garble of the fearful, the language that does not communicate, the secret language of the
truly lonely.

Karl Marx, building upon Aristotle, recognized well the inhuman quality of loneliness: "Man is a *zoon politikon* in the
most literal sense: he is not only a social animal, but an animal that can individualize himself only within society. Production by an isolated individual outside society . . . is just as
preposterous as the development of speech without individuals
who live together and talk to one another." Nothing is more
basic to man than his social existence, which is also his political existence. Without it, he need not speak, and as a creature
that does not speak he no longer meets the criteria of hu-
manness. One need only recall Gulliver's shock when he found
the Yahoos, speechless creatures in human form, living among

talking horses. It was not long before he found himself conversing with the horses and quite comfortably dressing himself in the skins of the Yahoos.

Speechlessness, the salient of loneliness, leaves men helpless, the potential victims of despotism. Arendt said, "What prepares men for totalitarian domination in the non-totalitarian world is the fact that loneliness, once a borderline experience usually suffered in certain marginal conditions like old age, has become an everyday experience of the ever growing masses of our century." The prognosis is clear: in loneliness men become atomized, and the atomized, defenseless creatures of the manageable herd comprise the mass, the tool of totalitarianism.

At the heart of the loneliness of business one finds the essence of the notion of property: competition. Men rise and fall, getting more or less goods and status. To mark the competition and to institutionalize it, the twin structures have been invented. Men closer to the leader have more status and usually more goods than those farther away; they do not give away their power, which is contained almost entirely in secrets not known to the outer layers. Men pretend strength, based not upon their own merits but upon the structure. If they knew each other, if they spoke honestly, as political men may, they would be naked, sharing according to a natural aristocracy as cruel as nature herself. They might also share in some egalitarian fashion, which had no basis in their innate gifts but considered them all men and all equal—some union contracts have been negotiated to produce that situation.

Within the ranked dual structures that reward competition, men are imprisoned in lonely isolation cells, lonely because they are never quiet, never cells of solitude, always, as David Riesman said in his famous oxymoron, the home of the lonely crowd.

We have been taught that those who fraternize with their inferiors to too great a degree can no longer manage them. In all the structures of Western civilization we accept the maxim: familiarity breeds contempt. How curious that fraternization (acting like brothers) should be frowned upon! How curious that we should fear that those who know us will hold us in contempt! One is led back to Diderot's criticism of modern society, to the absurd light in which his native of the South Seas placed our notions of unending work and competition.

Although capitalism has been saddled with the concept of competition, as if such warring were the invention of the capitalist system, one can find the same situation in socialist economies: Milovan Djilas was the first of the "dissidents" to demonstrate the failure of self-proclaimed socialist societies to achieve co-operation in the relations between men. It may well be that Rousseau, Marx, and Lévi-Strauss were not correct in their assessment of the relation between property and social structure, and that the causes of inequality may be more basic than most investigators of the question have been willing to admit.

The question for business, which is dedicated to efficiency in some economic systems and to the maximation of profit through efficiency in others, is whether it is best served by lonely men. Surely, lonely men are more easily managed: without allies, living as orphans without siblings in an unforgiving world, they are easily made over into mass man, who is more than manageable—he wishes to be managed, his very personality is malleable. But atomized men are also unable to speak in human language, the lonely are more mute than animals. Can men who live suspended between other layers, other levels, accomplish those tasks we set for human creatures? Is not every lie a loss? And is not every failure to say the human truth a lie? In the layers of isolation the essence of man, his ability to commune in the achievement of ends beyond his individual capability, is diminished.

ROOTLESSNESS

Thou didst reject the only way by which
men might be made happy.
                                        The Grand Inquisitor

Her hair had been very long; a general brown, she said of the
color, as opposed to a particular brown. When she was painting, she gathered her hair into a bunch at the nape of her neck
and tied it there with a ribbon or a rubber band or a piece of
string. The tying was never quite successful. Strands came
loose and fell along her cheek, escaping the knot as the day
wore on and the work came closer to completion.

We can't be married, she had said to him, because you're
too neat. When you wake up in the morning your hair is still
combed.

A painter and an engineer. If you marry me, he said, I will
take you away from all this and teach you to draw a straight
line.

She married him because he convinced her that engineers
could laugh. He married her because her hair came loose as
she worked, and the strands fell along her cheek. The marriage was announced in both newspapers in Springfield. They
were married in June in a white wooden church, and before
the month was over they had made love in Firenze in a castle
made into an inn on a street where Leonardo da Vinci had
walked.

Da Vinci was an artist, he said.

Leonardo was an engineer, she said.

He designed electronic control systems in Connecticut after they were married. She stopped painting in Connecticut. He laughed less. She laughed more. They built a house on a hill near a bay. From the living room window they could see the water and the moored boats.

He designed electronic control systems in California after the company transferred them from Connecticut. She swam in California. Their first child, a girl, spent her first year in California in a house overlooking a brown field with one tree not quite in its center.

In Oregon they bought a house made of redwood. He designed electronic control systems at the company's Seattle plant. She continued her macrame, which she had learned in California.

Their second child was born in Houston, where he tested electronic control systems in the company's facility near the NASA complex. She drank wine in Houston, he worked long hours. She laughed. He explained the dangers of vertical promotions: morale problems. She watched soap operas on television in the afternoons in Houston. He said the damp air was good for her skin.

She cut her hair in Florida, where they lived in a house along a canal and sailed their boat on weekends. He said she looked younger with short hair, very young. He was elected a vice-president of the firm. Their first child took up painting in Florida; she enjoyed putting the proper colors in the numbered areas. Her father approved. Her mother drank wine and watched television in the afternoons; she was pleased by the concept of the television network, which provided the same soap operas in every part of the country. She wrote a letter to the heroine of a soap opera.

He was promoted to manager of the company's largest plant, which was located in South Bend, Indiana. She said, I am thirty-seven years old and everyone I know is on television.

He said, I will be the president of this company in five years, but in order for me to accomplish that you must become more friendly with the wife of our chairman. She became the closest friend of the wife of the chairman. Together, she and the wife of the chairman drank whiskey sours in the afternoons and watched television.

Her mother died in Springfield. She went home for the funeral services, which were held in a white wooden church. All of her mother's friends came to the church to weep. They said to her, I've known your mother since we were in grade school. I remember when you were born. Your mother and I grew up on the same street.

A man, distinguished by his white hair and craggy face, said, If your father hadn't married her, I would have, because I've been in love with her since we were in Sunday School.

She did not go back to South Bend after the funeral. Instead, she rented a small apartment on a street only two blocks from the place where she had lived when she was a child. The rent was low because the neighborhood had deteriorated. She was able to support herself by working in a department store.

He came from South Bend to bring her back.

I cried at my mother's funeral, she told him, but not out of guilt. I cried because I envied her. I cried out of guilt.

It will ruin my chances for the presidency if you don't come back with me, he said.

She took up painting in Springfield, and let her hair grow long.

He watched television in the evenings in South Bend.

Authority opposes totalitarianism, not the authority of force or of the power of men or organizations, but the authority of culture, of human history. This authority of culture relies very much on a sense of place, for it is with places that we associate tradition, and it is or has been possible so far to develop the moral authority of daily life only when it is rooted in places. An obvious example can be seen in the unseemly behavior of many travelers: Fidel Castro, in one of his famously long-winded speeches, described the behavior of tourists in Cuba and the more than two hundred brothels that catered to their tastes. These tourists had not made brothels of Peoria or Hartford; only when they left the moral authority of place behind did they behave like pigs.

To be a stranger does not give men freedom, for to be without cultural authority does not make men free, it merely gives them license, it weakens them. Floating produces a kind of nihilism: with the cultural authority of place no longer binding a man to his moral roots, everything is permitted, there are no limits. A floating man can be moved in any direction, and there are no limits on how far he can be moved.

Yet floating makes men uncomfortable: to live alone in the space between the instants of action is agonizing; without an atmosphere to contain him a man can burst of his own inner pressures. The corporation or the bureaucracy relieves the pressure of the vacuum, it becomes a place, the cultural authority, the moral home of a man. The rules of the corporation become the rules of society, the future replaces history, and the organization becomes the family of the floating man.

The rootless man, who cannot count on the disapprobation of his family and his neighbors, behaves as the corporation asks, lest he suffer the disapprobation of the only family and the only neighbors left to him. By detaching him from the real world of place, the corporation becomes the world for him. He is relieved of options, his relation to the corporation is total.

It has been estimated that, on the average, 20 per cent of the population of the United States moves every year. In five years the number of changes of residence equals the number of households in the population. Entire industries have grown up around the relocation of middle managers in American business, solving (for a fee) the problems of finding a house, choosing a school for the children, etc. No industry has arisen to solve the problem of disequilibrium that plagues people without roots, nor has anything been found that can rescue a floating man from finding a solution to the agony of nihilistic limitlessness in the totality of the corporation.

THE CLASS WITHOUT A CLASS

> The crowd instantly bows down to the earth, like one man, before the old inquisitor.
>
> The Grand Inquisitor

There was his mother, holding her big cardboard box loaded with sausages, bread, and milk bottles filled with water. She could hardly reach her arms around the width of the box to hold it. Whenever he looked at the photograph he wondered how she had carried the box so far. Every year, at Thanksgiving and Christmas, when the family gathered in the dining room, where the picture had hung from the beginning of his memory, he asked her if she had been afraid.

You think I was crazy? Sure I was afraid. They didn't have just clubs, you know. Lead pipes they had. You could break a head with such pipes.

Don't let her kid you, his father always said, those goons took one look at your mother, and they were so scared they almost ran away.

He looked at the picture again. She might have weighed a

hundred pounds on the day the photograph was made. Perhaps it was just that she had dressed in her most feminine clothes: high heels, beads, earrings, a little feathered hat, and that huge cardboard box with the end of a sausage and the tops of four milk bottles showing over the brown sides.

Sure I got myself all gussied up, she said. You think I wanted them to think I was a man? I was worried enough as it was. You can get a guarantee on that.

I saw her from the window, his father said. I had a pipe wrench in my hand. As hungry and thirsty as I was—I'll tell you, I could taste my own spit already—if they had laid a hand on your mother . . .

What? What? she said. You would have been a dead duck.

And then his father always said in a whisper, choking with remembered sentiment, It was the women who were the heroes. We were locked in like rats. The toilets didn't work. We didn't even have a glass of water, let alone something to eat. The leaders were beside themselves. Sing, they told us. We didn't even have spit to wet our mouths to sing. But when we saw the women walking through those goons. So proud they held their heads. Then we sang!

Such were his holidays for as long as he could remember. Such were his children's holidays. He told them not to laugh when Grandpa and Grandma put their arms around each other's shoulders and sang "Solidarity Forever." It was history, he said, serious business.

He had never belonged to a union, although he had worked with union men when he was in the company training program. The utility of unions seemed to him to have been greatly diminished by their own successes, as well as by overbearing federal regulatory agencies. Moreover, he had begun to wonder whether unions were not responsible for inflation and poor productivity. In the salaried employees' dining room he listened to talk about unions ruining quality, sending the balance of payments into the disastrous outflow situation that had hurt the dollar without bringing about the expected increase in exports, breaking the back of American industry. He nodded. There were other problems, of course, but the unions could not be ignored.

There had been three strikes against the company during his sixteen years of service, but each time he had been in a field office, either in sales or district service. Those offices were manned entirely by salaried people, and only once had the union sent a lone picket to stand in front of the district service office. The picket had stood on the left side of the front door for three hours one morning, holding his strike sign, drinking coffee, and slapping his hands against his sides to stay warm in the chill late October weather. He had avoided the picket by using the back door.

Now, the situation was different. This morning, when he entered the building to take his usual place as central office sales manager, there would not be one picket, there would be hundreds, perhaps a thousand. He envisioned the tightly packed lines of pickets, the police standing along the lines to keep order. He had seen such lines in the news, he had heard his father's descriptions a hundred times. Would they recognize him? Would he meet his father's old cronies? Would his father himself be there, holding up his three-fingered right hand and using his hearing aid, as he had in the '54 strike?

He drove to the office in the company of his imaginings. The union was wrong, he knew, the company offers had been good, they would not have been willing to work so far into November if the company had not been making decent offers. It was the union that had broken off negotiations and called the strike. There wasn't even a wage issue, he thought. All negotiations now were over work conditions, demands for more paid holidays, longer rest periods.

He parked his car in the company garage. There was no attendant to wish him a good morning; the teamsters were honoring the line. The garage seemed to him more full than usual at that hour. Perhaps they had permitted the security guards to park inside. He walked down the ramp and out onto the street.

There were the pickets; not a thousand, but more than a hundred, two hundred at least. They were not singing or chanting, as he had imagined. The men and a few women walked slowly back and forth in the gray light. They carried signs. Some wore brightly colored union jackets with the number of the local under the acronym. Most of them were big men, with wide backs and heavy shoulders; yet they walked in pairs, like children at the end of recess, each one with his partner, his pal.

He walked down the line hurriedly, looking away from them, keeping the police between himself and the line of strikers. The cold did not bother him, but he pretended to be hiding from the weather by hunching down inside his turned-up collar and lowering his head to let his hat brim break the wind. He was still fifty yards from the entrance to the building when the insults started. Scab! You scab! You fuck! You scab-fuck bastard! Brown-nose! Ass-licker! Scab! Look at the fucking scab!

He stopped and faced the nearest picketer. He and the picketer braced themselves, as if for a fight. The picketer was a slight man, thoroughly bundled into a red and black plaid lumber jacket, a thick scarf, ski gloves with tubular plastic fingers, and a blue watch cap. The picketer's nose and the tips of his ears were red. His face was lumpy, in middle age still marked by acne scars.

Scab!

No. That's not right. I'm not a scab, he said with histrionic calm. A scab is someone who crosses a picket line to take a union member's job. I'm not a union member. My job is non-union. It never was union. The union never wanted it. I'm management. Can't you tell by looking at me? The way I'm dressed? I don't belong to any organization. I come to work myself and go home myself. I don't go to meetings or walk on picket lines. No one fights for me. I have no comrades, no brothers. I don't sing songs to get up my courage. I go it alone, the hard way, like a man.

Scab! Scab! All along the line they shouted. Scab! Scab! Scab! Some of them were laughing. A man and a woman began to dance. Scab! He saw a three-fingered man. He saw a man with a hearing aid. Scab! They were all laughing and dancing. They held hands and skipped to the rhythm of their insults. Scabscab! Scabscabscab!

A policeman took his arm and led him gently toward the entrance.

———————◆———————

Labor unions, which institutionalize class solidarity, have always been the first victims of totalitarian regimes. Hitler destroyed them immediately after taking power. Lenin thought unions would be a balancing factor in socialism, acting as a counterweight to government and the Politburo, Trotsky demanded "bureaucratic centralism" instead, and Stalin achieved it. The relation of classes to freedom was perhaps best expressed, although in negative fashion, by Stalin, who said, according to Deutscher, "Freedom for several parties can exist only in a society in which there are antagonistic classes, whose interests are mutually hostile and irreconcilable. . . . In the USSR there is ground for only one party."

Machiavellian republics cannot survive without the vigor of conflict generated by class as well as other interests, neither can Madisonian republics endure without the envigorating conflict of various interests. Lacking class identity, men have neither power nor the comfort of allies in success or suffering, they are alone, like the atoms Wittgenstein said could be removed without affecting any other atoms; they are entirely expendable in their social and economic existence, relying on no one and with no one to rely on them.

The middle manager and the white collar worker theoretically belong to the middle class, which is no class at all, but an economic grouping characterized by dissension and competition. There is no reason why those in the middle class must exhibit bourgeois behavior simply because they are neither rich nor poor: the economic middle class in America does, in fact, include blue collar workers, shopkeepers, managers, and technicians. Some of those groups have class identities while others do not; it is those who lack any identity who are prey to bourgeois life. The weakness of the bourgeois, his willingness to compromise all moral values, springs from his terrible loneliness. He has nothing but goods to make his life; he lacks fraternity, he despises equality, and he, being alone, will sell his liberty for whatever goods he can gain. Linked to goods as a measure of life, any material loss is intolerable to him—he sells out because he has sold out—as a man for sale he has no dignity.

As the corporation separates men from each other, making a class of competing atoms, it gains control over them. The corporate bourgeois has no political loyalties but those of the corporation, because whatever helps the corporation helps him by increasing his supply of goods. He contributes to the political action committee not because he has to but because he wants to. The political action committee does the work of the only group he can identify with, the surrogate for class, the organization that replaces fraternity.

It could be argued by followers of Adam Smith or Milton Friedman, two economists of past centuries, that the man who finds his identity in the corporation merely pursues his own self-interest, which, in the thinking of that school of economics, is the height of morality. The value of selfishness to man's moral worth can be dismissed by an understanding of morality as a way for men to live well together. More interesting is the question of whether a man who cedes himself to the corporation does so in his own self-interest. The cession of one's self to any outside entity destroys a man's autonomy and human dignity; it leaves him defenseless. With neither autonomy nor the strength of fraternity, a man depends upon the mercy of the organization—he does not negotiate, having already ceded everything he has of value, he obeys.

MOVEMENT

> The great conquerors, Timours and Ghenghis-Khans, whirled like hurricanes over the face of the earth striving to subdue its people, and they . . . were but the unconscious expression of the . . . craving for Universal Unity.
>
> The Grand Inquisitor

He had never traveled with a bodyguard before coming to Manila. Now a small brown man with a machine pistol accompanied him everywhere, even into the toilet of the restaurant, where he opened the doors of each of the stalls, hooking them with the toe of his polished black shoe and pulling them sharply outward. Only after all the stalls proved to be empty did the bodyguard motion him to come forward to stand at the urinal.

The president of the company laughed at the precautions, but he had difficulty urinating: it was too much like war. His sales manager had shown him a newspaper story about a man who had been robbed and murdered in the toilet of a Manila restaurant only a week earlier. In reply, the president had accused him of trying to get extra pay for hazardous duty.

Oh no, the sales manager said, I'm not afraid for myself. He laughed nervously, obsequiously. Although he was six and a half feet tall and heavily built, once a football player, the sales manager had been in the Pacific for almost twenty years and he had adopted the delicate gestures of the Orient. He held his hands together, the fingertips touching lightly, when he spoke, and he bowed at meetings and farewells. He seemed to be trying to make himself smaller, more in accord with the people to whom he sold his goods, but he succeeded only in making himself elephantine and effeminate.

You understand, the president told him, that I'm still opposed to this expansion. I don't like doing business in competition with the Japanese. I won't agree to rebates, bribes, or pimping. If the Japanese want to do business that way, to hell with them. I'll guarantee you a better product at a competitive price. You can sell that, can't you?

The sales manager shrugged. He managed to bow while sitting.

The president had opposed the expansion into the Pacific, but the board had overruled him. He had been given lectures in the utilization of plant and equipment. The chairman had talked about the failure to expand in a growing world market as an insidious form of contraction. He had destroyed the president's arguments against doing business in the Japanese style by calling them sanctimonious rationalizations.

Manila had been their first target market, and it had suddenly begun to look good. A member of the Cabinet had agreed to consider acting as a distributor for their products in the Philippines. And just as suddenly it had begun to look bad. The cabinet minister said the Japanese had also made an offer.

Jesus Christ, the president said to his sales manager, don't they remember World War II? Tell him MacArthur was my second cousin. Change your name to Wainwright or something.

The Japs give incentives.

Isn't profit an incentive in this goddamned country?

The sales manager bowed again, Things are different in the Orient: there are profits and incentives.

No bribes, no rebates, and no whores, the president said.

These Flips are horny little bastards. I know a place where we could take him to talk a little business.

The president terminated the lunch and went back to his hotel room. He said the flight had tired him and he wanted to have a clear head when he met with the minister at dinner. But when he got back to his hotel room he couldn't sleep. He lay on his bed listening to the afternoon sounds of the hotel: the laundry carts wheeled through the halls, the maids chatting in Tagalog, the machinery of the elevator somewhere in the distance. He chose not to use the air conditioning, preferring the breeze that came in through the louvered doors and window shutters. The air smelled of flowers and fuel oil. He drifted. Fears spoke to him: age, the numbers of his blood pressure, the chairman's capricious character, the fate of his predecessor. He thought of sending a postal card to his wife, of buying gifts for her and the children. In three years he had raised the company's productivity by 38 per cent, but it had cost too much: earnings were up less than ten cents a share. The stock analysts had labeled him too conservative, and the price of the stock had dropped to 17⅜. If the minister took the Japanese offer . . .

The door opened, the bodyguard peered into the room. His black pupils moved abruptly. He met the president's eyes, acknowledging his presence with a momentary stillness, like a bird's sudden stare. He smiled, bowed his head slightly, and withdrew it, closing the door softly afterward.

Was it an offer? The women of the Philippines were the most beautiful in the Pacific, his wife had told him so. And he had answered, But I don't love them. I'm not married to them. She had laughed. Her voice was low, with little squeaks in it when she laughed. Voices in the Philippines tinkled in laughter. He did not trust the sound.

He washed away the slight sweat of his drifting near sleep, dressed for dinner, and went down to the bar to meet his sales manager. The bar was filled with rich-looking Orientals, mostly Japanese, a few Koreans, and Chinese from Taiwan. They wore dark suits, mainly blue, in spite of the heat. He noticed the color of scotch in almost every glass. They adapted, he thought, like roaches. They were pushing him, swarming over him. He said to the sales manager, Humans are the only moral creatures.

And sometimes I wonder about us, the sales manager answered, following his words with a tinkling giggle, a Filipino giggle.

The minister was due to meet them in fifteen minutes. His car would be outside. They would be preceded by his bodyguard and followed by theirs. The sales manager recited the details, bowing and smiling. At the end of the recitation, he asked, Where do you want to take him? I know a little place. It's a crackup, a scream. They have girls who come around to your table and pick up dollar bills with their snatches. It turns my stomach, but I know it's the kind of place he loves, the best whorehouse in the Pacific. Take him there and you got him. The owner wouldn't let a Jap into the place. The war, you know; some of these people are still mad about the war.

The president looked around the room. His and the sales manager's were the only white faces. Everyone was drinking, dealing, bowing, smiling. He felt dizzy, nauseated.

Is there any other way? he asked the sales manager.

Not for this guy.

And if he doesn't distribute for us?

Nobody will. He's the minister who gives out the import licenses.

You take him. Tell him I've gone up to my room. I'm sick.

He'd be insulted.

The president finished his drink in a great gulp. He nodded to the sales manager that he was ready to leave. As he stood up, his foot turned and he stumbled forward. The sales manager and the bodyguard caught his arms to steady him. They stayed at his side, holding his arms all the way out through the bar and the hotel lobby, down the steps to the minister's car.

The best way to succeed in business was documented by Aristotle, who learned the system from Thales the Milesian among others. Thales leased all the olive presses in Chios and Miletus, having discovered through his knowledge of the stars that a great olive harvest was coming. He then leased out the presses at any rate he pleased. Aristotle commented on Thales' business dealings without great admiration: ". . . His device for getting wealth is of universal application, and is nothing but the creation of a monopoly."

Neither did Aristotle think much of people whose whole lives were devoted "to increase their money without limit. . . ." "The origin of this disposition in men," he wrote, "is that they are intent upon living only, and not upon living well; and as their desires are unlimited, they also desire that the means of gratifying them should be without limit."

This view of business compares with Arendt's view of movement in the totalitarian state, where she says power is never achieved finally: "Their [National Socialism and Bolshevism] idea of domination was something that no state and no mere apparatus of violence can ever achieve, but only a movement that is constantly kept in motion: namely, the permanent domination of each single individual in each and every sphere of life." In other words, total and universal monopoly, which as she and Buchheim point out, can never be achieved. Totalitarianism, like the modern corporation, has no end: either it grows or it dies.

In the dynamics of totalitarianism the desire for growth, for the impossible total monopoly, makes a juggernaut of the organization. Nothing can deter it, neither morality, nor reason, nor even self-preservation. The urge to dominate comes to dominate all those within the organization, men are but the means to movement, and movement is the only possible end.

The modern corporation, especially in America, with its antitrust laws, professes to eschew monopoly in favor of healthy competition, but every corporation wishes to expand, to become the industry leader, the dominant factor. Every corporation wants to be considered a growth company, every capitalist wants to put his money into growth stocks. If growth in a single industry has limits, due either to the health of competitors or the size of the market, the corporation can continue to expand, through diversification, by merger or acquisition, into other industries. The end, the universal corporation, cannot be achieved; thus the corporation, like the totalitarian state, develops an ideology of movement, putting the point of diminishing return always one step beyond.

Application of antitrust laws can no longer have meaning, for in a world of free trading nations competition has become internationalized, as in steel, automobiles, and electronics. The battle between corporations has escalated to a battle between nations, as Clausewitz said it would. The analogy between war and business has become a simulacrum, the two differ only in the choice of weapons—structures, ends, and the use of men are identical.

SUDDENNESS

> . . . Today, people are more persuaded
> than ever that they have perfect free-
> dom, yet they have brought their free-
> dom to us and laid it humbly at our feet.
>   The Grand Inquisitor

The one thing he knew about the management of the company
was that they valued him. They had told him so, he had told
her so. Whenever he felt unhappy with his job, whenever they
felt the pinch of inflation at home, she reminded him of how
he was valued by the company. It saw them through a bank
loan to consolidate and stretch out their other loans. It saw
them through their children attending public schools instead of
the country day school they had planned on. It saw them
through the fleabites and itchings of their lives.

They were not unhappy. She said he watched too much television on weekends. He wondered aloud if it was healthy for
her to watch television in the afternoons. A week before their
fifteenth wedding anniversary he bought a sex manual, but he
had second thoughts about it—she might consider it a criticism
of her performance in bed—and he left the manual on the seat
of the bus.

On Sundays they went to church. She collected money for
the United Fund, he did his best to hire minorities and women
in his section, they despised Richard Nixon after Watergate.
The evening of the day the car broke down he said to her that

life was not easy for decent middle-class people anymore.

But we haven't lost our values, she answered.

His hair was thinning, she had developed a varicose vein in her left leg. One night while they were in bed, he said, Time is passing.

It's not so bad, she said.

I don't know, honey, I think the Joneses have passed us by.

You have a good job, and it'll get better. You provide for us.

He kissed her. She wiped the moisturizing ointment from her hands before she touched him.

He was not an easy man to work for. Mistakes irritated him; he did not hesitate to point them out to those who erred. He believed people were happier when they did their best, and he told them so. Everyone was equal in his eyes: male and female, black and white. No one escaped criticism for an error, even if it came in the form of a long coffee break or an unexcused morning lateness. Some people said he was grumpy, an old woman rather than a middle-aged man. Neither was he an easy man to supervise: his ways were set, he knew what was best for the company, and he did not hesitate to say so. He did not deviate from the rules: there were no shortcuts, he abhorred cheating in any form, the thought of stealing a paper clip or a moment was odious to him. When he refused to reconsider scrapping a thousand gross of journey crosses because an indeterminate number had been forged with one side three hundredths of an inch too short, the vice-president congratulated him, taking responsibility for the error as his own.

His dismissal was the greatest surprise of his life. What did I do? he asked.

You didn't *do* anything, the vice-president said. You're simply not promotable in the job. God almighty, you must know that by now, man.

I like my job. I do it well. You told me I do it well. You told me how valuable I am to the company.

It's policy. We don't want any first line managers who can't be promoted. It's policy. I can't do anything about it.

But I haven't done anything. I don't steal, not even a paper clip, not even a piece of notepaper. I never let down on quality. I gave it all I had.

You can't argue your way back into the job. Make it easy on yourself. The vice-president offered his hand. While they shook hands, the vice-president took an envelope from his pocket. He said it was a check for fifteen weeks' severance and four weeks' vacation pay.

When he left the vice-president's office, he went to the men's room to wash his face with cold water, especially his eyes, which were burning and itching, as if he'd been touched by some industrial pollutant. He looked at himself in the mirror above the sink. It was an honest face. The thinning hair, the eyeglasses, the fold of flesh above his shirt collar, the beard so bluegray and steely on his white skin, the manly pores of the skin on his nose, everything about him was forthright, decent. He was an ordinary, hardworking American, veteran, tax-payer, husband, father, Rockefeller Republican, and he had been fired!

He cleaned out his desk and took the pictures off the wall behind him, sorting out what was his from what was theirs. He had three tins of aspirin. Was that wasteful, he wondered, or had the headaches been so bad?

Everything fit into his attaché case, the present his wife and children had given him the Christmas after his promotion. The case was scarred, one lock was broken, and he had put a piece of adhesive tape on the handle where the leather had come loose. The tape was gray now. He paused to consider it for a moment, the time was all there on the piece of tape, every morning, every evening, all the work he had taken home to do on the kitchen table. He slammed the case shut, closed the one lock that still worked, and left his office. He said good-by to no one. He had been a severe man, an honest man, who gave no quarter. That had been his value to the company. Even now, he wasted no one's time in farewells.

On the way home he tried to make a plan, knowing that a man couldn't go about looking for a job in a haphazard manner. Discipline was important. He would get up at the same time, he would shower and shave and catch the same train he always caught. He knew all the failings of weak men: he would not spend time in bars, he would not go to the ball game in the afternoon.

She kept coming to mind, more than the job hunting, more than the children. What would she do? What would she say? She would cry, she would think of the bills, she would hug the children. When they went to bed, she would not put ointment on her hands, saying they could no longer afford it. Late at night, after he had gone to sleep, she would permit herself to cry; he would know by the redness around her eyes in the morning.

At the station there was a woman selling orange and gold and rusty brown autumn flowers. He bought a bunch from her. They were only a dollar and they would look so good, so cheery on the dining room table. They were just right for the green vase.

He opened the front door and called out to her, Hi, honey! It was like every other evening. He smelled the food cooking in the kitchen, a chicken roasting; he hoped she had basted it with orange juice.

She came hurrying out of the kitchen, through the dining room, wiping her hands on her apron. Her hair was so neat, the same bangs she had always worn, the gray not spoiling it at all; her face was so sweet, made sweeter by the weight she had gained in the past few years. He held the flowers out to her.

It's an occasion, she said. She blushed, running the last few steps, embracing him, dancing him half a turn. It's an occasion! She leaned her head back to watch his face.

You know how valuable they say I am.

---◆---

Juridical man has dignity and entertains feelings of autonomy because he knows himself as a legal person, more than an animal or a thing, a person capable of beginnings, a person who must be considered in the special category of humanity. Juridical man exists in his own eyes and in the eyes of others, he leaves a mark in the world, he can engage in politics. In societies based on law, he expects to have certain rights: no one can do violence to him without breaking the law.

Totalitarian organizations seek to destroy the concept of juridical man in their search for total power. Things submit to domination more easily than legal persons. Things do not begin; there is no thing new under the sun. To do violence to a thing breaks no laws, even the murder of a thing does not call for punishment. When all persons are reduced to things, law has no meaning, all is permitted, without limit.

Night and Fog was the Nazi code name for the order that people who were considered security risks were to disappear without a trace. It implied that enemies of the organization were not legal persons. Stalin chose first to destroy those who opposed him and then to destroy those who agreed with him in order to rid the Soviet Union of the notion of juridical man. His method included concentration camps, assassinations, and the sudden dismissal of people who had performed well in their jobs.

Corporations, by turn paternalistic and cruel, teach their employees not to consider themselves juridical persons, with rights, living under the rule of law in human fashion. The sudden and apparently unprovoked dismissal of a few people or even of one person makes the rest docile. It teaches that the will of the organization is greater than the will of law or even of reason: the will of the organization is incontestable.

Men who live in such circumstances are not free, for there can be freedom only when law limits power. A man can be either a juridical person or a slave, he may have recourse against power or he may not. When men have no legal existence, when power may be exercised against them without the restraint of law, the social contract has been abrogated, human society has been replaced by the organization of things, all human values have been lost. The man who believes himself to be a creature utterly without rights belongs to a mass of disconnected atoms, no one of which has any unique value. That man obeys. He considers it his happiness.

ESPRIT

> Man was created a rebel; and how can
> rebels be happy?
>
> The Grand Inquisitor

The Piranha had been very close to death. He had been bleeding for days, perhaps a week, losing his strength, watching the color of himself pale away. Finally, the light did not come with the morning. He could not move. His wife was only three feet away in the other bed, but he could neither see nor hear her. He knew she was there. He knew it was summer. The early light would awaken her. He waited, praying: Hail Mary, full of Grace . . .

His sight came back in spots and streaks. He heard a low

hissing in his ears before he heard a true sound. He felt pains in his joints before he felt the pain of the needle in his left arm. Doctors and nurses stood by the side of his bed. His wife was somewhere in the farther part of the room; he heard her voice.

You've had a close call, the doctor told him after his blood pressure was near to normal again. What you have to do now is get that sore in your gut completely healed and then make sure it doesn't happen again. Diet will help, but you can't solve the whole problem with a bland diet; you're going to have to change your life-style. The problem you have is caused by stress.

I'm not under stress, the Piranha said. I cause stress for other people. That's what senior management is supposed to do. I tell my managers they've come to work for a Piranha, that if they don't perform I'll eat 'em up alive.

Is that effective?

They perform, the Piranha answered. No vice-president of our company gets more out of his people than I do. I drive them, and they perform, and they love it. My guys are happy because they're winners.

You could have died, the doctor said.

Country boys are tough, doc.

The doctor nodded. He seemed weary, as if he were also bleeding. He said he would come back in the late afternoon.

The Piranha's wife came to stand at his bedside. She took his hand in hers and squeezed it, not speaking, looking down at her pale husband. Everything was white: his skin, the hospital gown, the sheets, his thick, wavy hair. I was so frightened, she said. You were hardly breathing.

Don't worry about me. I'll be back at work in a week.

She shook her head: The doctor said it would be a long time.

A business doesn't manage itself, honey. If I stay out for a long time, they'll have to find someone else to manage my people. It's not that I'm worried about my job, nothing like that. But there's work to be done, the company has to keep moving. We're on the verge of breaking a billion dollars in sales. Think of it! A billion dollars. That's a milestone, like the Hall of Fame or the Academy Award or something. A billion dollars. We made something out of nothing, we put a lot of people to work. It isn't just making money, business is how people live. What do you think would happen to people without business? We'd all starve, that's what. We'd go back to living in caves. This world works on the power of business. We eat because we work, and we can work because we have businesses, structures that give us the opportunity. So we can't just slough off, coast along, you know what I mean. You've got to drive. Work, create goods, sell goods, make more, work harder. That's life, that's what we were put on earth for. The Garden of Eden is closed for the duration: men earn the good life by their own sweat. And that's what's right with the world. A guy can grow up in a hick town on the Canadian border and move himself from there to this office, to this view, the comforts of home and a fat paycheck too. Can you beat that? Can you match it anywhere else on earth? This is the best time in the best country and you're working for the best, fastest growing, most aggressive company in American industry. You're with the doers, the makers, that's why you can be a winner. This is your chance. Take it.

———————◆————————

Esprit de corps, Freud thought, derived from envy. At the turning point in *Group Psychology and the Analysis of the Ego,* the place where he describes man as a "horde animal" rather than a "herd animal," he describes the "reaction-formation" against the inability to excel, against envy, as the cause of equality, esprit de corps, and even the wish for justice. When he described man as "an individual creature in a horde led by a chief," he adumbrated the political situation that would take place in Germany only a little more than a decade after his publication of the description, for the Germans truly did become a horde and they truly were led by one man in a totalitarian state.

As we know from Nazi Germany, the wish for justice is not necessarily a part of the reaction-formation and the horde is not composed of equals but of layers and levels of equals. Envy contributes to the atomization of man, which permits the making of mass man in whom esprit de corps or internal motivation becomes a determining force. But envy does not disappear because men react to it by the formation of esprit de corps. The two exist side by side: men are loyal to the group but not to each other; esprit de corps becomes a means of rising above the others in the group to a new level of equals or a new layer of intimacy with the leader.

In totalitarianism the situation is greatly magnified, as Hannah Arendt explained: "Totalitarianism is never content to rule by external means, namely, through the state and a machinery of violence; thanks to its peculiar ideology and the role assigned to it in this apparatus of coercion, totalitarianism has discovered a means of dominating and terrorizing human beings from within. In this sense it eliminates the distance between the rulers and the ruled and achieves a condition in which power and the will to power, as we understand them, play no role, or at best, a secondary role."

Internal motivation has become a more and more common goal of industrial psychologists as salaries replace wages and knowledge workers comprise more of the labor force. The blunt truth of labor in exchange for money favored by many unionists has given way to the notion of the motivated worker. Well-meaning psychologists, in their haste to escape cruel authoritarianism, have dissected man and made his parts vulnerable to totalitarian management. While they have succeeded little, if at all, with blue collar workers, their task with those who consider themselves managers poses fewer difficulties, for managers and other white collar and technical workers belong to an inner layer of the organization; they are lonely, envious, but initiates in the circle. They identify with the leader to distinguish themselves from the outer layers. To save themselves, they become believers, and then are motivated by their beliefs. For them esprit de corps is an act of cession, the wish to be part of the horde.

TAKE AND GIVE

In the end they will lay their freedom at our feet, and say to us, "Make us your slaves, but feed us."
                                   The Grand Inquisitor

She did not want to cry. She refused to cry. A woman with an M.B.A. who earned twenty-two thousand dollars a year and supervised a staff of professionals should not cry, did not cry. He was wrong. He was the director. He was intelligent, experienced, a good judge of people, a fair-minded man in most instances, but every now and then he was wrong.

A month before he had been so decent, avuncular, even fatherly in confronting what she considered not only her failure but the failure of all the analysts. Then he had praised her effort, now he criticized her success. She listened to his words again, seeking some clue: Too slow, too much manpower. The project wasn't worth it. In the time it took your group to complete the project, the entire category lost its salience.

She closed the door to her office, went back to her desk, took the tiny mirror out of her makeup bag and carefully checked her mascara. With a piece of Kleenex, she dabbed at a spot under her right eye. It didn't come off. She wet the tip of the Kleenex on her tongue and rubbed lightly. There was nothing more to do. She put the makeup kit back into her purse.

There were no telephone messages, she had dealt with the morning mail. No one was waiting to see her. It was still an hour before lunch. She looked at the pile of clips on her credenza. The article on the top was from *Iron Age*. She would read it later, after dinner, in the quiet of her own apartment.

Had she made an error? Why hadn't he spoken to her earlier if he thought she was spending too much time on the project? He had seen her project report, he had initialed the memo.

When her group had misread the effect of the upward valuation of the yen on the electronics market, he hadn't been angry. He had said that no one could get inside the Japanese Government to predict that they would have chosen not to dump on the U.S. market. You can't be faulted for that, he had said; they aren't called inscrutable for nothing.

Now, when she demonstrated that big steel was cutting prices while demanding protection, he criticized her. He hadn't even noticed their success in getting the transaction prices. Mercurial, that was the only possible description of the man's behavior. Maybe it was his time of the month. She laughed to herself. A bad joke. A good way to get into trouble. She felt a slight chill. The outline of her spine was sharp against her skin.

She turned on the Dictaphone and addressed a memo to him. Then she shut off the machine. It would be better to talk to him in person. He knew things. He had connections, old friends in the business, he heard rumors. If she was going to

continue with the parts manufacturing project, it would be
best to stay close to him about it, to ask his advice, to be there
when he changed his mind, if he changed his mind. As the
Japanese said, she would read his stomach. She was pleased;
she had learned how to handle him.

———◄◆►———

The tactic was first recognized by Cicero, who described its
use by Caesar: "By a mixture of intimidation and indulgence,
he inculcated in a free community the habit of servitude." In
the Soviet Union the practice has been used both to keep from
softening the knife edge of terror and to keep citizens from
such utter despair that the difference between compliance and
noncompliance becomes meaningless.

To break the spirit of a person, to destroy any faith he may
have in his ability to be an origin, no system can work more
effectively than to praise him for failure and criticize him for
success. The tactic leaves its victim without faith in his own
judgment. It is a form of terror calculated to leave the victim
in a state of disequilibrium, so that he must look to his superior as the crutch that holds him upright.

The tactic is widely used in business, most often by managers who are themselves frightened and wish to keep their un-
derlings from having the opportunity of passing them by or
even of questioning their decisions. The result of applying a
tactic calculated to destroy autonomy is that any creative or
innovative capabilities the victim may possess are destroyed.
The victim has no choices but to become a sycophant or an
obstructionist, finding fault with every idea, every activity, in
order to avoid facing the unpredictability of his supervisor.
Yet even obstructionism will not save the victim, for his supervisor still has the opportunity alternately to praise or criticize
him for his fault finding. Eventually, the victim becomes a
mere thing, the kind of slave that Rousseau said loves his ser-

vitude, mass man, the creature who can neither rebel nor withdraw.

PLACED LOYALTIES

> They will understand themselves at last,
> that freedom and bread enough for all
> are inconceivable together, for never,
> never will they be able to share between
> them!
>
> The Grand Inquisitor

The vice-chairman had never fit into the company. He suffered from machismo, he wore blue blazers and brown pants to public meetings, he dyed his hair, and he was married to a woman younger than his youngest son. Moreover, he was a sentimentalist, the kind of man who could spend his nights at the bedside of a dying colleague. He did it because the man was a bachelor, he said, all alone in the world, with no one else to hold his hand.

There had never been an electrical engineer quite like him. His name was on seventy-three patents, and the men who worked for him in research and engineering said it should have been on another seven hundred and thirty, at least. There were stories about him that achieved the status of legend in the industry. To meet a contract delivery date he had invented a monitoring system for rocket engines while on an airplane trip from Florida to Ohio. Although he had no formal training in hydrodynamics, he had used his experience as a weekend sailor to design a new hull that increased by 20 per cent the speed of a ship the company was building for the navies of Argentina, Lebanon, and South Africa. His work in mathematics was more important, according to the sophisticated scientists in the company, but more difficult to explain in practical terms, because the machinery to prove out his theoretical work had not yet been built.

When he contracted Hodgkin's disease at the age of sixty-two, he responded as everyone expected: he took up the study of biochemistry, reading all day and into the night, complaining of the interference of treatment, questioning the doctors. I intend to find a way to kill this disease, he said, before it kills me. The doctors nodded gravely. His family physician said, If anyone can . . .

The disease weakened him. The treatments weakened him further. He lost weight, his hair fell out, he suffered sudden swellings and internal bleeding. He soon realized that he was dying. It's not the pain, he told his wife, but the lack of time that hurts me. If I had enough time, I could beat this thing.

As one kind of treatment after another failed to put the disease into remission, the doctors began to offer sedatives to him. I'll wait, he told them. The body builds up tolerances to sedatives. If I take sedatives now, what will I do when I need them? The doctors nodded gravely. They said he was wise to wait as long as he could. The nurses were instructed to give him Darvon as soon as he asked for it.

After the treatments were abandoned, he began to feel better. He ordered a desk and a comfortable chair for reading to be brought to his hospital room. Each morning, he put on a clean shirt and a freshly pressed pair of brown pants. He wore a torn cardigan sweater, as if he were at home, and he covered his bald head with a black watch cap, which he said was not only the cheapest but the best-fitting wig available.

In the course of dying, he began to have insights. He spent much of his time with mathematics, which he found more beautiful than ever. He made equations in shapes that were more like paintings than mere lines of numbers, letters, and signs. He called it the aesthetics of aesthetics, the form of forms.

I'm so old to be a Platonist, he said. I think now that my life has been misspent.

His wife also changed. The frivolity he had admired and loved in her was lost to seriousness. She read Russian novels and ontological philosophy. She too thought her life had been misspent.

Together, they listed the things they should have done:

Given more to charity.

Adopted a child.

Baked on Tuesdays.

Read the Greeks, Romans, Russians, Scholastics, Kant, and Marx.

Eaten less.

Spent a lifetime in another business.

Showed more kindness to subordinates.

Showed more kindness to domestics.

Worked on the world food problem.

Grown a beard.

Found a cure for Hodgkin's disease.

There is one more thing, he said to her, and it is the thing I am most ashamed to admit, even to you. But I'm dying, and even though my death is not yet so close that I sincerely believe in God or the afterlife, I want to make this confession: I should not have committed the murders, not any of them. It was self-defense in every case, but that is no excuse.

You're wandering, she said. Should I call the nurse?

He was pleased by her calm and competence, and he told her so. But he insisted that he was rational, in some pain, severe pain, but still rational.

Sit down, he said, stop being solicitous, and I'll explain. I will, in fact, explain my entire career to you. Yesterday, I had a visit from the two other members of the great troika, my chairman and our president. I offered to resign from the company. That's reasonable, don't you think, considering that I will probably remain in this room until I die? Not only did I offer to resign, I suggested that of my three possible successors only one was a sensible choice, a surprising choice, but sensible. You'll be surprised too, because I didn't suggest either my engineering or my research vice-president. I suggested the fellow who runs the computer section. He's a good mathematician and he's shown some fairly original thinking in the area of computer vision, which is the only way the company will be able to compete with Third World manufacturers in the next century.

But that's obvious. What's interesting is that they refused to accept my offer to resign. They said they might leave the job open. And to keep from hurting my delicate feelings, they told me why. They didn't want to destroy either of the men who didn't get the job.

That's what they said. Can you imagine that? The sons of bitches. The dirty sons of bitches, that's what they said.

He closed his eyes for no more than a second, but it was long enough for her to see how close he was to dying.

Now I know everything, he said. Now I know how lonely I was.

Competition in business occurs on both intermural and intramural levels. The intermural sort associated with capitalism may, as Marx argued, separate "individuals from one another, not only the bourgeois but still more the workers, in spite of the fact that it brings them together"; but it does not have the destructive effect of intramural competition. In the latter form, which is common to all political and economic systems, excepting a few utopian plans, men are pitted against each other like animals on an island of scarcity.

Men come quite naturally to the competitive situation. As Freud noted, "All relationships contain a sediment of feelings of aversion and hostility. These are less disguised in business." It is clearly a totalitarian tactic in business to set men against one another to arouse these feelings. Were it not for intramural competition, men in middle management and white collar or technical jobs might band together in co-operative fashion to create autonomous units made of autonomous individuals.

Stalin recognized the danger to a totalitarian system of any kind of equalitarianism, as Isaac Deutscher reports. He insisted upon a highly differentiated system of both material and psychological rewards, which he claimed were to act as incentives to greater efficiency, but which were, in fact, used to atomize society. Lonely men, Stalin knew, became mass men, who could not defend themselves against a totalitarian organization.

The use of competition in business on an intramural level is not new. It forces men to behave so savagely that Hannah Arendt made the following comparison in describing the murderous actions of despots: "Practically speaking, the totalitarian ruler proceeds like a man who persistently insults another man until everybody knows that the latter is his enemy, so that he can, with some plausibility, go and kill him in self-defense. This certainly is a little crude, but it works—so everybody will know who ever watched how certain successful careerists eliminate competition."

An advertisement for *The Wall Street Journal* showed the process graphically: a group of men were shown at the bottom of a diagram of a pyramid. As they marched toward the apex, men turned away at each level, until there was room for only one at the top. The newspaper was so certain of the understanding of the murderous nature of intramural competition by businessmen that it used this graphic portrayal in an attempt to gain new subscribers by promising them that reading the newspaper would improve their chances of reaching the top. It was a cruel way to use men's anxieties, but probably a successful one, because the advertisement was repeated often over many months.

Many managers set out to increase the intensity of competition among the striving equals below them, as in the preceding fictional illustration. They do so believing, as Stalin said he did, that efficiency would be improved and skills would be heightened. Stalin, of course, was viciously cynical, but many businessmen use this tactic of totalitarianism in the sincere belief that it will produce better results than a co-operative spirit. To hold that belief they must assume that men will finally be promoted or rewarded on merit. In fact, the atomization of men through artificially heightened competition leads as often to calumny as to superior performance, more often to anxious backwardness than to innovative work, and always to a loss of useful energy in the waging of internecine war.

Within the layers and levels of a corporation, each competitor at an inner layer or higher level heightens competition among those below him to weaken them so that they are less able to compete with him. War inside the organization thus takes place vertically, horizontally, and tangentially. A view of the corporation from a great distance would reveal a war unlike the grand maneuvers of classic battles. It would appear far more like a riot spreading through the narrow maze of streets and steps of an ancient city.

The difference between the riotous waste of totalitarian conflict and the enriching and stabilizing conflict of a Machiavellian or Madisonian republic comes in both the genesis and the end: totalitarian organizations direct a conflict of competition as a means of using men, while conflict in a republican democracy arises from the differences between men who seek no end but their own happiness. The latter enhances the political nature of man; totalitarianism aims at nothing more precisely than to atomize men so as to destroy the political part of their nature.

INTERCHANGEABLE DESPOTS

> So long as man remains free he strives
> for nothing so incessantly and so pain-
> fully as to find some one to worship.
> The Grand Inquisitor

The vice-president of human relations said that the change of chief executive officers had deeply affected his life: Fifteen years ago, I was vice-president of personnel; five years ago, I was vice-president of industrial relations; a year ago, I became vice-president of human relations. I sit at the same desk and do the same job. If I last through one more chairman, I'm sure I'll become vice-president of human interactions.

When the chairman was a Protestant, the Protestants were disappointed; when the chairman was a Catholic, the Catholics were disappointed. If we ever have a woman as chairman, the women will be disappointed.

It wasn't the chairman who failed the company, it was the oil crisis that failed the chairman.

Yes, it is foolish not to have names or even numbers on the doors to the executives' offices, said the chairman. It is also pretentious, confusing, and wasteful of people's time. But there have never been names or numbers on the doors.

I get paid three hundred and twenty-six thousand dollars a year to avoid precipitous change, said the chairman. As long as I do the inevitable, I'm the right man at the right time in the right job.

You're a powerful man, the interviewer said to the CEO.
In what way?
You have power over people. You could fire anyone in this company.
There are eighty-five thousand people in this company, the CEO said. Half of them are not giving us a day's work for a day's pay. If I fire ten per cent, it will decimate the company. What would you call it if I fired fifty per cent?

In the year of his retirement, the company lost forty-one million dollars and did not pay a dividend for the first time in twenty-seven years. The chairman's wife could not understand why he was despondent. After all, she said, you earned over seven hundred thousand dollars.

———◆———

The modern corporation differs from the tyranny of the single proprietor associated with classical capitalism at the center and at the apex of the dual structures. The corporation and the proprietorship compare in the same way as the monarchy and the tyranny described by Coulanges in *The Ancient City:* "It was not the custom to call a good prince *king* and a bad one *tyrant*. Religion was what distinguished one from the other. The primitive kings had performed the duties of priests and had derived their authority from the sacred fire; the tyrants of a later epoch were merely political chiefs, and owed their elevation to force or election only."

Like the sacred fire, the office of chief executive in the corporation or leader (by whatever title) in the state is the investiture, carrying with it power greater than the consent of the employees or the citizenry. Replacement of the leader makes little difference to the totalitarian organization. Most often, if not always, the leader will come from the inner circle of the onion structure; on many occasions from near the top of the authoritarian structure, when it nearly coincides at that level with the inner circle; i.e., when the party and the government do not diverge sharply outside the person of the leader.

Hannah Arendt presents a different point of view in *The Origins of Totalitarianism*. She contends at one point that the entire system fails with the removal of the leader, although later on in the same work she presents Hitler's view that the machinery of the Nazi state would function without him, even though he thought himself irreplaceable. Since the publication of Arendt's work, history has demonstrated that the totalitarian organization of the Soviet Union was able to survive the death of Stalin. There have, of course, been changes, but mainly in the tightening and loosening of the bonds of totalitarianism necessary to maintaining the population in a useful condition.

In corporations, the change of chief executives is common, while changes in basic policy and organizational structure are rare. Corporations, like states, may fail, and in the throes of failure great changes may occur. The first stage of change in a dying totalitarian organization is the rise to complete power of the onion structure and the concomitant murderous tightening of the bonds of the employees or citizens. Great numbers of people are eliminated, with loyalty rather than utility or efficiency the criterion.

When mere tyrants fall, there being no investiture, the organization is transformed, for the tyrant is only a ruler and not a philosopher; the force at his command is not sufficient to build a lasting organization.

MANNA

They will become timid and will look to
us and huddle close to us in fear, as
chicks to the hen.
                    The Grand Inquisitor

As a matter of course, he advised his clients, when approached
on the subject, to adopt a bonus system and to use it at all
levels of management above first line supervision. A CPA has
no credentials for discussing management policy, he told them,
let alone industrial psychology, but for what it's worth, I think
the bonus system is a great motivator. The financial benefits to
the company are easier to demonstrate. First, you keep the
money during the year, earning interest on it. And that can
amount to an appreciable sum. Second, you have the option in
a poor year to withhold bonus payments, which may be substantial. In other words, your management salaries become
much more on the variable rather than the fixed side. And
finally, you need never pay your people more in salary and
bonus than you would have paid them in salary. Give it some
thought, keeping in mind that just fifty bonuses at twenty
thousand dollars each amounts to a million dollars; it really
can make quite a difference.

Without fail, they asked if his company used the bonus system. To which he always answered, Yes, and very effectively.
Despite my awareness of its utility to the company I never fail
to feel enormous gratitude.

He did not tell them his dependence on the bonus system,

how he planned on a certain amount each year, based on the profits in his office and the overall performance of the company. Nor did he tell them that he had been driven by family circumstances to achieve an ever larger bonus.

This year, for example, he might have said, there were two incidents that greatly increased his needs. His daughter had matriculated at a private college in the East, and while a spoiled freshman romance had ruined her first year academically, he held great hope that she would recover. The problem with his son was unexpected. The city's new bussing program had brought a large number of blacks into his school, and it had been a disaster: the blacks had not performed at the level of middle-class whites, but the whites, including his son, had declined to the level of underprivileged ghetto students. Worse, his son had been "mugged" twice: once on the playground and once while walking home from school. He and his wife had decided to enroll the boy in a private day school.

Cleveland's best neighborhoods were declining, they had said to each other. Bussing hadn't helped anyone. Fortunately, the bonus would enable them to pay thirty-five hundred dollars a year to the day school. It couldn't be helped if the boy got snobbish attitudes from attending a private school; his future was at stake. They had to do what was best for him.

Events seemed to have conspired to help him, he told her. The new savings and loan account they had just taken on was the biggest mess he had ever encountered. He was putting in hundred-hour weeks, like a New York investment banker, trying to straighten out the problem before either the state banking commission or the federal examiners went over the books. The savings and loan had obviously been red-lining, and at the same time, they had been misrepresenting the quality of the loans they were making.

It'll be a very profitable year for us, he said, if only because I don't get paid overtime. Fortunately, they'll make it up in my bonus. He expected fifteen thousand. But sometimes at night, after his wife had gone to bed, he sat at the desk in the living room and calculated what he would have after taxes if the bonus came to seventeen-five or twenty or even twenty-five. Twenty-five wouldn't be out of line, considering the way things were going.

The recommendation for his bonus was made by the regional director, who sent it to the director of national operations, who made his comments and passed it on to the bonus committee. Three outside directors and two inside directors sat on the committee. None of them knew him, of course, although he had met the treasurer and the chairman of the board on several occasions, but it was not important, because they declared a bonus fund and then divided it up according to the recommendations.

On the day the regional director was to come to Cleveland (all bonuses were handed out personally, along with praise and promises for the year to come), he asked his wife to meet him at the office. Let's have dinner out tonight, he said. We don't have to go to an expensive place.

It was a ritual they practiced. The bonus checks were always delivered at that time of year. He always led her to believe the bonus would be smaller than it actually was. She always pretended to be surprised. And they always went to a very good restaurant, the same one they went to on her birthday.

The regional director arrived in the office shortly after noon. He didn't have time for a fancy lunch, he said, because he wanted to get to the Detroit office before five, and then drive to Toledo to spend the night. He made the usual speech, then took a white envelope from his pocket and gave it to his office manager.

The check was for seventy-five hundred dollars, less deductions for federal and state income tax and Social Security.

I think there's a mistake, the office manager said.

The district manager laughed, Do you think we need a good auditor?

It's the amount. I've had a hellish year here. We've made a lot of money, but it's cost me a lot. I'm tired. I've been working seven days a week for I don't know how long. You know what went on with that savings and loan problem.

We've all worked hard, the district manager said.

But this is the same as I got last year. I can't get along with this amount. I made plans. For God's sake, you know what I put in, is this what you recommended?

I don't recommend the amount. You know how the system works. All I can do is tell them that you did a great job, a marvelous job. I couldn't ask more from a man. In fact, I'm embarrassed by how hard you worked.

I only took one week of vacation.

I'm sorry. Maybe this year will be a little more normal.

They must have made a mistake. I think I should ask them.

The district manager shrugged. If you like.

The manager rubbed his forehead in the palm of his hand. He said, speaking to himself, What can they do to me for asking? It could really be a clerical error, not a mistake in judgment.

Send a letter to the committee. It's your decision.

You're advising against it, the office manager said.

It's between you and the committee. I made my recommendation. That's all I do, I make a recommendation in writing. They consider it along with all the others. Look, I don't even know those people. I don't know how they would react, and that's the truth. Now, you do what you want.

Were you surprised by the size of my check?

No one ever gets as much as he hoped for.

Did you? the office manager wanted to ask. Did you get a fat bonus this year or did you get screwed too? Instead, he asked, Will they take it out on me next year?

I would hope not.

What should I do?

Keep up the good work. I mean that, it's not just a platitude. If you let your attitude go to hell over one bonus, you'll just suffer for it next year. Forget this year, think about next year. He looked at his watch. I've got a plane to catch, he said. Keep your pecker up, and you'll be all right.

When the office manager was alone, he put the check in the inside pocket of his suit coat and went to stare out the window. To think. He looked at the city. It was the colorless time, before the lights and the neon signs began to come to life in contrast to the night sky. He heard an ambulance or a police car or a fire engine from somewhere below. He saw the bright tops of taxis. The streets were quiet, the city was sickly, failing socially, weakening economically, the streets were always quiet. He looked at the time and temperature sign. Snow was expected. His wife was coming to meet him in three hours and twenty-seven minutes.

———◆———

In large corporations, the bonus committee includes high executives and outside directors, the inner circle and the apex of the structure meeting to determine the rewards of men and women who appear to them as no more than terse recommendations hastily made on printed forms. The one who receives the bonus has no appeal and does not face his judges. He has no rights, he is not a legal person, and he has even less opportunity to negotiate his bonus than his salary.

Were the bonus administered with perfect justice, it would still be outside the power of the manager or technician, for the bonus pool depends first upon the profits of the company and the decision of the executives to allot profits, and only after those decisions are made does the performance of the employee have any effect upon his reward. From the employee's point of view, the corporation appears to be omnipotent, omniscient, and implacable: the bonus system achieves the totalitarian relation between man and organization, the circumstance that leads one to ask, "What can a man do?"

THE GREATER UNKNOWN

> We shall show them that they are weak,
> that they are only pitiful children, but
> that childlike happiness is the sweetest of
> all.
>   The Grand Inquisitor

For six years he had watched the man in the office across the hall. He did not deceive himself about his reasons for moving his desk to the left or having his telephone on the other side of the desk. He was spying.

Neither did he deceive himself about his motivation for spying on the man across the hall. It was self-defense, survival, important to his wife and children as well as to him. No one had asked him to spy, he reported his findings to no one, he kept no journal, dictated no reports. He was his own client.

He had worked in the company for twenty-one years before he was appointed manager of customer service and warranty administration. Only a year after his appointment to the position the market for small home appliances had exploded: food processors and blenders, popcorn poppers, coffee grinders, electric broilers, electric can openers and knife sharpeners, dehumidifiers, hamburger cookers, electric shoeshiners had all found a place in the market at approximately the same time.

His job was split: warranty administration was given to the man across the hall. They reported to the same vice-president, they each had two people in every district office. He had a small staff to write and revise instructional manuals that were supplied with the appliances. The man across the hall had a small staff to write warranties and warranty policies.

Neither of them hoped for the vice-president's job. It called for an engineering degree and manufacturing experience. They were destined to remain in their present positions until retirement. Equals.

But were they really equals? The question had haunted him ever since the man across the hall had joined the company. Each had one wife and three children. Each had been an officer in the Army, serving in Europe but avoiding combat. Each had attended a state university on the GI Bill after the war. He was taller by an inch than the man across the hall. His wife was better looking, especially now that the bosom of the other man's wife had taken a dive. It was difficult to compare children. He had three sons and the man across the hall had three daughters. Each had one in graduate school, one in college, and one in high school.

One of them, he suspected, earned more money than the other: the man across the hall. He had thought so from the beginning. New employees always came in at higher salaries. It was one of the rules of business. Didn't he do it? Didn't he have to hire at going prices? It made sense: you simply couldn't entice someone into taking a new job without offering more money. On the other hand, it had been a promotion for the man across the hall. The vice-president had said that everything was split right down the middle.

Of course, customer service was a bit more difficult. A manual was rather more complicated than a warranty. He had a staff artist, whereas the warranties were simply designed by the printer who won the bid. On the other hand, there was no denying that warranty administration consumed much more of legal staff's time.

In six years, his salary had been raised eight times. Perhaps there had been adjustments to equalize them, even if the man across the hall had come in at a higher salary. What aroused his suspicions was the difference in certain material aspects of their lives. He drove a Pontiac. There was a Buick across the hall. He wore a London Fog trench coat. A Burberry hung on the coatrack across the hall. He had examined his subject's shoes and he was certain that they were Johnson & Murphy's finest. There was a difference between those shoes and Florsheim's best, which he had worn since graduating from college.

He also noticed attaché cases, umbrellas, mufflers, and shirts. Shirts were much more important than suits. Anyone could afford a few decent suits, and who cared about suits anyway? A good-quality suit could be in style even when it was out. There was something individualistic there. But shirts! He could swear that the man went to Brooks Brothers and had shirts made to order. He had gone to the store on his lunch hour to study the colors and the cut of the collars. There could be no doubt: the man was paying twenty-five dollars a shirt and buying them by the half-dozen!

In every comparison he found himself slightly behind. An eight-room house compared to a seven-room house. A forty-five-minute commute compared to a fifty-two-minute commute. His sons went to Penn and Haverford. The daughters across the hall went to Bennington and Sarah Lawrence. Bennington!

Bennington was the clincher. A man who had three children, one of them in college and one in graduate school, and could send one to Bennington was earning more than forty-one five. Or he was up to his ass in debt.

His wife's theory was that *she* had some money.

He smiled at the theory. Pollyannaism!

He resolved to find out for certain. He transferred his account to the same bank used by the man across the hall, and every month, on the first and the fifteenth, he waited for the man across the hall to put on his suit coat and head for the bank in the lobby of the building. Then he threw his coat on and hurried after him. Sometimes he stood behind him in the line, sometimes he stood in the line next to him. He looked over his shoulder to see what was in his hand, hoping to read the numbers. He strained to hear some conversation with the teller. But the man across the hall was careful, obviously hiding his higher paycheck.

They had lunch together once or twice a week. At those meetings he always steered the conversation around to money, speaking of bills, college tuition, raises, inflation. But the man across the hall would give nothing away. There was no clue.

It was at lunch that he said his daughter was getting married.

Oh, that's good news, the manager of customer service said. A quiet wedding, I suppose.

Pretty quiet. We're going to hold it at the club. Dinner, a little dancing afterwards. But not her kind of music. If I'm paying, I want it to be something I can bear. What do you think?

The manager of customer service did not answer for several moments while he added up the cost of dinner for God-knew-how-many and a ten- or twelve-piece orchestra. Three to five thousand, he guessed. Maybe more. What do I think? he said. I hope you drop dead on the dance floor, you conniving son of a bitch.

———————◆———————

No totalitarian organization could exist without secrets. With sufficient numbers of secrets, an organization can divide men down into their smallest units and keep them separate, hostile to each other, and domitable. Mass man, that unenviable crea-

ture so easily molded, so easily frightened, is simply a man
who knows there are secrets all around him, and suspects that
some of the secrets are about him.

To make atoms of the mass, corporations have no more
obvious device than the keeping secret of men's earnings. It
spurs competition, makes the loyalties of class impossible, and
thus presents to the corporation a set of managers and technicians who have no ties to anyone but the corporate body as
personified in the leader or chief executive.

Curiously, the secrets of corporations are seldom active secrets, and often not even a means to hide unfairness. Men
may be paid similar salaries for similar work, but when their
salaries are not made public, the unknown works against the
employees, eliciting the bad dreams of envy.

Simone Weil noted that, "Generally speaking, the relation
between work done and money earned is so hard to grasp that
it appears almost accidental, so that labor takes on the aspect
of servitude, money that of a favor." And when the extent of
the favor is not known to be distributed according to clear, negotiated rules, as in a union contract, the recipients of money
begin to understand their salaries as signs of affection or even
love. Competition for the goodwill of the leader or primal father follows the patterns described by Freud, except that envy
generates esprit de corps, which, in turn, generates greater
envy. The horde becomes a mass, men not only permit themselves to become a means, they seek their own debasement in
the hope of winning secret favors.

THE WAR OF ATOMS

All will be happy, all the millions of
creatures except the hundred thousand
who rule over them.
                    The Grand Inquisitor

Production is the problem, the distribution manager said. We
don't have a decent product, and the customer knows it. He
can get the same quality in a discount brand and save himself
a dollar and a half.

The sales manager agreed.

The marketing vice-president swung his chair around and
stood up. He was not comfortable with anything he heard
these days: everyone had another excuse, no one had an answer. Sales were up, but share of market was down badly in
some parts of the country. He could go before the board and
show them a simple chart and be all right, but the pieces were
falling apart, they couldn't seem to co-ordinate their efforts.
He vowed to himself that he would get to the bottom of the
trouble.

Look here, he said, we got a problem, a big goddamn problem. We're getting the shit kicked out of us by the Japanese on
two coasts and the peewees are chewing us up in the Midwest.
We got nothing left to call our own but the South, and that's
cause we own the South, we are the generic name, the only
fucking name they know.

Now, I'll tell you what I think, boys. I been in this business
thirty-eight years. I was twenty-five years old when I started

peddling this shit. I seen every kind of trouble in this company all the time it was growing up, and I know the kind of trouble we got now. Gentlemen, we are not all singing off the same song sheet. Now, what the hell we going to do about that?

The distribution manager said, I don't know what the sales problem is. We have product on the shelves and in the pipeline. We're set up to increase share on both coasts and to hold our own in the middle. Advertising is following the pattern. It's co-ordinated. We're in on time, we're taking advantage of national rates in all media, cost per thousand is down, impressions are up. I'm right on the marketing plan.

The sales manager said, I can't sell on the Coast, where I've got more product than I need, but I can't move as much as I could in the Midwest and the South because I'm always short of stock. I'm getting cancellations, I'm losing sales.

You want to give away the major population centers to the Japs? the distribution manager asked.

I don't want to give anything away, the sales manager said. But you can't do it on the coasts. We've got product, we're getting window displays, co-op advertising, all we're not getting is sales. Jesus, they aren't even cheating me on the co-op. They're running the ads. We're giving a better markup than the Japs; they want it.

The problem's with product, the distribution manager said.

Product my ass! Public don't know turnips from turds when it comes to product! Now, you let me tell you something. One of you boys is fucking up, and I aim to find out which one. I been studying those sales reports till my eyes don't shine, and I'm just beginning to get a little light off the paper, you know what I mean? And it's all about co-ordination.

He sat down in his chair again and pulled it in close to the desk. You know what I think, he said, I think one of you boys might just be greasing the other. Like you think I'm just about at the age where I'm ready to chuck this shit once and for all

and go fishing. Don't you? And if I go fishing, I got to leave
somebody in charge of the store, don't I?

Two expressionless faces looked back at him.

Well, he said, don't I?

Both men nodded.

And one of you is sure to wind up sitting in this chair. You
think I don't know? You think I didn't go around with a hard-
on for this job for twenty goddamn years? For the love of
God, man, I even went to night school so I could get this job! I
was forty-two years old sitting in a classroom with a bunch of
tittysuckers learning how to do wrong what I'd been doing
right for seventeen years. I didn't have to fuck my buddy to
get this job, I earned it.

You boys aren't like that, are you? At least one of you isn't.
One of you is a serpent.

No, not a serpent. I'll tell you what one of you is. One of
you is a maggot, a fucking maggot. That's what a man is who
gets fat off another man's misfortune, a goddamn maggot.
Now, I'm looking to find that pasty white maggot color in one
of your souls, and when I find it, I'm going to cut it right out
of this company.

He spent the rest of the morning going over the sales reports, customer surveys, and advertising research with them.
Nothing was quite right, but nothing was quite wrong. They
just never seemed to have the right product in the right place
at the right time. Exactly at noon he pushed his chair away
from the desk, saying, I got better things to do than to keep
throwing my time down this rat hole. I'll see you boys later.

As they stood up, he looked very carefully at their faces.
They were his two fine young men, good boys, graduates of
good colleges and the best business schools, smooth young
men, good looking, well mannered, soft spoken, they could
stand up in front of a civic club and charm the pants off everybody in the room. They just couldn't work together. It was like
mules, maybe it was like mules. Sometimes you'd get a pair

that would pull together and sometimes you'd get a pair that couldn't stay in the same barn. Maybe they were like that, just their natures. They were both smiling as they took their leave, saying something—he didn't know what. He didn't hear them because he thought he saw a darkness in their smiles, something that spread through their faces, killing the light, like a cloud over water.

———◆———

Although his writing could only have been an adumbration of totalitarianism, for the technology necessary to accomplish it was lacking in his time, Montesquieu was intensely aware of totalitarian tactics. In *The Spirit of the Laws* he wrote: "Under despotism, it is necessary that the people be judged by laws and the notables by the caprice of the prince, so that the head of the lowest subject be safe and the pasha's head always in danger." He saw the method for accomplishing the vulnerability of the notables in Roman law: ". . . Their constant maxim was to divide. . . . The Roman senate declared that henceforth each city would be governed by its own laws, without reference to common authority."

In the corporation, the tactic of division applies to middle managers and technicians, those whom the corporation wishes to keep in fear of losing their heads. Co-operation replaces the common authority used by Montesquieu. Divided or atomized men become so intent upon competing that they cannot co-operate. They want the company to succeed, but not each other. As a result, they place their faith in the sort of magical formula proposed by Adam Smith, as if he meant it to apply to competition at the intramural level. Argyris, one of the many industrial psychologists who oppose any alienation from the organization, describes the woeful result of dividing the pashas and putting their heads at risk: "The nature of the formal principles of organization causes the subordinates, at any given level, to experience competition, rivalry, intersubordinate hostility, and to develop a focus toward the parts rather than the whole." An English translation might read: Men in fierce competition with each other forget about the larger goals of the business.

As in so many instances of totalitarian organization, the tactic succeeds in controlling the members of the organization but at great cost to its overall efficiency. Nazi Germany expending men and material to kill Jews while its armies were being destroyed on two fronts is the classic example of a totalitarian organization concerning itself more with despotic principles than with reality. Secrecy, atomization, and terror are the fortress of organizations founded in opposition to the political life of man; defense of the fortress can have no limit once it has begun, for the organization has no real foundation in the free association of autonomous men.

CORPUS DELICTI

And as man cannot bear to be without the miraculous, he will create new miracles of his own for himself, and will worship deeds of sorcery and witchcraft, though he might be a hundred times over a rebel, heretic and infidel.

The Grand Inquisitor

In his first years in the central office he had been pleased by visits from old friends who had stayed out in the plants. They admired his office, they took note of his success, they flattered him openly, preparing him for favors and protections that might one day be needed. He had enjoyed the reflection of himself in their eyes, telling them numbers of shipments, hinting at the size of his paycheck, amusing them by complaining of taxes and such discomforts as the height of the interior of the company jet.

He could not remember when his feeling about former co-workers had changed. Perhaps it had come with the failing of his memory of them, the paling of their names, the disguise time worked on their faces. Now they were an irritation. In New York for two days to attend a computer seminar or a course in new engineering techniques developed by the company, they seldom failed to stop in his office at the end of the last day of a visit to the central office. Often now, they asked for the favors or protections they had prepared him for over the last few years. As executive vice-president he was empowered to offer the dispensations they requested, but he thought it bad business. He rebuked them for leapfrogging their supervisors, then with a smile, he promised to say nothing of the visit, to forget that they had come to him.

I am not an unkind man, he told himself, I am a busy man; everyone wants a piece of me, and there is not enough to go around.

None irritated him more now than those who wanted only to share in nostalgia. The historians, he called them, dredging up names he had forgotten, telling tales of people no more meaningful to him than the stick figures that appeared in television dramas. He had reduced his own roots to a symbol, witticisms for the speechwriters. History bored him. Those who know history too well, he had told an audience of financial analysts in Chicago earlier that year, are condemned to live in the wake of progress.

The historian who sat before him had come into his office unannounced. Neither secretaries nor closed doors dissuaded him. He came as if he were a relative or a policeman, using given names, pushing into private spaces, sprawling over the room, talking, smoking, rearranging objects on the desk to soak up the energy of false hubris.

The historian spoke of the comptroller of the old plant who had retired the year before. The old plant. Which old plant? Did he realize how many plants the executive vice-president had worked in or managed on his way to New York? Which old plant? Indianapolis? Atlanta? Buffalo?

The man rolled on through his litany of Christmas parties, marriages, divorces, grandchildren, politics, promotions, dismissals, names and names and names. Do you remember Allen the detailer? he asked. Sad story, tragic. But then who knows if anything could have changed it? I hadn't heard his name for years when a fellow who worked in the Atlanta plant with me a long time ago sent me a newspaper clipping from a California paper. Drowned in the bathtub. I think it was suicide, but they say it could have been a heart attack. You never know. How many people have heart attacks in the bathtub? Poor man, poor man. After he was fired I think I heard from him once. Or maybe I didn't. People come and go. Time marches on, doesn't it?

Twenty-five minutes after his sudden arrival, the historian looked at his watch, declared that he had to catch a plane, and departed. Only then, in the humming quiet, did the executive vice-president remember the dead man. It was Indianapolis; yes, certainly, it was Indianapolis. The face of the dead man was not clear. He had no distinguishing features. Eyeglasses. Yes, eyeglasses, very thick lenses, horn-rims. The man had been a creature of the fifties, hidden unhappiness, frequent visits to psychiatrists, self-involved, myopic, thoroughly myopic.

Had he been married? Was he married then? Divorced? In the distance of memory, divorced seemed fitting.

The man had been fired. One afternoon, yes, it had probably been on an afternoon, the man had come around to say good-by. Had he been bitter? What had he said? What plans had he made? They never had any plans. People who are fired are always surprised in their incompetence. If they were perceptive enough to know they were going to be fired, they wouldn't be fired.

And the next morning there was someone else at the desk. Maintenance cleaned up the workspace, the department coordinator brought in fresh supplies, the department manager brought in the new man. No signs of the man past were left in the office. It was made to seem new. For the sake of the new man. No ghosts, no shoes to fill, a clean slate. Termination was quick and clean, as it should be—an antidote to memory. Sometimes they did not say good-by.

He was not surprised by the announcement of the death of the man, because the man had died a long time ago, on the day he left the company. Yes, it is a death, the executive vice-president thought, but we do not consider it death because there is no mourning. A man just ends, like the minute before this minute, gone forever, unheard, unnoticed, unmarked, like the tickings of the minute, which have no residue. Nothing is more dead than an end without a death.

He wondered if the dead man, whose name he could no longer remember, had been given a proper funeral, if anyone had sent flowers. In such matters the company had no obligations to former employees, including officers and retirees.

———◆▶———

"All executioners are of the same family," said Camus, and so it is with corporate and government killing: physically murdered or fired, the result is the same. The special quality of totalitarian murder is the absence of the body. Persons disappear, they do not die. Without the body, there is no proof that the person ever existed. The lesson to those who remain is clear: they are not human, for human beings leave a mark in the world, unlike all other creatures. Pyramids, cave paintings, poems, grave markers, funeral pyres, this book are all efforts by men to demonstrate that they changed the world, even if only in the smallest way, for only by changing the world does man prove he exists as an autonomous creature, capable of beginnings.

Corporations have become expert in eliminating the residue of human life. All executives are taught how to fire people quickly and to eliminate all trace of them. They argue that it is bad for morale if those who are fired stay on the job after they have been told of their dismissal. Such things as identification cards, building passes, keys, etc., must be returned immediately. Even the shame connected with dismissal works to make the dead disappear.

Nothing in a corporation is given the name or the face of an employee, unless he is the leader. All others are anonymous. Products carry the names of animals or verbs or acronyms, or they are neologisms; they never carry the name of the person who invented them or sold them or made them. The aim is never to permit a life to mark the organization so that there can be no deaths, except those of the leaders; all others simply disappear.

Hannah Arendt devoted a long section of her work on totalitarianism to describing and analyzing this peculiar form of assassination: "The murderer leaves a corpse behind and does not pretend that his victim has never existed; if he wipes out any traces, they are of his own identity, and not the memory and grief of the persons who loved his victim; he destroys a life, but he does not destroy the fact of existence itself.

"The Western world has hitherto, even in its darkest periods, granted the slain enemy the right to be remembered as a self-evident acknowledgment of the fact that we are all men (and *only* men)."

When she wrote of the Eichmann trial, she described the

need of the Nazis for his work: ". . . Totalitarian domination tried to establish . . . holes of oblivion into which all deeds, good and evil, would disappear. . . ." And Stalin himself told how totalitarian organizations must deal with death: ". . . The revolution is incapable either of regretting or of burying its dead."

Without children, works, or memory, the existence of a man is too brief to matter; if his death causes no grief, what was the value of his life? Every man the corporation causes to disappear negates the human existence of the hundreds and thousands who remain; every trace of human life it can destroy increases its power to dominate.

MODERN MORALITY

> We shall tell them that every sin will be expiated, if it is done with our permission, that we allow them to sin because we love them, and the punishment for these sins we take upon ourselves.
>
> The Grand Inquisitor

After the airplane had risen through the clouds and the ground was obscured, he turned away from the window and looked at the back of the seat in the next row forward. It was his time to think, to be with himself and without himself, suspended, like the airplane. Thoughts on the stairs, the French said. How curious that they thought while going downstairs and he thought while climbing in an airplane! Idioms should be adjusted for technological advance.

He invented titles for a drama about whistle blowing: *The Glory and the Controversy. Invitation to Revenge. The Regretful Moralist. King for a Day.*

The true ending to the story about the man who pointed out that the king wore no clothes came not in the demotion to reality of the king but in the demotion to penury of the outspoken hero.

Talleyrand was right, he thought: a man with a wife and children will do anything for money. He had read the quote in a book about the Pope's complicity in the Nazi death camps, and the quote had stayed with him. He had children. He had a wife.

An hour and a half to Chicago. Thoughts on the stairs were regretful, the French were dour for having to think their best thoughts while heading toward the fouled streets of medieval Paris. Thoughts on the airplane should be different, soaring, above the world, as high as metaphysics. The big picture. He laughed. What was original about telling the truth, not finding a new truth, just reporting what had happened? On the other hand, there was nothing original or exciting about lying. Morality and immorality were both banal.

She, of course, thought differently. He earned, she ate. A cavewoman had no need to be aggressive either. Nonsense, they lived together, they were a family, she and the children had as much to lose as he. She had more courage, she was more good; it had always been that way with them: freedom and virtue belonged to her, hard work was his.

He wore sneakers and she wore workman's shoes with steel toes. They carried hard hats. The pigs came on horseback, with plastic masks over their faces and long riot sticks in their hands, black knights of Daley. She took a bag of glass marbles from her knapsack and tossed handfuls of them at the oncoming mounted police. But the horses did not slip and fall, the union hall myths did not work in the age of war protest. The end of a riot stick caught him in the belly. He fell to the ground, unable to breathe, thinking he had been shot. Gut-shot, the bastards!

A pharmacologist was innocent, a man against disease, against suffering. He would not make war, he was useful. She wet a cloth with water from a passerby's canteen and waved the wet cloth in the air to cool it before she placed it on his forehead. She wiped his mouth with her shirttail, then she kissed him.

The hearing room was silent while he read his prepared testimony, pages approved by lawyers and lobbyists, the public relations of science. He had not been able to breathe and then he had not been able to control the quick, shallow breaths that made him feel drunk or drugged. He was sick. The room was too cold. He should have taken a tranq.

In the labs the drug had been something of a miracle. Ulcerations in mice, dogs, and monkeys healed in less than a week after administration of the drug commenced. The steroids were not, in one sense, artificial cures, they just aided the natural mechanisms of the body, hurrying the process, sparing the patient loss of blood, possible dehydration, and severe pain. True, the rats, dogs, and monkeys had behaved strangely afterwards, becoming withdrawn, quiescent, but the head of the department had assured him that the behavior was due to the healing process, the animal husbanding all of its strength to use in the fight against death. Surely, the department head had said, there was no need to include the obvious in his report. And later, humans exposed to small doses of the drug had shown no noticeable side effects. Only after the drug was approved for use in clinical situations and large doses were given to seriously ill patients did the effect begin to manifest itself: in one of every thirteen cases the patient experienced a severe psychotic episode. So far, the chemically induced psychoses had proved irreversible.

Had he known?

No.

Had he suspected?

No.

Had they been in a hurry to get the new drug on the market?

No more so than any company with a huge investment in research. No more than any company with an interest in saving lives and reducing suffering.

Had he been aware that three other drug companies were working on similar treatments for the same kind of ulceration?

There are always rumors in research. How many cures for cancer have you heard about this year?

Answer the question, please.

I heard rumors, nothing definitive. Gossip. I paid no attention to it.

What are the pressures on research pharmacologists in your company? I mean the pressures to produce drugs that can be sold, that can make a profit.

Our resources, including people, are limited. To waste them would be unconscionable.

Answer the question, please. Are there time limits? Does funding for projects cease after a certain period? Could you lose your job if you worked for a long time on a project that failed to come up with something the company could sell? Could you lose your job if some other company developed a product ahead of you?

There are no formal rules to that effect in our company. However, you know that every project and every man must be evaluated somehow. A researcher who constantly fails in his search for new methods or new products raises questions about his abilities.

In other words, you are under pressure to produce, no matter what the possible danger to the people who eventually use the product?

A man has moral standards.

Sir, that is exactly what is in doubt here. Your tests with

laboratory animals have been duplicated, with behavioral changes resulting in more than fifty per cent of the cases. What are your moral standards? That's what this panel would like to know. And what are the moral standards of your company? I think the almighty dollar is the only standard you live by, and because of your standards there are more than sixty people who are now in danger of living out the rest of their years in mental institutions.

His attorney demanded an apology.

We make mistakes. There is no evil in that, he had told his wife.

You winked, she said.

I wanted to save lives.

You did what they wanted, you winked. Tell them in Washington. Don't wink there.

She had not changed since Chicago. Her eyes were deeper, she had gained some weight, mainly in the shoulders. She drank vodka now, she was suntanned in summer, she read best-selling books written by angry women. The children were docile when she was with them. The dog cowered when she reprimanded it. She had become expert at sex, as precise as a surgeon at passion. Like him, she was not happy with Bob Dylan's new songs.

She mourned the deaths of Sylvia Plath and Anne Sexton. Nothing about Watergate surprised her. She defended the right of Third World countries to raise the price of oil. She said that when the revolution came they might be killed because they had become so middle-class, but she was willing to accept that necessity, if there were some guarantee that the children would be spared.

When the president of the company took the stand, he announced that he had a short opening statement. It is not the policy of this company, he began, to submit to the FDA for approval for use in human beings drugs that have produced serious or potentially serious side effects in laboratory animals.

In the case of the steroids in question, I submit the laboratory reports given to management of our company as evidence. Nowhere in these reports is there any mention of side effects or of unusual demeanor in the laboratory animals on this steroid therapy. I make no excuses. When this kind of error, potentially injurious to human beings, occurs, it is a failure of management. It should be noted, however, that in experimental dosages administered to human volunteers no side effects were observed. I also make those reports available as evidence, and I am willing to produce the names of every volunteer, if the committee wishes to examine them. The drug is safe in the recommended dosage. In every case where side effects occurred dosages beyond what we believe and what we said are permissible were given. Granted, the patients to whom the abnormal dosages were administered were in extremis. It was a matter of life and death, a calculated risk. Even so, I can assure you that the person or persons who submitted the incomplete laboratory reports . . . He spoke for more than half an hour. At the end of the hearing the members of the committee shook his hand.

The plane had turned north toward Chicago. He looked out the window, trying to imagine the terrors a psychotic might see in the sun-reddened clouds.

———————◄◆►———————

Totalitarian organizations seek to disrupt the moral equilibrium of men. They teach a perverse deontology, keeping secret the plans of the inner circle while demanding that the members of the organization obey a sham moral code. Thus the organization may act in ways that seem immoral, but which can be justified by a far-reaching plan; the converse, however, more often proves to be true. A citizen or an employee doing his duty according to totalitarian morality loses his own moral standards, being nothing more than a tool for secrets, a means to goals of which he has no knowledge. Any act he performs may turn out to have been moral or immoral, depending upon the secret plan of the organization. His own judgment has no value.

Helene Hanfstaengl, the wife of Hitler's social friend, explained to John Toland how Hitler knowingly kept even his advisors in the dark, refusing to confide in them, maintaining the secrecy of his plans. Isaac Deutscher reports the same thinking in Stalin: "An important part of Koba's [Stalin's] activities . . . developed inside that most secret redoubt [the technical branch] of the party, out of sight and beyond the control of ordinary members." Hannah Arendt similarly describes policy under Stalin: ". . . the constant zigzag of the Communist Party lines, and the constant reinterpretation and application of Marxism . . . voided the doctrine of all its content because it was no longer possible to predict what course or action it would inspire."

Secrecy extends to all parts of the organization in totalitarianism. Hitler issued laws, for example, that were not made public. Stalin raised and lowered production quotas without telling the managers of his factories his real goals; his secrets did not get beyond the NKVD.

Morality and secrecy cannot exist together; without the test of publicity, as John Rawls describes it, no one can truly know whether the justification for his acts can be understood by rational men as meeting ethical standards common to the society, the simple Golden Rule, or the more demanding categorical imperative. Without the test of publicity, men may delude themselves into thinking that their ultimate goals justify their actions, even though they would hardly wish for deceit or other forms of violence to become generalized in society.

The secrecy of totalitarian organizations creates moral disruption in the members or employees of the organization and beyond them into the general society. In a simplistic example: how can a child come to know that lying is immoral, violence done to the deceived, when exalted men and their organizations regularly deceive him and the rest of the public? Within the organization, of course, the disruption is far greater: in an immoral society a moral man is a stranger; his ethics come to seem foolish, even wrong.

NO HANDS

> We shall set them to work, but in their
> leisure hours we shall make their life like
> a child's game, with children's songs and
> innocent dance.
>
> The Grand Inquisitor

The girls asked him not to laugh when their friends were visiting. They said he squeaked like a mouse when he laughed, and a father should not sound like a mouse. He complied with their request reluctantly, sulking, refusing to come out of his basement rumpus room when the girls and their friends were upstairs in the living room or keeping to himself in the kitchen when they were downstairs in the rumpus room. For his part, the living room was wasted space: he liked to take his shoes off after dinner, and his wife said the odor of his feet stayed in the beige shag living room rug.

He acquiesced in these small demands of the women of his house, because he was fierce with them in all other things: the girls would not date until they were sixteen, skirts would not rise above the knee, lipstick was to be a modest color, brassieres were to be worn when breasts began to emerge, underwear was white, shoes were flat, budgets were adhered to, hats were worn in church, hot meals were on the table when he was hungry, white shirts were starched, handkerchiefs were ironed, television programs and movies were chosen by the man of the house, and the car was not a toy for children or a woman who had work to do in the house. He did not permit card playing, comic books, cursing, or complaining. Any grade below B was cause for punishment, any meal from which the leftovers could not be used was cause for lecturing about the economics of the household, with a reminder that the very word economics developed from the word for the household in Greek. Rock music was not to be played when he was within earshot. Gossip was a moral corruption.

Once, in tears over what they considered unfair criticism, the girls had accused him of being a martinet. He replied that he was serious about his duties as a father, explaining to them at length what moral strengths he hoped to instill in them. You will be virtuous women, good people, he said, or I'll know the reason why.

Afterward he had gone into the bathroom to look at himself in the mirror to discover what error of nature caused him to appear to his own daughters as a martinet. Was it his eyeglasses? He had chosen the rimless kind, even though the price was high, on the advice of the frame consultant, who said he should not obscure the evenness of his features with colored rims. Perhaps it was his hair, or the lack of it? God was his barber, and there was no denying he was a severe one. Perhaps it was the bland roundness of his features. Most people considered Northern European looks a sign of good breeding, the best. The girls had small noses, light eyes, blond hair, and thin, elegant lips. He did not have an artist's face, it was true; there was nothing bohemian about him, but there was nothing wrong, absolutely nothing wrong with being a hardworking, decent, God-fearing man.

He worked for a firm that manufactured small appliances.

Upon graduation from the local branch of the state university he had accepted an offer from the firm, and he had been there ever since, progressing from the accounting department to personnel to associate director of personnel. The firm had been good to him, he said, although it had not made him rich. He kept a picture of the president of the firm on the wall in his office and he bought one of each of the firm's products at 10 per cent above cost for use in his own home.

It was one of the firm's products, a milkshake and frothy cocktail maker, that brought him up from the rumpus room to the kitchen, where the girls and two of their friends were having difficulty making milkshakes. He took charge of the situation immediately: I suppose you didn't plug it in. But they had.

He pressed the On button and the Off button. He turned the dial to each of the speeds. Nothing happened. The motor whirred softly somewhere inside the plastic base, but the mixing blades remained fixed. The ice cream in the mixing container melted, turning into a watery fluid. He unplugged the cord, took the mixing container out of the base, gave it to one of the girls to hold, and then examined the inside of the base as best he could. He could see pieces of black metal, a spring, and something that looked like a paper clip. Get me a screwdriver, he ordered.

One of the visiting girls said, Your daddy works for the company, doesn't he?

Yes, his elder daughter answered.

Then he'll know how to fix it.

He held his hand out, palm up, like a surgeon waiting for his instrument, while he continued peering inside the base. He had never looked inside one of the machines before, nor had he been inside the plant to see them put together. He thought the motors came from somewhere in Asia: Taiwan or Korea. The box always said, Made in USA. But he knew that was just a trick: the box was made in America, not its contents.

His daughter put the screwdriver in his hand, firmly, as surgical nurses do. He said, curtly, Thanks. This was business, his business, the honor of the company was at stake before these girls, these customers and potential customers.

Now most of the ice cream in the mixing container had melted. Nevertheless, he ordered the girls to put the container in the freezer to preserve what was left.

It was his honor that was at stake, he confessed to himself. He had an urge to laugh.

With the screwdriver, he poked around inside the base. Something seemed to be loose, floating; it clicked when he touched it.

Have you found the trouble yet, sir? one of the visitors asked.

Loose connector, he said. As you know, those parts carry the power to the spindle, which is crucial.

Is that what you call the shaft that comes out of the motor? the girl asked.

That's our word for it, engineering talk.

He was sweating, melting like the ice cream. He did not know what was loose inside the base, but he thought he might poke around enough to push it back into place, whatever it was. But how would he know when it was in place? How should it feel? Was the part meant to be loose, to float?

None of the girls spoke, neither his daughters nor their friends. He could feel them watching him, like proctors at final examination, waiting for him to cheat, daring him. But he could not. The thing in his hands was a mystery, a Chinese puzzle. He turned the machine upside down. There was a small wiring diagram on the underside, a series of boxes and squiggles. There was also a trademark of some kind: the letters UL printed on an orange background inside a red circle. Upper Laos? Under Lease?

Of one thing he was certain, the blades would not turn unless the mixing container was attached. It was a safety device.

He ordered the container removed from the freezer and brought back to the kitchen counter. I may need a pliers, he said while he gave the container a half turn, affixing it to the base.

He put the plug back into the wall, then pressed the On button. Nothing happened. The motor whirred, but the blade did not turn. All the ice cream had now melted. Colors floated in the fluid, browns and creams, making strange patterns, like the paintings he had seen in an art appreciation class.

There were screws on the bottom of the base. He had a screwdriver. He could take the base apart, find the floating piece, and attach it to the proper part. He picked up the entire machine and turned it upside down to expose the screws. The blade spun. Watery ice cream flew out the top of the mixing container, brown and cream, thin, smelling of vanilla. The fluid sprayed over the sink, the dish rack, the counter, and the far wall.

Carefully, he set the machine down on the counter. The blade stopped turning, although the motor continued to whirr. But now the loose part rattled wildly inside the plastic base. He looked around at the girls. They were dappled with melted ice cream. It was in their hair, on their faces, being absorbed by the fabric of their clothing. The girls looked so solemn and so sloppy. He could not restrain himself. He began to laugh, squeaking loudly. It was the sound of a great mouse laughing.

His daughters began to weep. The salty tears passed through the splotches of melted ice cream like rivers at flood.

———————◄◆►———————

The middle manager, unlike the blue collar employee has no experience with things. He is like the service worker and the clerk, one who makes nothing, who recognizes nothing out of his own effort, who cannot see how the world is different because of him. The need to be a maker of things, stressed so often in recent years, is not new. Aristotle wrote, ". . . Existence is to all men a thing to be chosen and loved, and . . . we exist by virtue of activity (i.e., by living and acting) and . . . handiwork *is* in a sense, the producer in activity; he (man) loves his handiwork, therefore, because he loves existence. And this is rooted in the nature of things; for what he is in potentiality, his handiwork manifests in activity."

Adam Smith said, "The labor of some of the most respectable orders in the society is, like that of menial servants, unproductive of any value." The middle manager and white collar worker belong to such a respectable order; they are not makers but laborers. Their work begins again every morning as if the previous day had not existed. They, not the factory workers, are attached to the endless belt. The factory worker sees and touches the result of his work, no matter how small, while the manager and the white collar worker make nothing new, nothing lasting, nothing. If man's existence, as Aristotle says, manifests itself in his handiwork, then those who make nothing do not exist.

Middle managers make nothing but the organization, they exist in the organization. They must value the organization as they value existence. In becoming middle managers and white collar workers, they agree to cede the world to the organization, abandoning all opportunity for life in the natural, real world.

DIVIDENDS

Receiving bread from us, they will see
clearly that we take the bread made by
their hands from them, to give it to
them, without any miracle.

The Grand Inquisitor

He and his wife had always lived alone. They were proud people to whom punctilios were important. Their cat was Siamese;
its box was always clean and deodorized. He never wore the
same suit on consecutive days; she pressed the other suit with
an iron between wearings. They attended the opera eight times
each year; she preferred the French, he preferred the Italians,
they were united in their dislike of the Germans. Each year at
Christmas she worked as a clerk in a famous and expensive
leather goods store; it was their rule to use her earnings solely
for gifts—for each other, for his secretary, for her nephews, for
his aunt, and for his brother who was confined to a hospital in
Ohio.

She cooked for him with great pleasure and attention. Every
night they had one glass of wine each with dinner. They
bought wine by the gallon and decanted it into crystal bottles
that had been left to them by her mother. Wrong for the wine,
he said. But right for the wine drinkers, she said. In summer,
they repaired to a small house near the seashore, which had
also been left to them by her mother. They rented out the
house during the hottest part of summer, saving for themselves only the first three weeks in September. The tenants al-

ways made them unhappy, leaving behind a trail of nicks, scratches, chips, and stains, and failing to tend the garden properly. Of their three weeks at the seashore two were always spent in returning the house and garden to their original and proper condition. He had a talent for carpentry and painting, she prided herself on her green thumb. To have such work performed by hired help, they agreed, diminished the pleasures of living by the sea.

Children earned no esteem from them. Early in their protracted courting they had found to their mutual delight that neither of them wished to raise a pack of nasty brats. Furthermore, the low opinion they held of children extended to parents, nursemaids, schoolteachers, baby-sitters, and purveyors of real and metaphorical pap. He thought it very witty of her to have said that the trouble with children is that they sour the wine.

In his work he had long ago earned a reputation for intolerance. As manager of the office, he was, he believed, required to rage with equal vehemence over thefts, spots on the carpeting, broken furniture or machines, computer failures, tardiness, recalcitrance, disrespect, indiscreet modes of dress, and dubious expense accounts. Yet he considered himself a good and generous Christian. When a freckled black girl came to him to ask his advice about an unwanted pregnancy, he paid for an abortion out of his own pocket. When one of the boys in the mail room, a middle-aged, slightly retarded man, told him tearfully of a fire that had destroyed his two-room apartment and all his furnishings, he had permitted the mail boy to purchase certain items of worn office furniture at the scrap price. He never failed to give people ample time, with pay, to attend to illnesses and deaths, nor had he ever chastised a woman for failing to come to work during the first day of her menstrual period. As a result, he considered certain people as owing him more loyalty and therefore more nearly perfect performance, and he was more intolerant of their failings.

His superiors, as he called them, constantly disappointed him. They were men of little style or taste, aggressive, opportunistic, avaricious. He thought some of them less than adequate to their tasks and a few of them nothing less than benighted. Business as such held very little interest for him. He did not follow sales reports or stock market prices. He had certain responsibilities, which he exercised with care and concern for costs and appearances. Production, marketing, sales, finance, personnel, procurement, international were all the same to him, all equally uninteresting.

He did, however, have some special feeling for the chief executive officer, a man with a full, red face and thick white hair, a figure, the office manager said. It was the chief executive officer who had for some years borne the cultural responsibilities of the company: a seat on the board of the opera, fund raiser for the symphony, patron of the ballet. How many times the chief executive officer, forced to be out of the city on business, had sent his tickets to the office manager! How generous! How considerate of the value of the seats!

During twenty-five years with the company the office manager's salary had not risen greatly. In comparison to the rate of inflation, his after-tax income had actually fallen over the past several years; yet he did not complain. It was not necessary to be rich to be cultured, he told his wife. In fact, had he earned a great deal of money, they might have become bourgeois; money had that effect on many people of quality; he had observed it more than once, hadn't she? Even so, the economies forced upon them were irritating: they could no longer buy art books or eat endive; the quality of the wine they drank was not what it had been—they took risks on Italian wineries, experimented with unknown vintages; he worried that the lapels of his suit coats were just a bit too narrow; she sensed that everyone, particularly her husband, noticed the faint marks left by lowered hemlines; and their underwear had begun to gray.

They needed more money, she said. Perhaps she should

consider full-time employment. How often they had called from the leather goods store to ask her to accept a full-time position! Wasn't this the proper time to accept the offer?

He thought not. They would reward him at the office, he said. The chief executive officer was a cultured man, he was not unjust or unthinking. While the world was going to hell in a handbasket, there were still men of quality, companies of quality; he was fortunate enough to have cast his lot with such a company. At any time their problems would be solved. Meanwhile, the triennial increase in their rent could be accommodated easily enough; they had only to rent the summer house for two more weeks, taking their own holiday later, when the summer people had gone and the air was truly brisk and refreshing.

We are not poor, he reminded her, merely a bit on our uppers, and only in the most temporary way.

An envelope arrived for him in the company mail. It was marked Confidential and Personal. Inside it, he found a notice of his inclusion in the stock owner program. He was to receive ten shares of stock initially and then have the opportunity to purchase additional stock on a one-for-one basis: for each share he purchased, the company would purchase one for him. The record of stock dividends was included in the envelope. Over the last twenty years the company had never failed to pay a dividend. In the chart of stock prices he noticed that the stock had split four times since the company had first gone public.

He suffered an epiphany. It was suddenly clear to him that one who owned shares of stock in the company was more likely to profit by his labors than he. But why? They did not work. Ownership of such a well-managed company was hardly a risk. It was entirely unjust that they should be paid so much while he labored for a steadily declining salary, while his standard of living fell year after year, while his wife, a woman of quality, considered accepting a salesclerk's position full time.

And who were these persons who profited by his labor? Speculators! Jews, Mafiosi, union crooks, oil-rich illiterates from Texas, Arabs, Germans, Japanese, trash of every variety.

He took a piece of stationery from his desk, not notepaper or a memo form, but the best stationery, the rag bond, and wrote a brief letter to the chief executive officer:

Dear Sir:

It has come to my attention that the earnings of my labors over these twenty-five years past have, for the most part, been paid out to persons who have no interest in the firm, no connection with our operations, and no loyalty to our goals or products. These stock owners, who are, in actuality, mere speculators, have no right to the fruits of my labor.

Unless this situation is remedied post haste, I must submit my resignation effective immediately. I await your reply.

Shortly before five that afternoon the director of personnel telephoned the office manager, asking that he return his building pass, company credit cards, keys, and so on. I'm sorry you're leaving, the director of personnel said, because you would have been entitled to early retirement in only two years.

The office manager said, I shall put the items you require into the company mail immediately. As to your regrets, I can do without them, thank you.

The office manager packed his personal belongings, which were few, into his old leather briefcase and left the office promptly at five. There was no one to whom he felt he owed a farewell. On his way home he went out of his way to pass by the elegant leather goods store in which his wife worked during the Christmas season. It really was a lovely place, he noted, filled with rich browns and maroons, smelling of expensive leather, patronized solely by persons of quality.

The crime of capitalism, say its critics, is to earn money with money. In defense, the capitalists say they put their capital at risk, creating industry, jobs, more capital, more industry, more jobs, and so on in an ever greater economic expansion. The theory of this bigger pie holds that even the poor have a proportionately larger slice as the pie grows. Therefore, argue the defenders of capitalism, reward the risk takers, for from them flow all improvements in the standard of living.

But what of those who risk their capital not in opening new industries or expanding existing industries, what of the speculators, the second to the ten thousandth owners of the stock of a corporation? They risk money for money, and they are meanwhile paid dividends on the stocks in which they speculate. How do they differ from one who buys a house to speculate in the real estate market and collects part of the wages of the gardener, the painter, the plumber, the carpenter, the cleaning woman, all those who improve the value of the house while he owns it but do not share in the capital gain when he sells it?

Unionists, alienated from the corporation, have traditionally opposed the making of money with money. Meanwhile, they have been investing pension fund money in stocks, acting as speculators. Peter Drucker calls this pension fund socialism, warning us of the dreadful *ism*. It might more accurately be called the comedy of capitalism, for what could be more absurdly funny than workers exploiting themselves?

In the position of one who is exploited by speculators, the worker's alienation saves him, it enables him to feel moral outrage, to maintain the system of values by which he lives and strives to have dignity. Middle managers, having ceded themselves to the organization, have an opposite situation: they conspire in the goal of giving away ever greater amounts of their labor to the owners of speculative capital, daily laboring to increase their own loss. They are estranged from the products and the profits of their labor!

The middle manager cannot allow himself to be outraged by his exploitation of himself. He must wink at his own loss. Like a suicide, he abandons the limits of a system of morals and permits everything, even violence against himself. All this in the middle of his life.

RISK MIDDLE MANAGEMENT

> . . . Who can rule men if not he who
> holds their conscience and their bread in
> his hands?
>
> The Grand Inquisitor

The decision to revise the entire sales effort had been made by the vice-president less than a year before. In theory it was sound enough: to depend on a few large accounts rather than many small accounts was risky, liable to produce large swings in revenue. A great number of small accounts gave reliability to the market, making it possible to plan more carefully. The salesmen were instructed to devote no more than 10 per cent of their time to managing the large accounts they had been servicing for as long as twenty years, and to put their efforts into getting new accounts. The first few months of the program had been moderately successful. New accounts were brought in, although not in the anticipated numbers. But the signs of trouble were already appearing in sales reports. Several large insurance brokers and the risk managers of two of their largest clients had expressed dissatisfaction with the company's claims policy, the speed of its paperwork, and the general inattentiveness of the salesmen, who were known officially as "account representatives."

At the first sign of trouble the director of sales had gone to the marketing vice-president to discuss the situation. It was, he learned, not the decision of the vice-president; the board of directors had set the new sales policy.

He was astonished. The board! They were bankers, oil company executives, a university president, a black woman who taught accounting, chief executive officers of a food processing company, a construction company, and a foundering regional airline. What did they know about selling insurance?

There is a bigger picture, the vice-president had said.

What?

I don't sit on the board.

The policy remained unchanged, the complaints from the old clients increased, grew strident. The director of sales and the vice-president of marketing shouted at each other. Threats were exchanged. Within a month, three of the company's oldest and largest accounts moved the majority of their business to New York companies. An Omaha company took another and yet another went to a British company. Two more left near the end of the first year of the program. Although a large number of small accounts had come in, revenue projections for the coming year were down by 16 per cent.

Of the thirty-eight salesmen it was decided that seven would be fired, the seven who had previously serviced the large accounts that had been lost. The director of sales looked out at them, seven men in middle age, parents, husbands, members of civic organizations, golfers, and lovers; one played the viola in a string quartet, another was president of a Republican Club, and another walked on a mechanical leg that replaced the one he had lost on Saipan.

He called them into his office one by one. They showed no anger, no surprise. Some had already begun looking for other jobs, one had his resignation in his pocket. They asked about money: the retirement plan, separation pay, vacation pay, the business of being fired. All of them inquired about him, the safety of his job, expressing their appreciation of the difficulty of finding work at his level of pay and responsibility. He reassured them about his position; they seemed pleased.

How fortunate he was to be working with salesmen! He appreciated their resilience, their resourcefulness. A salesman never had a sure thing, a salesman never let the customer know his disappointment. They were actors, psychologists, unabashed optimists. Actors, each one taking a different role, making himself up to succeed in the eyes of his audience; they made great edifices of the straws of personality. He praised them, he promised them letters of reference, a fair shake on vacation pay, a week of severance for every year of service. They made it all so easy for him. The violist embraced him, the Republican promised to work for an administration that would give greater protection to the middle class, America's backbone, the veteran said he had been through tougher times and knocked on the wooden part of his mechanical leg.

At the end of the day the director of sales was surprised at how easy the terrible business of firing men had been. There had been no recriminations, no attempts to place blame where it belonged. The salesmen had accepted disaster as fate and begun to think of survival even as he gave them the bad news. He felt a sense of camaraderie with them, he admired them. For all that the world laughed at insurance salesmen, he knew what strong, decent men they were.

Shortly before five o'clock the fired men started coming into his office to say good night and good-by. They had little jokes to tell, sentimental words to follow, smiles to exchange. Actors, he thought, actors who authored and directed their own plays. He felt very close to them, as if they were relatives or childhood friends. When the violist came in humming the opening theme from a Beethoven Quartet, the sales manager was so touched by the man's character that he stood up to embrace him again. As the violist stepped into the open arms of the director of sales, he took a scissors from his coat pocket and stabbed him in the chest.

———◄◆►———

Morality depends upon the ability of men to initiate the actions for which they are responsible. Without that basic justice, moral systems are farcical. A world of responsibility without autonomy can only lead to nihilistic despair: everything is permitted them and nothing is permitted me, nothing I do makes any difference, I may do anything.

The critical issue in the Nuremberg trials was the question of responsibility. Men who ceded themselves to the organization had lost their moral being: they were willing to profit or suffer by the decisions of the organization, and they were willing to do anything. Once a totalitarian organization has destroyed the moral equilibrium of those it controls, the will of the organization becomes absolute.

In democratic societies, men may be made to suffer for the decision of their elected leaders, but the suffering results from one's own poor choice of leaders; responsibility cannot be completely denied. Democracy makes the theoretical burden of the categorical imperative a real burden. Business has no roots in democracy. The corporation puts men at the mercy of the executives; those who cede themselves to the organization, who lose the autonomy-giving power of alienation, condemn themselves to the ethical life of slaves.

LEADERSHIP

> Man seeks to worship what is established
> beyond dispute.
>
>   The Grand Inquisitor

A picture of the chairman hung on the wall of the treasurer's office. He often looked at the picture, a colored photograph printed on flat paper to simulate the importance of a painting. In the photograph the face of the chairman was serious, almost dour. The jaw was set, the dark blue eyes stared straight ahead, the vertical lines of age, wisdom, and stern forthrightness were marked in dark brown shadow. But he knew how the chairman could laugh at crude jokes and lose at poker and give the world, if she wanted it, to his wife, Maisie. No one but he knew when the chairman had taken two weeks to have a prostate operation. No one but he knew that on some days the chairman was so tired his vision blurred and his heart pounded in his chest like a piston. He was one of the very few to whom the chairman had confessed his awe of public officials, his reticence at attending meetings in the White House, the discomfiture he suffered in any dealings with the press. When he looked at the photograph of the chairman, he saw the man and the executive, and he was pleased that he knew them both, for he believed in them, he trusted them, he was loyal to them.

I don't believe in him the way I believe in Jesus Christ, he told his middle son, who was a skeptic, but I believe in his strengths and his virtues. The chairman is a good man and a good executive. He makes money for the stockholders, and he does it honestly, fairly, by managing the company well and giving the customers value for their money.

Bullshit, the skeptical son said.

He did not argue with his son, who had a graduate degree in English literature and wrote poetry when he was not earning his living as a roofer. There were some things that could not be understood by poets. In the ivory tower different virtues were practiced. The chairman was a man of the world. He told his son that poets never accepted leaders, for which he admired them, because it was their job to see the world beautifully and critically at the same time and never to accept anything on face value. However, he said, if you knew the chairman the way I do, if you knew the things I can't tell you, the private goodness of the man, you would think better of him. In fact, you might be willing to accept him as a leader.

Bullshit, the skeptical son said, for which his father, accepting the travail of parenthood, forgave him. Poets went their own way in life; they could not be expected to understand that loyalty begets loyalty.

Bullshit, bullshit, the skeptical son said, to which his father bent his head lovingly, for he knew the boy had not asked to be born into this world. He did not argue that it was through the good management and the generosity, yes, generosity, of the chairman that the boy had been able to attend Yale University: third-party endorsements had no effect on family life.

His wife liked the chairman, or so she said. The virility of power pleased her, although she often wondered, if not feared, what the chairman might do to her husband if either she or he said a wrong word or otherwise disappointed him. He was reputed to be a good man, churchgoing, hardworking, charitable, wishing the best for his employees, but he was also known as a man who sometimes acted impetuously. Some said he was bold in a job that required boldness, others said he was mercurial, his competitors and many of those who had not done well in the corporation said he was ruthless.

She engaged in something like a flirtation with him, although both of them knew nothing would ever come of it. What she promised in greetings, dances, farewells, glances over cocktails, offerings of food, and the pitch of her laughter was that she would always consider him a bit more virile, a bit more attractive than her husband, because he was the chairman. She humbled herself, the skeptical son said, and she responded by reminding him that humility was not a sin and admonishing him to be more humble in his own life and opinions, particularly his opinion of himself.

What use is poetry? she asked her son. How can you compare roofing to the making of steel girders, giant steel ingots, long rolls of sheet steel for cars and appliances, enormous steel gears, parts of generators and great turbines? Your father's business is at the very heart of the nation's economy, the world's economy. America is built on steel.

Bullshit, the skeptical son replied. Small is beautiful.

I don't like it when you use that kind of language, dear, she said. She could use the tone of her voice like a hatpin in the eye. He shrank away in argument with her; she could give him hives.

The treasurer had known the chairman for nearly twenty years. They had never been enemies, they had never been friends. As the chairman rose in the corporation, he had become the target of everyone's affection. He preferred old friends, however; and even when he did not give them high positions, he gave them high insights.

Money was the chairman's specialty, as it had been the specialty of the chairman before him and the chairman before him. They understood money in terms they were forever explaining to the treasurer, for they acted and he counted, they decided and he advised, they were men of breadth as well as depth. The treasurer's job was a dead end in the corporation.

He was the bookkeeper. No one was expected to carry home a fatter briefcase at night than the treasurer; he was the drudge, the slug who crawled over the print-outs and balance sheets, but he was also the man who knew more secrets of the corporation than anyone but the chairman.

Because of these shared secrets the treasurer and the chairman often spent their leisure time together. They did not travel as friends, but more or less like friends. The treasurer made reservations, drove cars, paid checks, left tips, and generally oiled away the irritants of travel. He also took responsibility for amusing and charming the chairman, the chairman's wife, and whomever they encountered along the way.

I do it because he carries all the other burdens, the treasurer explained to his wife. Look at it this way: if business were a crime, the chairman would be the criminal and all the rest of us would only be accomplices.

You work hard, too, said the treasurer's wife.

He gives his life, dear. He's like a priest, a cardinal; he's the pope of steel. Two hundred thousand people are dependent upon him for a livelihood, two hundred thousand! Think of it! As he's said many times, the power is nothing compared to the responsibility of the job.

She was also charming. She shopped with the chairman's wife for diamonds and furs and fine crystal. She introduced the chairman's wife to hairdressers and interior decorators, gynecologists and plastic surgeons; they went to cooking schools and spas together.

One day, the treasurer's wife said to him: We are flatterers.

It was a Sunday. The chairman was in Japan, the children were not expected. The treasurer had planned to spend the morning raking leaves and the afternoon sitting in the den, dozing and watching football games. He acknowledged his wife's pronouncement with a nod and went about his planned activities, but he could not dismiss the notion. Neither the crackling leaves nor the Pittsburgh Steelers could displace the sentence. He dozed and dreamed and lost track of the score of the game. His foot fell asleep, his neck was stiff, he drank a bottle of imported beer.

In the evening, he and his wife went to a nearby restaurant that served nothing but lobster. It was a very small place, dark, leathery, smelling of cigar smoke and butter by the end of each night. He liked to look at her in the mild light of the restaurant: it made her pink, it made her the age she had been when first he tasted success in life, when first he sensed that she was his wife.

He told her whenever they visited the little restaurant how it had taken many years before he comprehended marriage, before he loved loving her. She greeted his romanticism with shrugs and giggles, but her eyes shone and her bosom became flushed. The little restaurant was a private place for them; they never came with friends or family, they never brought the chairman and his wife.

You were right in what you said this afternoon, he told her. We are flatterers.

It makes me feel unimportant, she said.

In comparison to him?

Yes.

He cracked a lobster claw, chewed the meat he found there, and washed it down with cold wine. She watched him as he ate. He watched her. She wore golden earrings, a gold necklace. The rings on her fingers were gold, diamond, emerald. Her mink coat was thrown carelessly across the chair next to her. She licked the butter from her fingers without caring who saw that indulgence.

Each of us is important in our way, he said.

Bullshit, she said.

He put down his fork and his claw cracker. He felt betrayed by her. After all those years, after all that work, he thought. His head felt heavy. The butter was drying into sticky bitterness on his lips. He felt his belly pressing against the waistband of his trousers, he wanted to wash his hands.

She began to laugh, to bubble with laughter, to shake with laughter, to spill butter and rattle silverware and make her wineglass overflow with laughter.

He leaned across the table in full sight of everyone in the restaurant and put his buttery lips to hers.

The work of the leader differs from that of all others in the organization. C. I. Barnard provides a useful distinction: "Executive work is not that *of* the organization, but the specialized work of *maintaining* the organization." The distinction applies to executives in all forms of organizations, in both the public and private sectors. A further distinction between executives in totalitarian and other forms of organizations was made earlier: the totalitarian executive is not satisfied with power over the tasks of men, he desires to have power over the men themselves. Coulanges draws the distinction in historical circumstances between tyrants and despots, despots (kings) having the additional power of priests.

Hannah Arendt theorizes in *The Human Condition* that with the loss of the sense of beginning (the Greek word *archon* is associated with the concept of beginning or founding) from the concept of rulership the most authentic understanding of human freedom disappeared from political philosophy; but that sort of thinking may have to do with Arendt's conservative thesis of culture rather than her understanding of totalitarianism. Hitler, for example, was associated with the founding of National Socialism, and in the business world Ford and Watson (IBM) surely began their respective companies. In the real world, authenticity has more to do with man's sense of his own capacity for beginnings (his alienation sufficient to enable him to be autonomous) than with the originality of those who rule him.

He may, in fact, not be ruled by a single person or even a group of persons. Freud recognizes the possibility of a leading idea being substituted for the leader, giving the example of the Mosaic idea holding the Jews together as a people. In totalitarian organizations the idea always carries as much power as the leader in whom the idea is personified. Nazism and Stalinism operated in that fashion. In modern corporations, the organization itself becomes the leading idea, and the executive, whose work is to maintain the organization, serves as the high priest of the idea, the only one who can speak directly to God (the idea).

The only advocate of totalitarianism bold enough or mad enough to outline his program directly was Hitler. Three comments on leadership by Hitler follow, the first quoted by John Toland, the others from Hitler's own *Mein Kampf:*

> I alone lead the movement and no one makes conditions for me so long as I personally assume all responsibility. And I unconditionally assume responsibility for everything that happens in the movement.

> The leader is always appointed from above and at the same time vested with unlimited powers and authority.

> There must be no majority decisions, but only responsible persons, and the word "council" must be restored to its original meaning. Surely every man will have advisors by his side, but *the decision will be made by one man.*

Arendt has no disagreement with Hitler on the function of the leader within the totalitarian organization. It is worthwhile to compare her description of the position to his, however, to see how clearly Hitler understood what had to be done:

"The leader represents the movement in a way totally

different from all ordinary party leaders; he claims personal responsibility for every action, deed, or misdeed, committed by any member or functionary in his official capacity. This total responsibility is the most important organizational aspect of the so-called Leader principle, according to which every functionary is not only appointed by the Leader but is his walking embodiment, and every order is supposed to emanate from this one ever-present source."

With wonderful insight, she describes how the leader achieves power and keeps it: "His position within this intimate circle depends upon his ability to spin intrigues among its members and upon his skill in constantly changing its personnel. He owes his rise to leadership to an extreme ability to handle inner-party struggles for power rather than to demagogic or bureaucratic-organizational qualities."

A great many explanations have been offered about the willingness of men to live under despotic conditions. Marxist explanations of the economic reasons for the rise of great corporations abound. Dostoevski's explanation of the weakness of men in "The Grand Inquisitor" is transmogrified by Freud in his study of group psychology. Perhaps Carlyle gave the reason most succinctly: "Society is founded on Hero-worship." Yet another theory will be offered in the final chapter of this book.

But what of the men themselves? In the modern corporation, responsibility is assigned in totalitarian fashion, leaders are appointed from above (by the board of directors), and surely chief executives rise to their positions more through their abilities to deal with factions than through any technical or managerial skill. Men in these positions do not seek to divest themselves of totalitarian power or to avoid totalitarian methods; rather, they seek always to expand their powers, expand the corporation, aiming toward impossible ideals of power within the organization and without. The problem may lie in the nature of power and the strains it places upon men's moral qualities. Aristotle said, "The saying of Bias is thought to be true, that 'rule will show the man.'" Kant offered an unhappy and uncharacteristically worldly assessment: "The highest master should be just in himself, and yet a man. This task is therefore the hardest of all; indeed, its complete solution is impossible, for from such crooked wood as man is made of, nothing perfectly straight can be built." Without limits, set by law or enforced by the alienation of men from organizations, the crooked wood men are made of cannot be expected to build organizations that are perfectly straight.

ONIONSKINS

> . . . Man is tormented by no greater anxiety than to find some one quickly to whom he can hand over that gift of freedom with which the ill-fated creature is born. But only one who can appease their conscience can take over their freedom.
>
> The Grand Inquisitor

Some men are pleased to give orders and some men are pleased to take orders. There are a few, however, who wish neither to give orders nor to take them, but to live in the between of the world, where the pleasure is in knowing the orders. Such men ordinarily become scholars or journalists, the true detectives of this world; and a very few live in corporations, in the role of confidant, advisor, and ghost speaker.

They are the intellectual beadles of business, those who know.

Like many beadles, he smoked a pipe, dressed in severe suits and white shirts, walked about in vest and shirtsleeves whenever he was deep in thought, lacked the composure to speak in public or even to large groups of employees, and strived very hard to appear wise, for he was ruthlessly self-aware, and he knew that the appearance of wisdom gave him power.

When he was a young man, working in one of the subsidiary companies, he had learned that wisdom was a form of magic, of foreknowledge. Wise men, he had written in one of the notebooks he kept in his youth, truly wise men are in danger of appearing foolish in an irrational world. He determined therefore to limit his wisdom to what he knew with certainty of the future. Gossip, eavesdropping, reading upside down, and artfully phrased questions were his early methods. As he became more subtle in his understanding of the company, he learned to read between the lines of memoranda and the company newspaper. He even gleaned information from press releases and executive speeches.

He did not rise to a high position quickly, as some technologists and financial experts do; he moved slowly from job to job within the company, always using the inside understanding of the newest job to demonstrate his capacity to achieve the next. He predicted, he knew before others at his level, he even knew before the man directly above him, he was always the wisest man at his level in the corporation. People came to him for advice, and he used what he learned in one discussion to give him greater insight for the next. He became encyclopedic. The rumor of his brilliance rose to the executive floor.

Public relations, personnel, planning, government relations, siting, and study groups were the jobs he was given. He avoided production and marketing jobs, in which the restrictions of numerical evaluation were, in his opinion, too limiting for a man of his special talents. In the main, he was a kind of

conduit, a confidential man who described himself as a cata-
lyst. His description of himself was curious, for his true function was to slow the movements of the corporation, to keep actions under control. Whatever happened quickly upset him,
for he liked his predictions to be dramatic, long-range views.

In time, he came to be part of the inner circles of management, not the innermost circle, perhaps, but very close. He
separated himself from other employees by his knowledge of
secrets. He was slightly aloof, as if his emotional distance were
a necessary device for the protection of secrets. He enjoyed the
position, describing himself to his wife and children as one of
the few men who did not suffer executive loneliness.

When they asked him to explain the phrase, executive loneliness, he said it was something no one outside business could
understand, that it had to do with one's distance from the
chairman, who was the only true friend one could have in the
corporation. His family did not understand. They did not like
his business. They were interested in expensive schools and expensive stores. Their favorite hotel was the Gritti Palace. They
flew tourist class because they were annoyed by the attentions
of the cabin attendants in first class. They rode horses and
knew the vintage years of a remarkable number of wines. His
wife was beautiful, his children were charming. They tolerated
him and his business. He did not spend a great deal of time
with them.

He harbored fantastic ambitions, aspirations to the presidency, the chairmanship, some special designation within the
corporation, or a government position, perhaps as head of
some commission to study a certain social or political problem; but he understood his fantasies for what they were. He
was an inside man. Publicity would destroy his usefulness
within the corporation.

Contentment did not become him, he said. He liked to fret.
He held up the chewed stem of his pipe to demonstrate his
tendency to worry. Nevertheless, at the age of fifty-six he con-

sidered himself a man still on the rise, albeit with clouded goals.

It amused him when the vice-president for labor relations and personnel asked if he were going to write the president's farewell address. He laughed: Only newspapers and angels write obituaries in advance. The vice-president looked puzzled, but he said no more.

Later in the day, following an administrative committee meeting which he attended as an ex-officio member, he walked down the hall with the president. There's a rumor that you're resigning, he said to the president; I don't think that's good.

It's not a rumor.

No one told me.

I'm sorry, the president said. May I have your permission?

He had a dozen questions: who? why? when? It was vital to know the name of his successor. But they had arrived at the door to the president's office, and he turned in without another word.

Left alone in the hallway, he began to think that they might have excluded him for a very specific reason: he was the choice. They were polling other members of the executive committee and the board before coming to him. He should have known, he should have known all along. The chairman was gregarious, a good speaker, a first-rate financial man, the vice-chairman was a brilliant operating man, a thinker, a wise man was needed to complete the picture. Wasn't the outgoing president Phi Beta Kappa, holder of three advanced degrees, the most educated man who had ever held a senior management position in the corporation?

He went to his office, nodded to his secretary, then closed the door to his inner office to permit himself to sit in the quiet of the wood and leather, to fill and light his pipe, to think. In that room, where subtleties floated in the air like the wind-borne seeds of autumn awaiting the grasp of his willing hand, the fantasy failed. It was not him. It could never be him. They knew the histrionic quality of his wisdom. They were the makers of secrets; his power lay with the receivers. No. It was not him. They only used him. It was not him, it would never be him.

He filled his pipe, packed the tobacco with his tar-stained thumb. The odor of the tobacco was familiar, there was no more excitement in the blend. He lit a match and held it over the bowl of the pipe, drawing the flame down into the tobacco. The smoke was bitter, it irritated the tip of his tongue. Perhaps the bowl of the pipe was burnt out. His hands were trembling. He felt a knot of constriction in the left side of his chest. He could not guess who would be the next president.

———◄◆►———

Here is Hannah Arendt's description of the layers of the onion: ". . . The sympathizers in front organizations despise their fellow citizens' complete lack of initiation, the party members despise the fellow travelers' gullibility and lack of radicalism, the elite formations despise for similar reasons the party membership, and within the elite formations a similar hierarchy of contempt accompanies every new foundation and development."

At the higher levels of the organization (the innermost layers) the distinctions become increasingly subtle, the layers paper-thin, and the tensions nothing short of terrible. There are no rules at the center of the onion, secrets abound, all relations are of the nature of plots, no one can ever be certain of the layer in which he works and lives.

The danger of the layered structure has been described by Arendt, but the cause of this danger to both the organization and its members was told earlier by Madison in *The Federalist:* ". . . where there is a consciousness of unjust or dishonorable purposes, communication is always checked by distrust in proportion to the number whose concurrence is necessary." This, according to Arendt, produces the following result: "Through a carefully graduated hierarchy of militancy in which each rank is the higher level's image of the nontotalitarian world because it is less militant and its members less totally organized, the shock of the terrifying and monstrous totalitarian dichotomy is vitiated and never fully realized; this type of organization prevents its members ever being directly confronted with the outside world, whose hostility remains for them a mere ideological assumption. They are so well protected against the reality of the nontotalitarian world that they constantly underestimate the tremendous risks of totalitarian politics."

The risks are of two kinds: totalitarian organizations fail, but during their existence they destroy men and society. In business, the failures brought about by this series of concentric circles around the CEO leading to a front of the uninitiated are also of several kinds: businesses may perform clearly antisocial acts, such as selling unsafe products, publishing deceptive advertising, or violating health and safety standards; the insulating quality of the layered organization may cause severe errors in manufacturing and marketing, as well as moral judgment, leading to economic failure; but more important are the destructive effects upon individual men and upon the general society that inevitably follow on the isolation of power.

We may, with the ease of smugness, ascribe these failures to the moral failures of the men in power, but to do so would be to forget Kant's admonition about crooked wood. No Nietzschean supermen, combining the qualities of Christ and Caesar, are in charge of corporations or countries. Human beings become leaders and members of the innermost layers of totalitarian organizations; the flaw lies not only in the leaders, but in the failure of men to recognize totalitarian traits and to provide forms to guard against them.

FORCED EMIGRATION

> . . . With us all will be happy and will
> no more rebel nor destroy one another
> as under Thy freedom.
> The Grand Inquisitor

It had been decided almost a year before. The question was how. When would not be an issue once they had decided what to do with him. Sometimes I wish the son of a bitch would drop dead, the chairman said. And I hate myself for thinking that way. For God's sake, the man is my friend.

The meeting in which the question of how was to be resolved was not held in the office. The chairman, the president, the vice-chairman, and four outside directors met in a motel room at O'Hare International Airport. They ate a small, very polite buffet lunch of cold cuts and salad, not beginning their deliberations until the table had been cleared and each man had a cup of coffee before him.

One of the outside directors, the president of a small midwestern college, asked if the directors were to be paid for this special meeting. Silence greeted his question. He withdrew it, with the comment that academics were more hardheaded than industrialists by virtue of their commitment to altruism.

The chairman began the meeting: Since we fail to constitute a quorum of the fifteen directors of the corporation, this meeting is adjourned and will be reconvened on the second Thursday of March in the boardroom of our headquarters building. The secretary will notifty the members. He leaned forward, resting his elbows on the table. I don't believe there's any question about what has to be done, he said. Are there any suggestions?

Have we given him enough time? one of the outside directors, the president of a bank, asked.

Three years, the chairman replied. We should have seen some improvement in three years. Every index says the situation has either remained the same or deteriorated. The quality index is down three points, repairs are up, productivity is static on a constant dollar basis, discounted for inflation sales are declining slightly. If we don't do something, we're looking for real trouble.

Ask for his resignation, the college president said.

The president of the company stood up. He was a year away from retirement, and he had begun to show signs of wear, like a machine beyond repair: too thin here, creaking there, failing at the core. His voice had lost its force. I've known the man since he was twenty-seven years old. I saw him come up through the ranks. I know the hours he's put in, the hardships it's worked on his family. I know the man's loyalty. Those are factors that can't be overlooked. He sat down.

We have to consider the public relations effect, the chairman said, especially in the financial community. When the executive vice-president of a company suddenly resigns at the age of fifty-three, people ask questions.

There's the question of kindness, the vice-chairman said. He was known inside the boardroom as the company communist. How would you want us to behave if you were in his shoes?

The conversation went on for nearly an hour before the chairman presented the solution he had brought to the meeting. I think it's been agreed, he said, that in his best interest and the corporation's we don't ask for his resignation. And I think it's also agreed that we have to get rid of him. So I'd like to propose a compromise: change his responsibilities to executive vice-president for development and send him overseas.

Give him no line responsibility, but set him up in our Latin American headquarters in Bogotá.

He'll rot there, the vice-chairman said.

He'll rot the whole goddamn corporation if he stays here, the chairman answered.

The decision was made. The next day the chairman called the executive vice-president to his office to tell him of his new assignment. They had known each other for a long time. They spoke for a moment about children, about the chairman's first grandchild, who was in his first week of kindergarten. Such conversations were infrequent now. The executive vice-president seemed to be enjoying it.

A telephone call interrupted the chairman's end of the conversation. He turned away to speak. When he turned back, his face was set hard at the mouth.

Bad news? the executive vice-president asked.

No. Well, we'll see. I asked you down here to talk about a change of assignment. I want you to take over development. It's headquartered, as you know, in Bogotá.

Have I done that badly since I came back?

Things seem to go better for you in the field.

Bogotá isn't London.

The UK is sinking. Latin America will be our fastest-growing market through the end of the century.

That's not why you're sending me.

Stick to the question, the chairman said.

It'll be hard on the kids. What the hell will Louise do in Bogotá? I think you're really screwing me with this deal. The action is here, this is where there's a chance to do something.

Take it or leave it, the chairman said.

And if I decide not to take it?

The chairman did not answer. His mouth was a flat line, his eyes were opaque. He sat completely still, even his breathing was silent, imperceptible.

The executive vice-president nodded his head slowly. He

said nothing. The nodding continued, as if he were keeping time to a cadenced and unmelodious inner music.

———◄◆►———

The meaning of exile can be understood best with the perspective of history. Coulanges gives this explanation in *The Ancient City:* "The ordinary punishment of great crimes was exile. Exile was really the interdiction of worship.

"Having no longer a worship, he [the exile] had no longer a family; he ceased to be a husband and a father. His sons were no longer in his power; his wife was no longer his wife . . .

"It is not surprising that the ancient republics almost all permitted a convict to escape death by flight. Exile did not seem to be a milder punishment than death. The Roman jurists called it capital punishment."

In totalitarian movements, deportation has always been used as a major tactic in the demoralization of those designated as enemies of the movement. Both the Nazis and the Stalinists, and according to the best information available, the Chinese Maoists, used deportation to reduce large numbers of people to the state of disorientation and disequilibrium that makes death seem a useless commonplace. The Cambodian Government deported the populations of entire cities, using deportation to destroy society and culture as a first step in building a new society according to the principles of the Pol Pot government.

The effect of deportation seems to be the destruction of the will, even the will to suicide, the last possible act of an otherwise erased personality. Suicides were not common in either Nazi or Soviet concentration camps, nor is there any evidence of suicide among those deported by Pol Pot or Mao.

The same result occurs in business. Those who are deported to branch offices or less important posts do not quit their jobs to seek others, even when they are capable of finding other employment. Exile supplants death in the corporation as it did in the ancient city. Exiles remain; they do not escape, because there is no escape from exile except return; they do not commit suicide, because capital punishment has already been visited upon them; and they do not rebel, because the dead cannot rebel.

Two kinds of persons suffer exile in business: those who fail at the inner layers of the onion structure, and those who seek greater power, even a coup, and are defeated. Those who fail in the other structure of the corporation, the pyramid of authoritarian management, are fired or, if they fail at low levels, they are filed away in jobs without opportunity for promotion. One might say that in business only friends can fall into the role of enemies and be condemned to exile.

NOT COWARDICE

> They will marvel at us and will be awe-
> stricken before us, and will be proud at
> our being so powerful and clever. . . .
> The Grand Inquisitor

He arrived in New York in the late afternoon, a big man, going skinny in late middle age, bending like a stalk of wheat in a steady wind. His voice was thin and cracked. He spoke slowly, with an Ohio twang and an Indiana twang and a drawl befitting his demeanor. He liked to laugh and to drink good whiskey, and his fingernails were black from working with greased machinery even though he had been a plant superintendent for seventeen years. When describing himself to a reporter from the company newspaper, he said, I'm American, Protestant, Republican, and a damn good engineer out of Ohio State.

The taxi took him midtown to a hotel near the company headquarters building. He carried a large black portfolio containing a series of cardboard placards filled with numbers and drawings, and a new unbreakable plastic suitcase packed with one complete change of clothes and fifteen copies of the placards reduced to regular sheets of paper and stapled into blue folders with the company name printed in raised letters on the front. He called it a mission; he intended to ask the company to spend $8.6 million to modernize the plant he had managed over the last seventeen years.

His chances of getting the money were good, he thought. Heat exchangers and a small computer to turn all the machinery off and on simultaneously would reduce the fuel bill; he projected a four-year payout at current gas and electricity prices. He would have more trouble because of the longer payout on an electric induction furnace and an automatic laser device for hardening the valve seats in the gas compressor pumps built in his plant; but they would come across if he was a good salesman. The rest of the changes he wanted to make were more or less optional: soundproofing, a new paint booth, devices to monitor grinding equipment, a numerically controlled milling machine to improve the deep dies.

He did not expect to get it all. The executive committee never gave anyone all that he asked; that was their job. He would be satisfied with 80 per cent, 60 per cent, if it was the right 60 per cent. Sixty per cent for a sixty-year-old superintendent, he told himself; that was the minimum. It would take almost five years to design the equipment and get it installed and working. When he retired, if they let him go to sixty-five, the plant would be up-to-date, sort of a model plant, if he said so himself.

The crowd at the registration desk surprised him. It looked like the shift change, everyone hurrying, carrying little packages. But these people were not factory workers. The women wore furs and many of the men wore expensive suits, although a few did not wear ties, but had their shirts open practically down to the belly button. He wouldn't let the men in the foundry do that, much as they liked to in summer; it was a safety hazard—a man could get a helluva burn that way.

He ate dinner in the coffee shop of the hotel: liver and bacon and spinach to give him strength and settle his nerves for the meeting the next day. Not that his nerves were bad, considering the importance of the meeting. It was just that he didn't want to disappoint the people back at the plant. Of course, if he made a fool of himself, they might, just might decide to retire him early, and he couldn't afford that. Ginny had come home after eleven years of marriage and four kids. Somebody had to care for those kids. Sure as hell her goddamn wop husband wasn't going to do it. Four kids. He estimated that it would cost him four hundred thousand plus in constant dollars to see them all through college.

After looking at the dinner check, eleven dollars and eighty-two cents, he thought about revising the estimate upward.

He went for a walk on Fifth Avenue after dinner, stopping in a bargain store to buy gifts for the grandchildren: two liquid crystal watches, a camera, and a small telescope. The department stores were all closed, so he went into a bookstore and bought an art book for his daughter and a French cookbook for his wife. He gave a quarter to a blind man with a mangy dog and bought two pencils from a legless man who sat on the sidewalk stroking a pet rabbit.

It was only nine-thirty Indiana time when he went up to his room. He washed and put on his pajamas and watched television for a while before he put his partials in a glass of water to soak overnight, urinated, shined up his shoes with a chemically treated paper, and went to bed. It was quiet in the room, the bed was hard, the linen was fresh and only a little scratchy, but he could not sleep.

He got up, turned on the light, picked up one of the folders from his suitcase, and took it back to bed with him. All the pages were in order, all the typographical errors had been corrected. He studied the material. The numbers were right. His estimates were on the conservative side. Would they think he was too radical? Was he acting like a foolish old man? The plant was turning a profit, a good profit. It had been a money-maker since his second year as superintendent. Maybe they would think he was a fool to want to spend $8.6 million.

For a while he practiced the speech he had made up to go along with the charts. He always talked off the cuff, he liked to talk, people didn't frighten him. Maybe he would have done well to have written out this speech? He could get lost up there in front of the executive committee, forget his best points, repeat himself, just go blank. It wasn't unheard of for a man to go blank in front of the executive committee.

He closed the light and went back to bed, but he could not sleep. He thought of his wife, of Ginny and the children. Pictures of them came before his eyes in the dark. He smiled at them. An hour passed. Still he could not sleep. He felt warm. These New Yorkers always kept it too hot in their houses. He kicked the covers down and lay stretched out on the bed with his feet reaching almost to the edge. He began to perspire. His ears rang. He felt his heart pounding in his chest. His chest was like a great steel drum, amplifying the sound and the pounding. At first, he thought it was a heart attack, but there was no pain. His chest tightened, he had difficulty taking in air, but still there was no pain.

He lay quietly on the bed, waiting to die, surely to die. His whole body clanged. His heart had no certain rhythm. Something had closed the valve to his lungs; he could pull no air into them. He tried to think of his wife, his daughter, his grandchildren, wanting to have them in his thoughts as he died, but he did not die. His sweat turned cold, his ears rang, the pounding of his heart shook his chest, but he did not die.

Never in his life had he been so filled with fear, not even in Belgium when the German artillery found the range of his squadron and he saw the tanks up ahead burning, exploding, throwing men and pieces of men into the fiery air. Now he was alone and old and the explosions were inside him. But he did not die.

He was not a cowardly man, nor was he unresourceful. He needed someone to help him: his wife, a doctor, someone. He lifted the telephone receiver from its cradle and dialed the operator.

After many rings, a voice said, Operator.

Help me, he said. His voice was only a whisper.

Operator.

Hello.

This is the operator, sir. May I help you?

Yes. Hold my hand. Please send up someone to hold my hand.

———◆———

The men and women who work in middle management and technical jobs in corporations suffer from fear, but not from cowardice. Their ability to endure fear in the struggle to achieve happiness as it has been defined for them proves that they are not cowards. They lack options. They may move from corporation to corporation, but the systems in which they live do not change with the change of employment. As they grow older, even that illusory option disappears. Then they must choose between human alienation and their accustomed standard of living.

Fear makes them weak, timid people, and each generation

becomes successively weaker, as in Plato's description of timocracy. They are bourgeois, as Arendt defines the bourgeois: each is a compromiser, one who will do anything to maintain his bourgeois economic position; the morality of an externally defined happiness becomes the only morality for such a person.

Lack of due process, lack of any immutable rules or body of laws to define proper behavior and the proper response of those in power to specific kinds of behavior leaves the middle manager and the technician in a world without limits, without control over his own destiny. Being human, he fears the unknown, and the unknown is his daily life in the corporation. He cannot predict with certainty the response to any act. He can be demoted, transferred, or dismissed without notice or reason. He exists as a productive, economically sound creature at the sufferance of the corporation.

The plain fact is that the most important element in any totalitarian organization is the power of the organization to assign or withdraw the means of earning a living. In that situation, men do not face obedience as a question; they obey out of necessity. Like the concentration camp guard cited by Arendt, they will do anything, because they know the meaning of not carrying out their responsibilities to their wives and children by earning a living.

Fear runs up and down the layers and levels of totalitarian organizations. One fears the next higher level or inner layer and the levels and layers beyond, all the way to the leader, and reflects that fear upward, reinforcing the fear of those above, like a mirror in which a man may see the signs of his own sickness and become frightened by what he sees. In the other direction, subordinates feel fear in the form of indecision, conservatism, and the possibility that they will be made the scapegoat for any errors made by their superiors.

No amount of inner strength or goodness will spare men from this suffering. As Aristotle said, "Those who say that the victim on the rack or the man who falls into great misfortunes is happy if he is good are, whether they mean to or not, talking nonsense." The bravest of men in fearsome circumstances suffers until he loses all will to resist and becomes what those he fears want him to be, and remains that way, because he never knows if his capitulation will suffice to spare him.

Stalin used fear, according to Isaac Deutscher, in perfect totalitarian fashion: "Stalin's raging wrath," Deutscher writes, "burst over people's heads not merely to punish past transgressions but to stifle any new impulse to disobedience." Montesquieu called fear "the principle of despotic government." He said, "A timid, ignorant, cowed people does not need many laws."

The effect of fear was also noted in the jargon of industrial psychology by McGregor: "Arbitrary management actions, behavior which arouses uncertainty with respect to continued employment or which reflects favoritism or discrimination, unpredictable administrative policy—these can be powerful motivators of the safety needs in the employment relationship at every level from worker to vice president."

Every employee outside the innermost layer in every corporation suffers the fear described by McGregor. Trade unions can mitigate that fear, but even a union cannot keep a plant from shutting down or an industry from dying.

"It is much safer to be feared than loved, if one of the two has to be wanting," said Machiavelli. "Men have less scruple in offending one who makes himself loved than one who makes himself feared; for love is held by a chain of obligation which, men being selfish, is broken whenever it serves their purpose; but fear is maintained by a dread of punishment which never fails." Corporations do not take unnecessary chances.

THE UNIVERSAL SPIRIT OF BUREAUCRACY

> They will have no secrets from us.
> The Grand Inquisitor

There were many secrets he did not know. There were many secrets he only imagined. He could not distinguish between real secrets and imagined secrets; it was logically impossible so long as both remained secret. Like an ambitious man, like a fearful man, like an ordinary man, he gave much of his time to wondering about secrets of both classes. He liked to think, however, that he gave the most time to the real secrets, not that he knew, but it pleased him to think so.

When at last he was made a senior officer of the company in charge of administration, many of the secrets became available to him. He did not pursue them immediately, preferring to wait a decent amount of time before prying. Some secrets came to him as a matter of course in his new position: the perquisites he had imagined were, in fact, real; the forward-looking research projects he had suspected were best kept secret, for there were none; the facilitating payments to agents of foreign governments were greater in number and smaller in amount than he had suspected; and so on.

No secret interested him more than his own personnel file, part of which was open to his inspection and part of which was available only to senior executives. It included the results of a security check by the Department of Defense, personal letters from other executives, health records, performance data, and various criticisms that had been accumulated over his years of service.

He asked the director of personnel, who now reported to him, to bring him the files of all the senior executives for his review. Half an hour later, the files, in correct alphabetical order, were on his desk. All were marked *Confidential.* He pulled his own file from the stack, opened it, and began reading. There were no surprises. The secrets he had imagined were only imagined.

He began to wonder about himself. Was he a dull man? A drudge? A bore?

If there were no secrets in his file, why was the file a secret? What is the purpose of secrets? He considered declaring all the files open, ending the secrecy. But he did not, for he knew, in an automatic way, that without real secrets there could be no imagined secrets. He sent the files back, keeping the secret.

———◆———

Secrets are betrothed to lies. The keeper of the secret implies that he will lie to keep the secret from being discovered; and the liar always makes a secret of the truth. In her book *Lying,* Sissela Bok listed the three claims used to support the keeping of secrets: "First, that we have a right to protect ourselves and those close to us from the harm that might flow from disclosure; second, that fairness requires respect for privacy; and third, that added respect is due for that which one has *promised* to keep secret."

In a rational society, no other claims can be made. Totalitarian organizations, however, are based on irrational and impossible certainties. Secrecy per se has value in an organization that opposes freedom, that cannot exist without blind obedience. Secrecy inspires fear, the precursor of the necessary obedience. But most important, secrecy cloaks the infectious madness that causes people to participate in their own destruction. "Secrecy," Marx said, "is the universal spirit of bureaucracy." It is the basic structural element in totalitarianism, containing the threat, the promise, and all the badges of rank in the organization.

The rationale for secrecy is seldom stated overtly, although Stalin did say, ". . . Nothing could be more dangerous to tyrannical authority than the people's curiosity." In business secrecy from competitors, the press, and regulatory agencies is connected with Bok's first claim and sometimes with the second, but it is carried to a totalitarian extreme. Any disclosure to anyone may be considered harmful to the possessor of the secret. Since all who are oppressed are potential enemies of the oppressor, it is rational within the irrational structure of oppression to make Bok's first claim on everything.

Secrets in business are kept according to the layers of the totalitarian structure rather than on the levels of authoritarianism, for power is distributed according to the layered structure, and secrecy creates and defends power. As Arendt said, "Real power begins where secrecy begins." The leaders of corporations use intermural and intramural secrecy to gain power for their organizations and for themselves.

NECESSITY'S REALITY

. . . Thou didst think too highly of men
. . . for they are slaves, of course,
though rebellious by nature.
                    The Grand Inquisitor

He and the boy walked along the river. The boy no longer
pleased him. Once, not very long ago, the boy had wanted to
please him. They had been friends, they went to football
games together and smoked the same pipe tobacco. In many
ways, he thought, that had been the best time of his life.

There was ice in the river. The trees along the bank were
bare, the trunks were gray and the boughs were nests of sticks.
There was no snow. It had melted, leaving the ground deeply
muddy. The river was brown with mud, running fast. There
was dark mud on the floating ice. Sticks, logs, cans, and paper
floated in the river. The man and the boy wore rubber boots
and tucked the bottoms of their trousers into the rubber tops.
The man smoked his pipe. The boy ate seeds from a plastic
bag.

In the distance, over the meshed sticks of the treetops, four
tall chimneys spoke dark gray steam. Water vapor, the man
said. Poison, the boy said.

The man glanced often at the boy, thinking of his childhood. The boy had been away for three and a half years. Soon
he would be a graduate of an eastern university. It had cost a
great deal to send him there. The money had not come easily.
At times, the man regretted sending the boy to the eastern uni-

versity. He regretted the money and the distance and the way the boy had learned to hate the company. Once, the man had said to the boy, The factory paid for your education. If you're an honest man, you won't forget that. And the boy had answered, Because I try to be an honest man, I have to forget it.

This river is filthy, the boy said. The fish are all dead and the water is no longer potable. The effluent comes from the factory. It's a shameful thing, a criminal act.

The water is dirty because the melted snow washes mud into the river, the man said.

One of us is a liar, the boy said.

The man looked off at the chimneys of the factory in which he had worked for almost thirty years. He was but for one man the ruler of the place. It had been good to him. It had sent his son to an eastern university and bought his family a fine house and two cars and three trips to Europe. He played golf, his daughters rode beautiful horses and sat them more elegantly than Spanish riding masters. His wife had never lost the girlish song in her laughter.

He looked steadily at the boy for a moment. They looked alike in many ways. Their noses were similarly small and pointed at the tip, their eyes were exactly the same color, their chins were similarly squared, both had crooked eyeteeth. He and the boy had argued over the river before. There was nothing more to say.

Are you going to answer me? the boy said. Will you tell me the last time a fish was caught in this river?

The man turned up the riverbank toward the road.

———⟫◆⟪———

Hannah Arendt makes the connection between unreality and totalitarianism in the following excerpts from *The Origins of Totalitarianism:*

"The outstanding negative quality of the totalitarian elite is that it never stops to think about the world as it really is and never compares the lie with reality."

"The ideal subject of totalitarian rule is not the convinced Nazi or the convinced Communist, but people for whom the distinction between fact and fiction (i.e., the reality of experience) and the distinction between true and false (i.e., the standards of thought) no longer exist."

The position of business about reality is clear: all critics are hostile; either they are hostile because they are misinformed or they spread misinformation because they are hostile. The only reality is that decreed by the leader and his inner circle, a group of men who are severely isolated from reality both inside and outside the organization. This is not to say that the leader necessarily wills the divorce between reality and the organization's perception of reality. The velocity of his life separates him from the real world and the structures of his organization impose his reality upon all those below him. Some of the leaders of corporations are aware of this lack of connection with reality and the dangers of it both to their employees and to the ultimate survival of the organization, but they are helpless to combat it.

The leader in New York must rely on the man in Chicago to tell him about the situation in Peoria. The man in Peoria distorts reality to please the man in Chicago, who further distorts it to please the leader, who then decrees to the entire organization the reality he perceives. The informal and formal communications machines of the organization enforce the leader's perception. Finally, the man in Peoria learns that his lie was the truth, the reality by which he must abide, if he is to earn a living for himself and his family. He must defend his lie to critics, lest he betray the organization. The circle continues at ever increasing speed. Only those who can put aside thought and misconstrue experience survive. Reality and the time to consider it become the greatest dangers to the organization from the point of view of the organization.

ACCORDING TO THE RULES

—some impossible *quidproquo* . . .
The Grand Inquisitor

His first contact with the product came on a visit to the labs. He was assistant product manager for the window cleaner, and he had gone to the chemistry building to talk about a possible change in the formulation of the product caused by the change from aerosol to manually operated pump dispensers. A young fellow who worked with synthetic waxes showed him what he called the most extraordinary breakthrough in woodcare products since bees began making wax. The chemist sprayed an unpleasant-smelling liquid onto a piece of dull wood and asked the assistant product manager to observe what happened. The drops of sprayed liquid spread across the surface of the wood forming an even coat of whitish translucent glaze. The glaze slowly lost its sheen as the liquid seemed to be absorbed by the wood. As the color of the wood returned to its previous state, the liquid seemed to have completely evaporated.

Touch the wood, the chemist said.

He did. It was dry to his touch and slightly warm.

The chemist put the piece of wood down on the worktable and asked the assistant manager to watch carefully for the next three minutes.

As if by magic, the wood began to shine. The reflection became brighter and brighter until, after the full three minutes, the assistant product manager could clearly see his face reflected in the shining piece of wood. There was a red and black tie, a gray suit, a white shirt with maroon stripes. He bent closer to the wood to examine the color of his eyes in the reflection. On the surface of the brown wood were two black circles surrounded by blue.

Fantastic, he said, absolutely fantastic.

The chemist nodded. It has problems, he said. It's too expensive, the stuff stinks, as you may have noticed, and the manufacturing process will be very difficult.

I think you've really got something there.

Actually, the chemist said, we're all pretty excited.

What's the next step?

We go to management, get a product manager, and take it to market.

I'll take it to market for you, the assistant product manager said.

A moment of laughter and camaraderie followed. The chemist who worked on the window cleaner confessed to the assistant product manager that they had been hoping he would have a positive reaction. They wanted a young man to handle the product, not one of the old farts who always moved so slowly that competitors beat them into the market. There were warm handshakes, hands round each other's shoulders, more laughter. They went outside the research center to have a lunch of celebration in a nearby German restaurant. They drank great steins of dark beer, covered their food with applesauce, and predicted a shining future for themselves and for all the wood floors of America and the world.

He went to the vice-president for marketing to ask for the assignment as product manager on the new magic wax. After all, he said, there was nothing but caretaker work left on the window cleaner. It had 97 per cent distribution and a 66 per cent share of market.

What about closing out the aerosols? the vice-president asked.

The formula stays the same, the product costs us almost six cents less, and it tests out at the same price as the aerosol.

And the use rate?

There's more product in the spray pump container but the delivery system is less efficient. It all depends on what's left in the bottom of the bottle. We're estimating that it will remain the same, plus or minus 2 per cent.

Four per cent is a lot of bottles of window cleaner.

I don't think we can get closer until we go through a full repurchase cycle.

The vice-president smiled. The young man pleased him. You've got the wax, he said. Keep me informed on the development. I don't want quarterly reports, either. Let me know what's going on at every step. If I can help, I will. Don't be afraid to ask for help; that's what I'm here for.

It was a good time in the new product manager's life. His salary was raised, he moved his family into a new house, he was invited to join a country club, he and his wife spent their first vacation in Europe. He had a sense of well-being, he put money into a savings account, and he began to read the stock market reports. His new office was elegantly furnished; for the first time, he was consulted on the colors and styles he preferred—he asked that a picture he did not like be removed from the wall and replaced with something more brightly colored and optimistic.

Development of the product moved quickly. The smell was changed by the addition of a masking lemon odor. A miniature manufacturing process was designed to produce the product in batches large enough to sustain a test market. Package design, market positioning, pricing studies, everything moved forward quickly. An advertising agency was appointed. He made trips to New York, where he ate in French restaurants and attended the theater. Everyone who came in contact with the new wax with the magical properties was excited by it.

He reported the results of the first test with consumers as

phenomenal. The advertising tested equally well. A computer model of the market indicated a 40 per cent share could be achieved in a year, given 75 per cent distribution, heavy sampling, and only a modest advertising budget for media.

The first test market came that spring in Milwaukee. He went with the salesmen on their calls to buyers for supermarkets. The salesmen carried a sample piece of wood with them, but they preferred to demonstrate the wax on the buyer's desk or the floor of his office. Distribution exceeded 75 per cent. The repurchase rate was astonishing. Women bought one bottle to try out the wax and came back to buy enough to wax every floor in the house.

He went home from Milwaukee to plan the national rollout for that fall. There were packaging orders, sampling and advertising schedules to co-ordinate with sales and distribution, thousands of details to attend to, and there was the conversion of a plant to be watched, for the sales reports and computer modeling had convinced management to make the investment. Meanwhile, his salary had been raised again. Some people said he was a young genius for having recognized the potential of the new product. Nice words, congratulatory words were sent to him in memos. Promises were implied.

The national rollout began in September. Sales were as expected at wholesale and the product moved off the shelves even faster than predicted. He had been purposely conservative. He understood company politics, he had ambitions.

Suddenly, sales of the wax stopped. The repurchase rate dropped to zero in market after market throughout the Northeast and Midwest. The pipeline filled and then overflowed. Production at the new plant was slowed and then stopped. He sat in his office, day after day, staring at the walls, examining the brightly colored, optimistic picture he had requested. The nice memos no longer arrived in the mail. People he met in the halls and in the dining room had little to say to him. Something was wrong with the product, he was certain, but he did not know what. He took bottle after bottle off the shelf in his office, trying them on various kinds of wood and wood finishes. In every case, the magic wax worked.

He took the family to his in-laws' house in Vermont for the Christmas holiday. It had promised to be a week of skiing and good times in the big A-frame house, but he had no spirit. The whole family felt his distress. The children fought and cried, his wife caught cold. To cheer him, his mother-in-law bought a bottle of the magic wax at the supermarket near the ski lodge. Immediately upon coming home with the groceries she went to the living room of the house and sprayed all of the wood floor that was not covered with rugs.

When he came into the room to accept congratulations for the magic wax that saved his mother-in-law from polishing the wood floors, he saw it. Near the fireplace the floor shone and near the front door it was covered with a gray film, as if someone had laid a very thin sheet of waxed paper over the wood. He knelt down near the door and touched the gray film. It felt as smooth as the rest of the floor. He tried to wipe it away with his fingers, then he tried to polish it away with his handkerchief. After a long time he was able to rub the wax away, leaving the floor dull and unpolished.

Something had gone wrong in the plant. The product needed heat to work. The exothermic reaction he had felt in the lab had been lost in the reformulation that had brought down the cost. He was standing on a disaster. All around the country there were floors turning gray as winter touched them. He stood there for a very long time, looking down at the floor. He did not know what to do. He was glad the floor did not shine in the place where he looked, because he did not want to see his own face.

———◆———

Rewards in business are said to be based on performance, but in most instances, the cause of reward is not performance, but some other circumstance or combination of circumstances. Even the commission system for salesmen tends to deliver more reward to a salesman for having a good territory than for being a good salesman. In the white collar, technical, and managerial spheres, determinations may be made on a purely personal basis or on the ability of one man to appear responsible for the good work of others.

Punishments in business rarely have to do with performance. In the now famous Ford/Iacocca story, Ford is reputed to have told Iacocca that he just didn't like him. Ford suffers the bluntness of befuddled kings, but his comment describes the situation throughout business and government: careers rise and fall on such irrational judgments.

Even more commonly, men and women in one part of a corporation suffer because of errors in another section or because of new laws or changes in international affairs or public tastes. For example, the failure of U.S. industry, in general, to modernize its plant following World War II, preferring instead to distribute profits to speculators (and to themselves, for most executives are paid in large measure in stock and stock options), has resulted in lowered quality and productivity and the consequent loss of markets, including internal markets, to other industrialized nations. But the burden of that failure is borne always by people outside the highest layers and levels of business—from middle management to production workers.

The complexity of large business, a direct result of size (divisional responsibility, single mission plants, etc.), eliminates the possibility of clear claims on success or failure. Good work and goodness alike belong to the organization, which assigns punishment or reward arbitrarily, resulting in the moral disruption of the members of the organization, who have no choice but to abandon themselves and give over all moral responsibility to the organization. The moral imperative to those who have no control over the results of their own actions is duty first, what philosophers call "kitchen Kant." It is an easy morality in that it does not require thinking of men for whom thought can be of no use.

SUBTOTALS

> . . . We shall triumph and shall be Cae-
> sars, and then we shall plan the universal
> happiness of man.
> The Grand Inquisitor

In some corporations gentlemen still prevail. They are often lawyers, and they are usually from Boston, unless they are Southerners, in which case gentility is a function of size and age and gray ghosts. Gentlemen drink. And even when they are drunk they speak clearly and well, in long sentences, with too much punctuation. A gentleman's hair is always gray, and if he is bald, he is completely bald; a gentleman's hair does not embarrass him.

There is no need for gentlemen in corporations. The style of them makes no special contribution. A woman can do the same job as a gentleman and a man jumped up from the ranks holds a special attraction for his followers and his fellows. Terse, tough men are valued most highly. Gentlemen sometimes seem superfluous because of the habits of gentility. Their insistence upon correct grammar, for instance, is viewed as old-fashioned and even unproductive.

These troubles of gentility had followed the assistant general counsel for all of his career. He was a good lawyer in the opinion of his peers, and he was marvelous at dinner parties, poker games, golf matches, and vacations; an entertaining man, a reminder of times before men died too young from workdays that consumed all their waking hours. Women liked him, weary men found him restful, ambitious men often asked him to hurry up, to get on with it, and every year every supervisor he had ever endured called him into his office and suggested that he be less formal, more aggressive, more in tune with the methods of modern business.

He called himself a country lawyer, he traded in commodities, although unsuccessfully, and he liked living far from the city, in an area of farms and woods, where he could sit a horse lazily and watch his dog running alongside in the tall autumn grass. All his children were daughters, and they all went to school in the South and married architects, lawyers, or engineers—he advised them against doctors.

When the corporation merged with a smaller corporation, he approved. It added stability, he said. He approved of the purchase of other companies, although he wondered how managers could manage unfamiliar businesses. When the corporation became very large, having merged and acquired to do so, it built a great office building and gave him an elegant office on the top floor. He was not a director, but his office was no more than a few steps from the boardroom. He sometimes invited friends or business associates up to his office so they could admire his furnishings and his view and his company's new boardroom equipped with remote control audio-visual facilities.

He aged as a gentleman should, with grace. He put on weight, he wore darker suits, his speech slowed. His pink cheeks and thick white hair caused women of a certain age to flutter their eyelashes. He kissed the hand of the chairman's wife and he taught the president's wife to ride.

The announcement of a tender offer for a controlling portion of the stock of his corporation by a larger corporation made him laugh. They were simply too big to be swallowed up like a little fish. There were questions of antitrust. He had some friends in Washington, boys he had gone to school with who would see to it that a big, fat conglomerate didn't effect an extremely unfriendly takeover of their integrated, profitable company. Besides, the man who ran the voracious conglomerate just wasn't a decent fellow. He was a cost-cutter, a man who fired other men on whim, a crude man. He said to all who would listen, This fellow doesn't just squeeze a company for profit, he squeezes it to death.

Everyone knew he was talking about himself, his own death in the form of dismissal; the head of the larger company had an aversion to gentlemen. Business magazines described him as a rough-and-tumble entrepreneur, a brawler, a street fighter. The only lawyers he ever hired were Jews and Greeks who showed pieces of white calf when they crossed their legs.

As the ordinary legal maneuvers to avert takeover failed, he began to think of daring, unusual, even faintly unethical ways of saving what he called the tradition, the quality, the sound management, and the fine people of their company. The general counsel was amused by his first bouquet of innovative, if impractical, ideas. By the third series of proposals he became irritable. You surprise me, he said. I never expected you to turn into a Kamikaze.

My great uncle, who disdained Mr. Stuart's cavalry, died while charging up a hill on the orders of Cousin Pickett.

I don't understand your point.

It's not relevant. Call it musing, a personal recollection, perhaps a joke, too arcane to succeed, but intended as a joke.

Three months after the effective date of the acquisition by the larger corporation he was asked to take advantage of the early retirement plan, which was far less generous than that of the now absorbed corporation in which he had spent almost all of his working life. He considered a lawsuit, but did not carry through the idea, knowing that the costs were more than a retired man could bear. He sold the horses and the farm and moved to Florida with his wife and his dog.

For several months he considered taking the Florida Bar examination and opening a small practice there, but the heat and the dampness and the very weight of the casebooks tired him. He and his wife moved to a retirement community. Dogs were not permitted there. They had far too much furniture for the small white stucco house. He drank gin and learned to play pinochle while sitting outdoors with his shirt open, exposing his belly to the sun.

———◆———

Arendt, Buchheim, and others have written about the need of totalitarian states to expand continually, seeking the impossible, ultimate totality of domination. But Aristotle's description of this quality in the human character bears repeating, for it offers even greater precision: "Some persons are led to believe that getting wealth is the object of household management," said Aristotle, "and the whole idea of their lives is that they ought either to increase their money without limit, or at any rate not to lose it. The origin of this disposition in men is that they are intent upon living only, and not upon living well; and as their desires are unlimited, they also desire that the means of gratifying them should be without limit."

The economy, according to Aristotle, is the public household; and by living well he meant living as a free man, a political man. He opposes the sense of limits of a moral person to the wish for unlimited means of gratification of the person who is not intent upon living well. He opposes the free political man to the man without limits. The Greeks were not unaware of despotism, nor were totalitarian tactics unknown in Aristotle's time (according to some, the reading of the *Republic* would have exposed him to the most totalitarian organization of all), and human nature had already been formed, revised with the invention of writing, and revised again with the coming of both science and philosophy.

The desire to expand without limit, the goal of totality that can never be achieved, belongs as much to the modern corporation as to the totalitarian state. The Aztecs of Mexico conquered other tribes and used them in the conquest of still others. Caesar used the same tactic. Hitler fueled Germany's aims of world domination with the blood and materials of conquered nations. The Soviet Union follows the same pattern. All totalitarian organizations grow by agglomeration, like the modern corporation seeking the security of size, market share, oligopoly, and eventual monopoly. The desire to achieve the impossible totality overwhelms the moral sense (of limits to means), and the enemy becomes the resisting nation, the recalcitrant group within the nation, or in the case of the corporation the limiting laws enacted against its aims. Despite the regular protestations of their love for competition by the leaders of totalitarian organizations, nothing could be more inimical to their goals and their need to move incessantly toward them.

NEGATIVE INCLUSION

> We shall persuade them that they will
> only become free when they renounce
> their freedom to us and submit to us.
> The Grand Inquisitor

They had entered the training program on the same day nearly six years before, two women in economics in a time when there were few women in the field. One was pretty and one was not. The pretty one was also rich and well connected; she had come to the firm through the suggestion of her mother, who was the cousin of the chairman of the board. The plain one was thought to be the brighter of the two, but in truth, there was little difference between them in that regard; the plain one enjoyed the prejudice of her supervisors, who were all men of an earlier ethos.

The appearance of them in the Wall Street offices of the old bank was startling. The wood-paneled walls had never seen such colors as the clothing the two young women carried into meeting rooms: fuchsia, orange, carmine, green, purple, rose, yellow. The cooks who served the dining rooms in the pent-house came out of their kitchens to look at the young women. One of the old gentlemen of the trust department rose from his chair and bowed deeply at the waist when first he saw two women in the dining room. The women, amused, curtsied in response.

Although one was plain and went home every night to a small apartment on the West Side and the other was pretty and lived with her family in a brownstone between Madison and Fifth, they became friends. It was not the kind of true friend-ship in which the distinctions between altruism and self-preser-vation become blurred, but rather more like the friendship of countrymen meeting abroad, conversing in idioms that have the character of coded messages between allies.

One went to the trust department and the other went to the economics staff following completion of the brief training pro-gram. They moved from department to department during their first three years with the bank, then the pretty one settled into economics and the plain one settled into the foreign department. They worked on different floors, traveled to dif-ferent places, but remained friends, lunching together often, annually buying subscription seats together for the ballet. Nei-ther of them married, neither wished to marry, neither was happy, neither was sad; after a while they began to take note of the years, which led them to embark upon longer love affairs and to play tennis with greater frequency.

The pretty one's work took her to Washington often. She met other economists there and she went to many Washington parties, spending her leisure in the company of highly placed officials and sinister foreigners. Out of these meetings came an interest in public service, and she accepted a position in the Department of State because it offered opportunities for travel. Her friend at the bank said she was sorry to see her leave. We established a beachhead together, she said, having learned to use male metaphors to communicate her thoughts more precisely.

There's no reason why we can't remain friends, the pretty one said.

Now that you're in State and I'm still in the foreign department we'll probably have to move our lunches to Zurich and change our ballet tickets to the Bolshoi.

For the first few months after she changed jobs, the pretty one was very busy learning the routine of public service. She felt grand, for she no longer dealt with corporations, she dealt with nations and consortiums of nations; the old bank came to seem very small in the eyes of a woman of State. She did not see her plain friend for three months.

They met in the dining room of the Hay Adams, embracing, touching cheeks in the kiss of friends. Seated, each with a glass of white wine in hand, they spoke of apartments and parties and men. When they felt caught up as intimates, the plain one asked, What have they got you doing?

Analysis.

Is the data good?

Oh, very. And you, are you still working on forecasts?

As usual.

Japan?

I expect to be visiting there in about six weeks.

But hasn't the bank made a major . . . ?

Oh, you know all about that.

Not as much as State should.

Remember the fellow I was seeing last year, the one on the trading desk? He asked me to move in with him.

Are you losing interest in your work? the pretty one asked.

It's not that . . . She did not know what to say to complete the sentence. Her eyes shimmered with sadness and secrets.

"Whoever is not expressly included is excluded," said Mussolini; in characteristic fashion coming very close to a revelation, but missing it. Inclusion does indeed play a powerful part in controlling masses of people, but positive inclusion exerts far less force than negative inclusion. In other words, whoever is not expressly excluded is included. The leader uses his position far more effectively by setting the boundaries for the organization through defining its enemies.

Hitler wrote in *Mein Kampf:* "They must not fear the hostility of their enemies, but must feel that it is the presupposition for their own right to exist. They must not shun the hatred of the enemies of our nationality and our philosophy and its manifestations, they must long for them." Nationalistic propaganda uses negative inclusion almost exclusively, as do all totalitarian organizations.

All negative inclusion involves the concept of competition, either as war or war's sibling, economic competition. The competitor is by definition an enemy, a clear and present danger to one's life or livelihood. By creating a border of enemies, the organization instills a siege mentality in its members: they have no choice but to look to the organization for safety, to huddle together in fear. If they leave the organization, or worse, if they are cast out by the organization, what hope will there be for them? Outside the organization there are only enemies.

In this aspect totalitarian organizations imitate tribalistic thinking (to concede a point to Karl Popper), for all tribes have special gods, who minister only to those tribes; and one who leaves his tribe for another abandons the gods of his fathers, the gods who have guided and protected him, so far, in life. The totalitarian organization, like the primitive tribe, encompasses everything in life, even unto the distinction between heavenly and hellish destinies.

No one in a corporation can escape the power of negative inclusion: the act of competing defines every other similar business as an enemy, the hostility between business and the press and government defines another border, and the open warfare between business and consumer groups defines yet another. Labor organizations announce their status as enemies of management and non-union employees; and the customers of every business are fickle traders, always demanding higher quality and lower prices—there are no satisfied customers.

The middle manager, the white collar worker, and the technician live under siege; they have no fortress but the corporation itself, for it has convinced them that everything that is not expressly excluded is included. Thus they live in psychological tunnels, compiling secrets. And if they fail, the organization will dispose of them as ancient tribes disposed of those who broke the rules or grew useless with age: it will set them outside the tribe to die at the hands of enemies or of exposure to the hostile elements.

THE LAW OF MOVEMENT

They will marvel at us and look on us as
gods, because we are ready to endure the
freedom which they have found so
dreadful and to rule over them—so awful
it will seem to them to be free.

The Grand Inquisitor

He thought of his wife, imagining her reaction. She would be
frightened, then the absurdity of the situation would make her
laugh, and finally, her anger would shake her, and him, and
their marriage. She would make threats. He would sulk. She
would make more threats. He would have no choice but to
threaten her in return. She would blame him, he would blame
her. Perhaps this time one of them would carry out a threat.

A newspaper lay across his belly. He propped himself up on
his elbows to read it. He could not. The newspaper was written
in Spanish, printed in Bogotá, Colombia, by a group of rebels
who favored better relations with America and American
companies. He found that part of his situation amusing—
whoever had put him in this place, which he assumed was a
basement, judging by the height of the windows, had a crude
but clear sense of irony.

He did not feel ill, nor did his head ache, nor did the room
shimmer—it was not like the movies at all. He was simply stark
naked in a basement somewhere covered over with nothing
more than two pages of a Spanish newspaper. It was a helluva
way to treat a Princeton man! On the other hand, he had been

fifty-eighth in his class at Columbia Law: maybe it was all he deserved.

Well, the company had been investing ten thousand dollars a month in the paper, he thought. It was only right, only just—his lawyer's training corrected him—that the paper should provide him a bit of modesty.

His feet were cold. He wriggled his toes, as if that would make them warm.

He could not remember what the company wanted to do in Colombia. Nothing came to mind about the country but bananas. Ten thousand a month would buy an awful lot of bananas! What *did* they want? Oil? Minerals? What the hell was in Colombia? A law school? No. Spelled differently.

The predicament erupted in his thoughts again. They hadn't harmed him, they had simply put him to sleep somehow and taken away his clothes. Maybe they had taken pictures of him? Maybe he had done something terrible while he thought he was asleep? Why the hell did he have to be the bag man? Is that what lawyers do?

Corporate law. A vest. White shirt, wing tip shoes; seersucker and bow tie in the summer; best clubs year-round. He should have joined a firm instead of a corporation. What the hell was he doing in a basement?

When a man is fifty-eighth in his class the best firms don't seek him out.

Look, honey, he had told her, it'll be great. International travel. We'll get off the company jet at Heathrow, stay at Claridge's. You can spend the day shopping and visiting the British Museum. At night, we'll go to dinner, the theater, and a gambling club. Now, in Paris we'll concentrate on the restaurants. And in Rome . . .

So far, he had made thirty-one trips to Bogotá and eighteen trips to El Salvador. He had never come home from El Salvador without a fever and something bordering on dysentery. In both countries he had participated in negotiations to buy

controlling stock in local companies. In neither case had he
succeeded. His Spanish was improving; his intestinal tract was
deteriorating.

He laughed softly. The poise of a Princeton man. F. Scott,
Old Nassau, and all that stuff, Tiger.

The floor was cold against his back, reminding him of his
predicament. It wasn't so bad. He would wrap the newspaper
around his private section, go to the door or the window, get
someone's attention, tell them he had been robbed, and ask
them to call the police. When the police came, they would
wrap him in a blanket and drive him home. It was a warning,
nothing more. He would write a memo when he got back to
the office. They would transfer him to another section. No big
deal.

He looked around to find the door to the basement. There,
behind him and slightly off to his left, were his clothes. His suit
was neatly folded. On top of it were his shirt, socks, underwear, wallet, wristwatch, tie, everything. His shoes were
placed neatly at the foot of the pile, as if he had left them outside the door of his hotel room to be shined while he slept.

He became so frightened he could feel the trembling of his
heart.

American business exists in constant conflict with the law.
Business takes the position that the laws of the land should not
apply to it, that no law exists but a kind of law of the jungle
more fearsome and less moral than anything imagined by
Adam Smith or his liberal brethren of eighteenth-century economics. Not all businessmen subscribe to this will to be above
the law, but more and more they are led to it by the Milton
Friedman school of economics and bourgeois morality, and by
their own desire for expansion. Friedman, the Nobel laureate
who went to Chile to advise the Pinochet regime, champions

self-interest as the only morality on the part of corporations consonant with their obligation to serve the self-interest of shareholders.

The opposition to law may be found not only in the overtly illegal actions of such corporations as ITT, Gulf & Western, the electrical equipment manufacturers involved in price fixing, and so on; but in the response to all laws governing market share, health and safety on the job, protection of the environment, financial disclosure, facilitating payments (bribes), etc. Corporations may not wish to make unsafe products or force their employees to endure unhealthful working conditions or bribe foreign customers or foul the environment, but they want to make their own rules in all these areas; they do not want to be limited by external laws. To that end they employ large legal staffs, lobbyists, public relations experts, and brilliant accountants; and everything that can be kept secret is kept secret. Growth is the goal, and everything, including profit, must be subsumed under that single objective.

They oppose law because it is by definition a limit. All laws describe behavior and distinguish between that which is acceptable to civil society and that which is not. In their opposition to law, corporations exhibit the essential feature of totalitarian organizations: the will to totality—unlimited size and power. Since achievement of the goal is impossible, only movement toward it will partially satisfy the organization. Anything that impedes movement or sets limits on it distresses the organization.

"The greatness of a movement," Hitler said, "is exclusively guaranteed by the unrestricted development of its inner strength and its steady growth up to the final victory over all competitors."

Hannah Arendt made the connection between lawlessness and motion: ". . . The term 'law' itself changed its meaning from expressing the framework of stability within which human actions and motions can take place, it became the expression of motion itself." She was describing the lawlessness of Nazi Germany. No American business wishes to do the insane work of Hitler's organization, but the will to move constantly toward the impossible "final victory over all competitors" determines the character of the organization and the tactics it uses on its journey to the unattainable totality.

SHARED SECRETS

> The most painful secrets of their conscience, all, all they will bring to us, and we shall have an answer for all.
>
> The Grand Inquisitor

Nothing made him more unhappy than the hatred he felt toward his boss. In church, in God's own house, with his children and his wife by his side in the pew, he thought not of Him, but of him, and he hated him.

He hated the way his belly pressed against the buttons of his nylon shirts, he hated his garrulousness and his wheezing laughter, he hated the way he adored eating. From the first day he had hated him. The man was critical of every action of every man and woman who worked for him. He praised no one. He peered into everyone's work, he applied the rules of business with grinding strictness. No one who worked for him was ever promoted, no one left his department. The boss grew fatter, he belched, he oiled his thinning hair.

In church, in God's own house, with the gentle, forgiving words of Jesus Christ in his ears, he hated.

He dreamed of escaping, of transferring to another department, of moving to another company, but there were files, evaluation forms written by him year after year, forms without praise, with lists of errors, failures, opportunities missed. Who would take a man with such a record, what company would want a man who could not succeed in the place he had chosen on his first day after graduating from college?

One wife, three children, a dog, a mortgage, car payments. His mother was dying. He was forty-six years old. Do not hate, he told the children. Did they overhear him speaking to his wife of the hatred he felt for the man? Did they pass by the room where he slept on Saturday afternoons and hear him talking in the vulnerability of sleep?

What hope was there for him? What hope for the people who worked for him? If he was kind to them he was criticized for it; if he praised them, he was told his standards were too low. He was not kind to them, he did not praise them. He did what he had to do. His wife and three children sat beside him in the pew. His mother was dying.

Some men work on Saturdays, the boss said, some men work on Sundays after church. It's how they get ahead. There are signs of ambition.

He had been getting ahead, before going to work for him. No one in the corporation had been rising faster. Now, eight years had passed without movement. He was tired. He did not speak easily or forcefully. He felt sleepy in the middle of the afternoon. He had many colds, his stomach was uncertain, there was a gnawing fullness in the left side of his chest. He read articles about stress.

If you rent a headset on the airplane, don't put it on your expense account; the company doesn't pay for your entertainment.

It was Sunday afternoon. Sunday.

A soldier is on duty twenty-four hours a day, seven days a week.

This is not war; it's business.

You see your problem, don't you? I don't have to tell you. It's right there. Listen to your own words. Believe me, I hate to hear it, because I think you've got a lot of potential. Attitude's important in business. Ninety per cent. And you've got an attitude problem. That's my evaluation. If you disagree with it, you can always go over my head.

He hated the man. He wished him ill, evil, disease, death, a painful death. In God's house, singing a psalm, he wished for a fire that would destroy the headquarters building of the company, with all its records, with all the evaluation forms in his file.

He and his wife and children were singers of psalms. They sang sweetly, they prayed for deliverance.

When the psalm was completed and the vibrations of the male voices and the great organ had faded, he stepped out of the pew into the aisle. He was alone, standing, walking slowly up the aisle to the pulpit, mounting the steps. For a moment, he and the minister looked at each other. What is it? the minister asked.

He did not answer. He knelt there in full view of the congregation. His eyes were raised to heaven, his lips moved in silent communication.

What is it? the minister asked.

He did not answer. He lowered his eyes and bowed his head. Order was lost in the congregation. It erupted in gossip. Children laughed.

His wife hurried up to the pulpit. She called his name, but he did not answer. She and the minister knelt beside him and lifted up his head. His eyes were dull. He chewed on his tongue, slowly, with bovine regularity, as if it were the most ordinary of life's pleasures.

The employee evaluation form or efficiency report functions like the more ominous *dossier* in controlling members of the organization. It removes the privacy from men's lives, reduces men to objects, converts the human complexity of them to pale generalizations, and stores away this arbitrary reduction of a human being to be used against him later. The evaluation form institutionalizes observation; and when it is shown to the employee, it serves to force him to participate in the violence being done to him.

The evaluation form serves no positive purpose. Any employee can be told that he works efficiently or poorly without the evaluation being committed to paper and stored for future use. The suggestion that the employee be promoted or given a higher salary does not necessitate reducing him to a series of check marks on a form.

Because the form is stored and can be made available to various people, according to the will of the organization, it constitutes a profound violation of the employee's privacy. The form can be read while he works, when he goes home, while he sleeps, during his holidays, and even after he leaves the firm. The stored form itself becomes a secret police apparatus, a permanent end to the human privateness of the employee. As Arendt observed, people without privacy are like slaves—no longer human.

The stored evaluation form differs from the personal history of a man, which also follows him, in that he does not initiate the form, whether it be an accurate assessment or as is so often the case a biased and unfair view of him. In the form, the man is an object, a thing, not himself, but another man's creation; and that is the essence of slavery, the antithesis of autonomy.

UNSHARED SECRETS

> They will tremble impotently before our
> wrath, their minds will grow fearful, they
> will be quick to shed tears like women
> and children, but they will be just as
> ready at a sign from us to pass to laugh-
> ter and rejoicing, to happy mirth and
> childish song.
>
> The Grand Inquisitor

He read the file carefully, glancing up at the man across the
desk as he came to the end of each page. The face above the
gray suit and careful tie was unreadable, a mixture of responses thickened and disguised with middle age. The eyes
were hurt, the mouth was angry, but overall there was a
smugness, an unaccountable satisfaction in the whole of the
face that faced him. He noted that the man had a Connecticut
nose, an American perfection.

The file was thick. It had not been culled for outdated material. He was looking at a man from Princeton and Wharton, a
man who had served as an officer in the Navy, played tennis
on his college team, married at the right age, had children
properly spaced. A Connecticut man sat opposite him, neither
speaking nor smoking nor even moving uncomfortably in the
awkwardness of the situation. He looked up at the man again.
Not only was his nose perfect, his eyes were blue, his cheeks
had the darkness of a man's beard and the underlying blush of
good health, and his hair, dark blond, had begun to gray at the
temples.

Was there no promise in the man? What did he lack? What had he lost? For a moment the president of the company considered asking personal questions, probing for the failing. He checked himself: he was an engineer, not a psychologist, he measured men by their performance.

The record defended the man. His performance was never described as less than satisfactory. He was praised for his articulation, his manners, his education, his style, his sociability. He was a man of gracefulness. Either he was courageous or he was fearless. His calm in difficult moments was admirable. His staff admired him, his supervisor liked him. He worked within the allotted time.

He had been fired.

You were right, the president said, and I apologize for that. The evaluations weren't great, but they were all okay.

Then why have I been terminated?

The president looked down at the termination papers. He read the comment below the instructions on reasons for dismissal. The box next to the words *Would not rehire* had been checked. He read the comment aloud: Lacks initiative. No imagination. Does not seem to really care about his work. No chance for promotion. He would do best to try and make a fresh start somewhere else.

What caused the sudden change of heart? Could it be that I threatened him? There is, after all, a difference in our backgrounds, in what we bring to the party, so to speak.

What would you like me to do? Would you like me to reinstate you?

That would create an impossible situation.

Yes.

There was nothing more to say. The president looked down at the file on his desk. He touched the papers, neatened the stack, put them inside the folder with the man's name on the tab. He shrugged. You've been badly treated, he said. I'm sorry for that.

I was deceived.

I think that's possible.

To what purpose?

Maybe he wanted to be kind to you, maybe he wanted to give you a chance. It's very difficult to speak of a man's failings.

He didn't hesitate in the termination paper.

Yes, I read it, the president said. He did not like the turn of the conversation. Why did the man want to put him in a corner? What had he done? Hadn't he consented to talk to the man after he had been fired? He stood up and extended his hand across the desk, terminating the interview.

Good luck, he said. I'm sure you'll land somewhere and make a great success in your next job.

You do admit I was treated unfairly.

I admit nothing, the president said. A man tried to be too kind. It's no crime to be kind.

The man with the Connecticut nose mocked forgiveness with a smile. I hope no one is ever that kind to you, he said.

The interview was over. The man went out and the president sat down in his chair and put his feet up on the desk to think about what had happened. The intercom buzzed. He took calls. His secretary brought in the mail. He took more calls. A week later, while flying to London, he realized that the man with the Connecticut nose had irritated him. A man who reacted with such calm to being fired was admirable in many ways, but not suited to their style of doing business.

———————◆———————

In totalitarian organizations words do not mean what they say. Symbols and jargon mask secrets. Everything must be interpreted, and all interpretations are dubious. The lies exceed the truths so that even the truths become lies by the interpretations of those who are accustomed to dealing with lies. The purpose of the tactic is to reduce men to a controllable state, to take away all of their defenses, including that most basic defense against enslavement by inclusion—alienation.

To show a good evaluation to an inefficient worker constitutes a perfect example. On the surface, it would seem to be a kindness, but it is truly a means of gaining complete power over a man. The deceitfully evaluated employee has no defense, he cannot improve his performance because he does not know where he has failed to deliver what is demanded of him. The employee is an organizational cuckold, deceived into loving the very one who has wronged him.

The process of alienation in which one becomes a complete and unique person, able to be autonomous, to have dignity, requires the existence of something real outside oneself. A man alienated from himself is mad, according to the classic definition of madness. A man alienated from something that does not exist is also mad, for he alienates himself from his own imagination, which is nothing more than a part of him. The tactic exemplified in the deceitful evaluation forces a man to choose between madness and cession. It is the tactic demonstrated by Kafka in *The Trial*. In psychological terms we may call it instilling paranoia, but in the language of politics it is the elimination of all possibility of politics, an act of violence.

In the nonexistent world made of deceit, no man can have a dignified life. He must cede himself to his deceivers, for he knows that their ability to deceive him gives them power over him. He cannot, for example, disagree with what his deceivers tell him, because he can never know what they are saying. If he disobeys them, he may actually be obeying them. He can only agree, he can only give himself over to his deceivers, and that is not an act of consent but of cession; he abandons himself and remains estranged from that which devours him; he accepts the political life of a slave.

EXURBAN ATOMS

No science will give them bread so long
as they remain free.
                                    The Grand Inquisitor

He lived with his family in a town beside a river, along a thin
road, far from the highway, farther still from the railroad, surrounded by hills skied by children in winter, cooled by old
oaks and stands of pine in summer. The town was by choice
without a store, a doctor, a lawyer, a fire department, or a
school. There was no center in the town. It was a space between farms and forests, six miles from the nearest church,
four miles from a gas station with two ancient red pumps. The
country club was the soul of the town; everyone who lived in
the town was a member. All the events of the town took place
at the country club: weddings, parties, celebrations, even the
town meeting.

Before the moving van had brought the things of their life
to the restored white farmhouse, he had joined the country
club. His children had enjoyed the swimming pool, he had
played the golf course, and his wife had become a member of
the potters' circle. They had found more than a home, he
proclaimed on their first evening in the farmhouse, presiding
over a dinner of cold cuts in the room filled with rolled rugs,
boxes of dishes wrapped in newspaper, and stacks of pictures
in shallow cardboard crates, they had become part of a community.

They raised their cardboard containers of Pepsi-Cola in a

toast to home and happiness, to friends and neighbors. The goodness of their new lives so moved his wife that she raised her container of Pepsi-Cola a second time and proposed another toast: God bless America for letting us earn this good life. The children reported suffering goose pimples over the corny sentiment, but they admitted to similar feelings of gratitude, comfort, security, and good prospects.

I suppose this is the wrong time for me to say it, because everyone doesn't have it as good as we do, he said, but I think we owe something to the free enterprise system. I'll tell you, kids, and your mother will bear me out, I never dreamed we'd be living this well.

At night, in the quiet of their bedroom, after his wife slept, he shook with fear. He was, without question, the poorest man in the town, a fraud, a gate crasher, something—he did not know what name to apply to his crime—akin to a thief.

At the country club he described his place in the world carefully, elevating himself through modesty: I'm just another bookkeeper. We're a small company, trying to get along, hoping not to be swallowed up by one of you giants. No one pays much attention to me. If I thought a company like ours had any power, I'd worry about misusing it. We're having a super year, just super, and I'm glad to be going along for the ride.

His politics, discussed in The Nineteenth Hole and in the steam room, were straightforward: government regulation was inflationary, wasteful, the usurpation of the rights of business under the free enterprise system; welfare cheats had to be stopped at all costs; taxes had become confiscatory, weakening the country, inhibiting investment; capital formation had declined to a dangerous level, severely reducing the opportunity to give impetus to growth and greater productivity; economic education of the general public was vital; and while he favored doing business with the Soviet Bloc nations, he also favored a strong military. Bubble up served no one in the long run, while trickle down made America great: the bigger the pie, the bigger the slice. Deregulate oil and the market will conserve.

The men of the country club liked him. He was agreeable, affable, modest, bright, ambitious, and even though he himself lacked wit, he was quick to laugh at other men's jokes. The women of the country club liked him. He was attentive, tall, quite good-looking, although his hair was laboriously combed to hide its meagerness, and he never ever made old boy remarks. He seemed to appreciate women, not as mere objects, but for themselves.

His wife was tanned in summer. Her hair was blond and cut short. His children had good manners and straight teeth. Even his dog was polite.

He enjoyed the town and the house and the country club. No one from his office, no one from his field lived in the town but him. He banked in the city, and he paid his loan payments in the city. His wife sewed the children's clothes. He ate only expense account lunches. He walked from the train to his office, he cheated on his expense account, he gambled that his tax returns would not be audited, he kited checks, shined his own shoes, prayed for a raise or a bonus, dreamed of a promotion, and lay awake at night in fear of devastating winds that could come out of the darkness.

In his office he worked quietly and often alone. He spoke softly and agreeably to customers and colleagues. His life was in other places. Office politics did not interest him. He was loyal, punctual, serious, diligent. He drank too much coffee and sucked on commercial antacid pills to quiet the sour suffering in his gut. There were periods of sleepiness in his days: after expense account lunches and always at three-thirty in the afternoon. He slept on the train; it distinguished between his lives.

He told his wife, Sometimes I feel like Walter Mitty. If those people at the club knew what I did . . . A sales engineer is not an important man; they're top-flight people. I played golf last Sunday with three CEOs.

You're younger, you'll catch up to them.

He knew he would not. He did not tell her. He was afraid to leave her dreamless.

When the name of the executive vice-president of his company was put up for membership in the club, he thought it was a punishment visited upon him by heaven. For several days he drank martinis instead of coffee and refused to speak more than a few cordial words to his family. He thought of suicide, he called employment agencies to find out if there were other jobs available in his field, he chewed antacid pills. He was sick: his nose ran, his gut betrayed him, he could not control his bowels.

I am like a Japanese, he thought. I must save face.

He called his family to attention during dinner, tapping a spoon against his water glass. I have an announcement, he said. Since we moved into this house, in that short time, the value of this house has increased by darned near fifty thousand dollars. Now, that's a lot of money, even in inflated dollars. It's enough to pay for two college educations. And you know, if I take that much money and invest it in treasury bills, it'll pay for three college educations. Now, it just so happens that everything has come at the right time for us. I'm being transferred to the Atlanta office. We can buy an even better house than this one down there, and we can still have the profit from this house, every cent of it. Now, what do you think of that?

The children put down their napkins and left the table. Not one of them spoke.

When they were alone in the dining room, his wife said, After I heard who was moving in, I told them to expect we would be moving out.

Did you tell them why?

Sort of, she said. I told them it wasn't any fun to have your boss around after working hours.

It was easy to get the transfer, he said.

I'll miss this town, she said, especially the club.

He patted his carefully arranged hair more firmly into place. I don't suppose the children guessed, he said.

She sighed. Weariness showed in her eyes and the coarsening of her hands. She asked if the company would pay their moving expenses.

Yes, he said.

In a few years I'll be forty, she said.

———————◆———————

Suburban life would seem, on first glance, to produce class identity, for suburbs are single-class cities, fortresses against economic, social, and cultural pluralism within the polis. Certainly, they have functioned that way within the general society, as voting patterns prove. But the problem of the use of totalitarian tactics is not generalized in American society: it belongs to organizations within the boundaries of the nation. These organizations are affected in opposite fashion by suburban life.

Business and governmental organizations encompass much of the employee's life: providing for social, economic, and potential political existence. Since the structure of these organizations is the double hierarchy described earlier, they would seem to be places of clearly defined classes and class loyalties. The classes are defined, but there are no loyalties within them. The business day ends with the ionization of the classes, the members each going to their separate places in their separate suburbs.

After a day designed to separate every level into competitive atoms, the night offers no opportunity to heal the slights and wounds of the struggle for praise and promotion. Men who might learn from living together outside the struggle of the office to have brotherly consideration of each other's lives as men of family and culture, struggle with each other as strangers, sharing nothing but the struggle itself.

A class has a political life in its relation to other classes. But there is also political life inside the class; the cohesion of the class is itself a political act. Politics, however, cannot be practiced when the sphere of action is limited to economic life, which the Greeks may have recognized when they said that politics should be practiced by men of leisure. Economic life reduces men to symbols as currency reduces goods or labor to symbols. Symbols cannot practice politics: it is the life of complete men only.

Men who work in the same organization could, of course, live in the same suburb, enabling class cohesion to take place; but they regularly choose not to, for the struggle of life within the organization is so telling, so divisive, that few men wish to continue it outside the office. The atomization of the day causes the atomization of the night, which preserves the atomization of the day—men are cut off from the power to alienate themselves from the organization by their own lives in the organization.

A QUESTION OF MEANING

They will see at last, the foolish children, that, though they are rebels, they are impotent rebels, unable to keep up their own rebellion. Bathed in their foolish tears, they will recognize at last that He who created them rebels must have meant to mock at them.

The Grand Inquisitor

He expected a promotion. No one had told him, there was nothing official, but he knew, he had a feeling, something like anxiety, lacking only the dread. The feeling came to him like an itch in an unreachable place; it could be salved, but not by him. If there was any pleasure in this expectation, it was lost in the helplessness of the situation. A man who expects a promotion, like the sufferer of unreachable itches, neither initiates nor completes the situation, he waits.

The signs of promotion were subtle: an invitation to join a new committee, questions about the competence of the people under him to take on greater responsibility, the sudden availability of information that had previously been kept secret from him, an unexpected salary increase, and a change in the way his supervisors spoke to him, an approving softness, an invitation in their voices. He felt he was being seduced, but he did not know exactly who was seducing him or for what purpose.

He was invited to lunch with the executive vice-president, but they spoke only of football teams and inflation. He was invited to lunch with the president, but they spoke only of football teams and taxes.

Although nothing of his situation was discussed at the lunches, he understood them as initiations. He felt himself part of management. Complaints from people on his staff annoyed him, he became easily angered by mistakes, he asked people to take work home to meet schedules. When an article criticizing the company appeared in a newsmagazine, he told his wife that the reporters were liars. She responded by asking him not to shout at her.

He waited. He thought about luck. Two months after his lunch with the president he began to dream of heroic acts.

———————◆———————

Melvin Seeman describes meaninglessness as follows: "When the individual is unclear as to what he ought to believe—when the individual's minimal standards for clarity in decision-making are not met." All totalitarian organizations use meaninglessness as a tactic for keeping men from opposing the organization. The logic of it is simple: men who do not know the meaning of what they are doing or what is being done to them cannot oppose any action or even any statement.

To live in a world without meaning is to suffer the most terrible isolation, to be unable to think, to be cut off from politics. The process of making a meaningless world begins with removing all clarity from the simplest acts and statements. In business or government bureaucracies, for example, one may be *promoted* into a less important job, or praised in equivocal language, or constantly exposed to sudden reversals in patterns of behavior. After a short while, one learns that nothing is what it appears to be, yet continues to live in a world in which appearance is the only ostensible reality. The world as it appears has become, in Camus' term, absurd. To avoid going mad in such a world one must become fatalistic or attach mystical interpretations to all actions.

Some men, but few, have the courage to live in an absurd world; i.e., to understand that the world is absurd and yet to behave as an autonomous creature, with a system of morals independent of absurdity. Those who do not have such courage must either leave the world or cede themselves to it. Totalitarianism prefers cession, but will accept extinction (for those it does not wish to include the totalitarian organization practices extinction). In no circumstance can a totalitarian organization tolerate members who are sufficiently alienated to be autonomous, for given the goals of the totalitarian organization autonomy is opposition. Revel quotes Brezhnev to that effect: "An Opposition prevented the creation of an emotional bond between the people and the Government."

The inefficiency of creating a meaningless world cannot be overestimated: its inhabitants cannot possibly accomplish anything without errors of misunderstanding and lack of co-ordination. The use of meaninglessness as a tactic in eliminating opposition creates a company of buffoons. The misjudgment that leads to the use of the tactic of meaninglessness results from the belief that enough buffoons, operating without the constraint of morality and with the power of technology, can achieve total domination.

A CROWD INSIDE

> Men rejoiced that they were again led
> like sheep, and that the terrible gift that
> had brought them such suffering was, at
> last, lifted from their hearts.
> The Grand Inquisitor

She had wanted to see the Mayan ruins since her college days. The names of them had caused her eyes to shine and her voice to quaver since the first time she had read them aloud from a textbook: Uxmal, Copán, Bonampak, Chichén Itzá. The Maya were a mystery to her as God is a mystery to most people.

He arranged the trip for an anniversary present, not that he was uninterested by the Maya, but it was her dream, his gift to her—he had hoped to be a poet. It was long ago that they had dreamed together; now there were three children, he carried an attaché case and rode the train into the city and she raised the children and read stories to other people's children in the small public library in the town where they lived.

The trip had gone well from the beginning. They did not think about the children, the jungle heat did not bother them, he worried about the office, but found no convenient telephone service in Yucatán, Chiapas, or Guatemala. It was on their way out to Copán that she had become ill. They were sitting on a bench outside a roadside restaurant when she turned away from him and vomited blood.

For eight days they had kept her in a hospital in Guatemala City, giving her whole blood and trying to find out what had caused her illness. On the ninth day she was put aboard an airplane and flown back to New York. An ambulance met them at the airport, and she was given another transfusion on the way to the hospital. Her condition had stabilized, the doctors said, but her fever had not abated completely and she still needed transfusions of whole blood, although far less frequently.

He stayed with the children at night, worked during part of the day, and visited her during his lunch hour and in the early evening before catching the train home. Every day he conferred with the doctors and every day they told him she was improving, but that they did not know what had caused her illness. They had not been able to decide whether she had been attacked by a parasite or suffered an organic failure. All they knew was that the bleeding was not clearly localized, surgery was not indicated. They collected samples of her, analyzed them, and found nothing they could understand.

A routine developed in this new life. He grew closer to the children and he devoted himself to his work, reasoning that absorption in work improved his mood, relieved some of his anxieties, and made him a better husband to her in this difficult time. He never failed to visit her, although he telephoned her less frequently from the office, and he sometimes went two or three days without speaking with the doctors, who never had any news anyway.

When the call from the hospital came, he was in a staff meeting. He did not leave immediately, because he had not yet made his report and he had to turn over the information to one of the other section managers. By the time he arrived at her room the doctors were inside and he was not permitted to enter. He asked the floor nurse what had happened, but she volunteered no information. All she knew was that the doctors were treating his wife.

He sat on a bench in the hallway to wait. After a while the odors of the hospital disappeared in familiarity, he ceased to be startled by the paging system or even to hear it. There were problems in the office, in his section, with his people. He heard them, his people, while he tried to think of his wife. The company was with him in the corridor. He worried, but he did not know whether he was worrying about her or about the problem in his section. He tried to clear his head, to give himself to her. Bits of conversation were repeated in his hearing, office talk. Plans occurred to him, he created options, practiced words, speeches; he imagined the reactions. Where was she? A pay raise. The smile of the boss. Copán. If he fired his sales analyst, he could reduce his budget and still get the work done by transferring pieces of the job to other people in the section. But why had they telephoned him? Who would put the pieces of the analysis together? Was it his job? Was she better or worse? Had they found something? The cause? It was probably the man himself rather than the organization of the section.

A long time ago, when he had dreamed of being a poet, he had sat with her near the river on an autumn afternoon to watch the boats and feel the sun and kiss her without caring who saw them, no more modest than butterflies, and she had told him in her saddest girl's voice that the world was not always what people wished it to be. He had thought her profound, as touching as history. She had spoken of ancient times, worlds fallen, stones broken by trees, grass covering the arts of man. Was he away too much? Too often? Costs had risen in the section.

What was he thinking about? A poet could concentrate on

his wife. He loved his wife. The sales analyst had problems at home, probably affecting his work.

He had decided to marry her that afternoon on the river-bank. Now he decided to quit his job, to become a . . . To be . . . He was going deeper into debt every day even with his job.

There was an answer, a line of poetry to clear his head of the office and make him completely as he wished to be. He sifted through the lines he had collected in his memory. There were fewer now.

I am the absent husband, part-time father, and late poet who married the woman in the room I cannot enter, he thought. How had his report been received? He told the floor nurse he would be back in a few minutes, he had to call his office.

In a pocket of his wallet, long forgotten or hidden, as guns and poisons are hidden from children, were the words of John Milton he had copied out of a mildewed book found in a dark store one evening when it had become too cold to sit any longer by the river and he had preferred being with her in the dank stacks to leaving her at the door of the women's dormi-tory.

> . . . he who would not be frustrate of his hope to write well hereafter in laudable things, ought himself to be a true Poem; that is, a composition and pattern of the best and honourablest things; not presuming to sing high praises of he-roic men or famous Cities, unless he have in himself the ex-perience and the practice of all that which is praiseworthy.

That night, sitting on the side of his bed, he went through his wallet, taking out all the old things, cleaning out the closets of his life. When he came to the yellowed paper on which he had written Milton's words, he read them once, then let the tatters of the paper fall into an ashtray. He was conscious of the sentimentality in his action. Were it not for the discipline of business, he thought, he would have been a foolish man.

———◆———

The most effective way to abolish freedom is to crowd it out. Hannah Arendt described how the Nazis kept the death camps crowded, even slowing down the rate of killing to keep the inmates from having "the one essential prerequisite of freedom." Her observation about the physical abolition of freedom has an analogue in the mind: The same space, the same capacity for motion (in the form of changing ideas) must exist or freedom is inconceivable.

Karl Deutsch makes the point about interior space in the joke about life under totalitarianism: everything that is not forbidden is compulsory. He says that in a totalitarian society everything—one's free time, his home, all of his goods—must be devoted to the cause. There must be no open time or space. Totalitarianism occupies men just as it occupies nations.

The Nazis used terror to fill men's heads, thereby driving out the possibility of freedom. Business uses the anxiety of competition and insecurity as well as the simple filling up of available time. The middle manager uses about twelve hours a day going to his job, working, eating lunch with business associates, working, going home from work. Sometimes he has business dinners or breakfasts in addition to lunches. Often he takes work home. For many businessmen the newspaper and television news affect the corporation. Advertisements by direct competitors or competitors for attention affect the corporation, making radio, television, and magazines a part of the job. Much reading is also related to the job. Travel usually takes place the night before a business meeting or very early in the morning (for short trips), further extending the business day.

When time permits other thoughts, anxiety or real fear

crowds them out. Men who are not secure—and no one but the leader of a business or a union member in a stable industry is secure—cannot be free. Stalinism and Nazism use terror to cause insecurity, corporations use competition. Both methods succeed in abolishing freedom, both destroy the capacity to think by filling up that space of solitude beyond the world, where thinking can take place.

Internal crowding absorbs men in two ways: it successfully inhibits alienation, which requires stepping back from the world, the state, or the corporation to think; and it so fills men that they become the same inside as outside. When this happens men cease to be differentiated from their environment and it is not necessary to have laws that suppress freedom of action or expression, for men no longer have anything of their own on which to speak or act.

SILENCE

> Didst thou forget that man prefers peace, and even death, to freedom of choice in the knowledge of good and evil?
>
> The Grand Inquisitor

Because you were different, she said on the day she left him. You were funny. Don't you remember? I guess it was because you were a little bit overweight then, but your smiles were deeper, you had dimples.

You're a handsome man now. In your herringbone overcoat

and silk muffler, with your fine leather briefcase and your deerskin gloves, you are the handsomest man on the street. You won't have any trouble finding another woman. You'll get someone younger, blonder, and slimmer. You're now the kind of man fashionable women want. I'm not worried about you, dear.

And please don't think I'm being facetious or trying to practice some subtle cruelty. I mean every word I say. I still love you, but more for what you were than what you are.

Remember how the words used to bubble out of you? No one was more open than you. We all used to laugh. He wears his heart on his sleeve, my mother said about you, and she meant that for a compliment, because she believed in emotion. Maybe it was because she was part Italian; you know how those people are.

More in sadness than in anger, believe me, because that's the truth.

I used to be afraid that you would run away with another woman. All those business trips, all those pretty young girls around you in the office. Oh, how I used to worry! I don't know exactly when I stopped worrying about that. Five years ago. Maybe seven. You left me in a different way, a way I never expected. But I think you left everyone, not just me. You're still here, but you went away, if you know what I mean.

I'd give anything for an argument, a real knock-down, drag-out, With-Out-Papers fight with you, both of us shouting and slamming things down on tables and maybe breaking a little of the crockery. But that would be rude, wouldn't it? Not that you aren't rude. But a real fight, with real words, would be informal, a gut thing, a sweaty belly thing. And you don't have a belly anymore.

Oh, how I wish you were a little fatter! I think men's hearts shrink when they lose weight.

Aren't you going to say anything, even now? Aren't you

even going to warm up to losing your wife and your family? Won't anything get a rise out of you? Are you so completely frozen? Did you die?

Cat got your tongue?

You were the noisiest lover imaginable. Oh, God! how you used to embarrass me! Do you remember? The words you said, the sounds you made! Did you use them up?

You're so professional now, a sex machine. I feel like I'm fucking a mute.

Are you unhappy? When did you become unhappy? If you told, if you talked, maybe I could help. At least, at the very least, I could listen. This isn't the office, for God's sake. You don't have to be afraid to speak to me. I'm your wife—I'm not the chairman of the goddamn board.

One night, about a week ago, when you were asleep, I put my ear on your chest to listen to your heart just to see if there was some human noise inside you. It started out as a joke on myself, something to cheer me up because I couldn't sleep. Then I thought about what I'd done and why. That's when I decided to leave you.

That's it, dear. End of report. Cordially, your former wife.

He looked at her very directly. I'll see that you're well provided for, he said.

———————◆▶————————

Silence pervades the corporation and the government bureaucracy, either in the form of physical silence or a constant babble containing nothing human. It is the chief ingredient of most other totalitarian tactics, the insurmountable barrier to life as political man, and in the latter form, the acme of loneliness. Silence is the substance that catalyzes and maintains atomization.

Silence results from fear and the inability to think of meanings and silence causes fear and inhibits thinking. Silence imitates death, and the silence of inhuman babble imitates the most terrible death.

The meaning of silence has been known since antiquity. Montesquieu said, "Since the principle of despotic government is fear, its goal is tranquility. But this is not peace; but the silence which falls upon cities about to be occupied by an enemy." And Simone Weil reached back to the beginnings of Western civilization: "Nothing is more difficult to know than the nature of unhappiness; a residue of mystery will always cling to it. For, following the Greek proverb, it is dumb."

Marx recognized the silence of inhuman babble: "Our objects in relation to one another constitute the only intelligible language we use with one another. We would not understand a human language, and it would remain without effect. On the one hand, it would be felt and spoken as a plea, as begging, and as humiliation and hence uttered with shame and with a feeling of supplication; on the other hand, it would be heard and rejected as effrontery or madness."

This silence, so well known to all who have thought about the predicament of man, is the sound that crowds out freedom, thought, and human life; it is the sound of the unhappiness of seeking a happiness not one's own.

SKIPS AND DOTS

> Did we not love mankind, so meekly ac-
> knowledging their feebleness, lovingly
> lightening their burden and permitting
> their weak nature even sin with our
> sanction?
>
> The Grand Inquisitor

The amounts were intolerable. It was not a question of three-
martini lunches or theater tickets, the man was spending over
fifty thousand a year, more than the travel and entertainment
budget for the entire regional office. And of course he had re-
ceipts for everything but coatroom tips. One issue that might
be brought up was whether any of the expenses were legiti-
mate: he entertained only federal officials, senators, and
congressmen, and they did virtually no direct business with the
government through his division.

On the other hand, the man had been assistant to the under-
secretary of the Navy during a previous administration. He
knew his way around Washington, and the office products division sold everything from paper clips to file cabinets to the
government. But the man was assigned to him, and his division sold machinery to manufacturers and parts suppliers.

Fifty-one thousand dollars! He stared at the print-out, awed
by the numbers. No other salesman in the division, perhaps in
the entire company, spent one tenth of that amount. The man
was exactly as the comptroller described him, The Thief of
Sans Souci.

The comptroller had other news, as well. He had flagged the print-out of the T&E costs for the region at 173 per cent of budget. There would be trouble. Profit for the division was adversely affected, production for the region was down. A management review was indicated. The comptroller had advised him to get started on his written report to the senior vice-president in charge of marketing.

It was nearly seven o'clock. He had been sitting at his desk with the Dictaphone in his hand for nearly an hour. The office was empty, but for him and the cleaning women who passed through the halls with their carts and dustrags. He stared at the square microphone in his hand, then moved his gaze over to the print-out, and back to the microphone. He was afraid to speak.

Why had he not spoken to the man? The expense accounts passed across his desk, he initialed them, every one. Hadn't he realized what was happening? Why did he permit a man to spend three, four, even six hundred dollars for dinner night after night? Was he out of his mind? Was he getting some sort of kickback? Something was very wrong, perhaps illegal, certainly illegal.

He could hear their questions, he imagined their conclusions, for they were the same conclusions he would reach, given the evidence. He did not know what would happen to him if he did not explain, and he did not know what would happen to him if he did explain.

Fifteen months ago, when the man had first been moved into the Washington regional office, with responsibility for several major accounts in the Baltimore industrial area, he had spoken with him about the rules for expenses. And the man had replied, Yes, I understand that those rules apply in ordinary situations, but my situation is not quite ordinary. You see, I have a dotted line reporting relationship with the vice-chairman. Government relations reports to him, but I don't report to him through them; I'm doing something directly for him. By the way, the sort of thing I'm doing doesn't come cheap. I'll be turning in some very large expense accounts. It's Washington, you know. You can't impress a U.S. Congressman or even his administrative assistant with a bowl of chili and a handful of crackers.

We set sales goals, you know. No matter what you do for the vice-chairman, you'll have to meet your sales goals.

That may be impossible, the new man said.

In this division we meet sales goals or I'll know the reason why.

You'll have to take that up with the vice-chairman.

If the vice-chairman's so interested in you, why aren't you on his staff? He could put you in public relations or finance or government relations. What the hell are you doing here?

The new man smiled indulgently. I guess he wants to be careful about his lobbying costs.

Well, maybe I ought to have something in writing from him on this.

The new man laughed aloud.

Now he wished he had let his naïveté save him. Now he had either to put the whole story in writing in a report that could be subpoenaed or take the blame himself. Should he have known how to handle the situation? Should he have fired the man? What if the man had been lying, if he didn't have any dotted line relationship to the vice-chairman? Should he have known how to bury the expenses? Should he have brought the whole situation to light a year ago?

He turned the Dictaphone on, but he said nothing. The vice-chairman could destroy him. He turned the Dictaphone off. He did not know what to say. He had never been so afraid.

———————◆▶———————

Dotted line and skip-level reporting relationships are so common in business and government organizations that anyone who doesn't have at least one such relationship considers himself marked for failure. These reporting relationships comprise the second structure of organizations, the onion's layers described by Hannah Arendt as the more significant structure of a totalitarian organization.

By superimposing the onion structure upon the pyramid of efficient organization, the leader creates a nest of spies and informers. No man in the organization can ever be secure in anything he says or does. Dread fills him up. He fears the role of originator, knowing that safety lies in immobility. His life becomes a cautious stutter.

It is a curious aspect of totalitarianism, for it limits growth and inhibits innovation. In this respect totalitarian organizations are like the tribal organizations of neolithic man: locked in the circle of stasis. Were the organization to have achieved its impossible goal of totality, the immobilizing tension between the two structures would serve to maintain the status quo; but in the drive for growth the tension of the dual structures produces a contradiction that cannot be other than the seed of destruction of the organization.

JUSTICE NOW

> Thou wouldst go into the world, and
> art going with empty hands, with some
> promise of freedom which men in their
> simplicity and their natural unruliness
> cannot even understand, which they fear
> and dread—for nothing has ever been
> more insupportable for a man and for
> society than freedom.
> The Grand Inquisitor

The South Africans had been very different from what she had
been led to expect. Instead of boorish Boers, she had been
confronted with cool, sophisticated Englishmen, all of them
openly concerned with the plight of the blacks, many of them
willing to operate outside the letter of the law of Pretoria to
enable their black employees to have better working conditions and greater opportunities. Perhaps more important, they
accepted women in the professions. No one seemed the least
bit surprised when she announced herself as the mining engineer sent from the Chicago office.

She had asked to visit Soweto, and she had been taken to
Soweto. It was hardly paradise, she had commented to her
hosts, but it was not nearly so wretched as the slums she had
seen in Mexico and the Philippines. She was amused now,
thinking back on it, at her surprise over the way the blacks
exploited each other inside the ghetto. What had she expected?
Was it so different from Chicago's ghetto?

Meanwhile, there were metals coming out of the ground of South Africa that could be found nowhere else but in the Soviet Union, unless there were some great finds in Brazil, which her company was helping to explore for minerals, and where she hoped to go soon.

She let her seat go all the way back and stretched out her legs under the seat in front. She liked flying, especially first-class; and she very much enjoyed getting on a plane wearing engineer's boots and twill pants, shocking the stewardesses, letting them think she was a lesbian, catching them in stares and whispers. Once, on the way back from Mexico City, she had taken one of the stewardesses aside and lectured her on the need for women to show their abilities in the world of men.

I guess I'm just not a radical, the stewardess had answered.

She had laughed. Radicalism of one kind or another had driven her all her life. The civil rights movement had taken her out of school for a year to help register voters in Mississippi. During the Vietnam War she had made speeches and marched in demonstrations; twice she had been arrested. Now she gave part of her free time to the women's movement, working for adoption of the Equal Rights Amendment.

The company supported her in her efforts on behalf of women. She went to high schools and colleges to recruit women for engineering and to recruit women engineers for the company. She was living proof that women could become engineers and succeed in the business world. To demonstrate that women could work in the field she showed slides of herself working on construction sites and in mines, not only strip mines but down deep, bent double in a coal mine with her way lighted by a miner's lamp and standing next to a drill operator deep in a Bolivian tin mine.

She had new photographs to add to her lecture now, pictures of herself deep in a South African gold mine standing among black men whose naked, sweating arms and backs shone as if they had been oiled. It was clear in the photographs that she, a woman, was the person in authority, that these great muscled men deferred to her.

The slides were important to her recruiting for the company. They showed that she was not a token woman, beholden to affirmative action for her job and salary. When she put the slides up on the screen, she talked about the kind of company she worked for, the commitment the company had to equality and justice.

This is real justice, she said, not taking advantage of a law, but making a law work by your ability to do the work.

The plane droned on. She closed the window shade, and taking a pillow from the stewardess, she sank into sorrowful dreams.

———◆———

Among the tactics of totalitarianism that create moral disruption in the members of the society is the situation in which one carries out orders contrary to his own values. In the extreme, a man gives evidence against himself, as in the Moscow Trials, where men once of good sense had so thoroughly ceded themselves to the organization that they conspired in their own destruction for the sake of the state.

People carry out orders that conflict with their own values out of purely bourgeois motives: to avoid pain, hunger, failure, loss of status; to have a job, to get a job, to get a better job. All are the motives of men who have accepted a definition of happiness not of their own making, for if the definition were their own, it would not include actions that contradicted their own values.

Aristotle offers an estimation of one who suffers such an affront for bourgeois motives: ". . . To endure the greatest indignities for no noble end or for a trifling end is the mark of an inferior person." And Kant says: "None but the virtuous or he who is about to become virtuous is capable of . . . pure moral discontent. . . ."

Can one who carries out orders contrary to his own moral values be discontent? In the beginning of bourgeois life, one suffers moral discontent, but the insidious aspect of accepting an imposed definition of happiness is demonstrated in the moral failure that inevitably accompanies the habitual flouting of one's own system of morals. A circle of self-justification supports the actions of the bourgeois: each moral failure lessens the unhappiness generated by those failures that preceded it, culminating in a perverse deontology in which the organization prescribes all duties.

The extent to which the organization seeks to disrupt man's human system of morals can be seen in this quote from the French industrial psychologist Fayol: ". . . The higher laws of religious or moral order envisage the individual only . . . whereas management principles aim at the success of associations of individuals and at the satisfying of economic interests." Without moral order, there can, of course, be no human society; and nothing recognizes that more fully than the higher religious principles expressed by Moses, Christ, Buddha, Confucius, etc. Fayol describes two moral systems, explicitly incongruent, therefore competitive. Men succumb in what they mistakenly consider acts of self-defense.

ARBITRARY EQUIVOCATION

> Nothing is more seductive for man than
> his freedom of conscience, but nothing is
> a greater cause of suffering.
>
> The Grand Inquisitor

A week before he was scheduled to testify before the Subcommittee on the Environment he received a memo from the chairman of the board. It said: As our chief of engineering you are the man in this corporation most qualified to testify on the practicality, in terms of cost/benefit, and the technological feasibility of meeting the proposed standards for stationary sources of pollution as they affect our industry. Your testimony must be clear, honest, and with regard for the public interest. My only cautionary advice is to remind you that you will be speaking to a group of laymen. You will have to explain basic concepts in chemistry, physics, and mechanics if you are to succeed in communicating your position to them. Good luck.

Since there was no comment on his draft testimony, he went ahead with the second draft, polishing the grammar, adding explanatory passages, and comparing his figures to those his staff had been working up for him. He broke his conclusion into five simple points:

1. An electrostatic system was feasible, although unproved under operating conditions in the industry.

2. The use of electric induction furnaces was possible, but with present technology the furnaces were still too expensive by a factor of four, assuming the sharp rise in rates for electric power predicted by the committee's own economists.

3. Increasing the height of the stacks by 200 per cent could be expected to halve the concentration of gaseous and particulate pollutants in the areas adjacent to the plants, given prevailing wind conditions.

4. A study of achievable levels of pollutant concentrations compared to the available medical data indicated that the proposed reduction would eliminate all potential health hazards, both long-term and short-term.

5. The cost of meeting the standards, based on a five-year depreciation of the capital investment and including operating costs, was approximately one dollar and six cents per ton of refined ore, which would narrow the gap between their price and the price of imported ore, but which would still give them a slight price advantage, unless there was a price restructuring by foreign or American-owned foreign-based competitors. Therefore, barring the need for electric induction furnaces and assuming the success of an electrostatic system for removing particulates, the standards could be met without irreparable damage to the domestic industry, although with some added inflationary pressure due to the cost passthrough.

The day before he was to leave for Washington he received a draft of a speech the chairman was to deliver the following week to an industry conference in New Orleans. In his speech the chairman planned to say: "Sometimes I wonder who those people in Washington are working for. The proposed standards for emissions will literally strangle this industry. We cannot now meet the standards with any proven equipment. And if the equipment works, the capital and operating costs will destroy us. What are we doing in this country? We are setting standards based on incomplete medical evidence. We are forcing up the prices of our own goods, giving every advantage to our foreign competitors, putting our own people out of work, destroying the value of our own currency, hurting our own poor and aged people by destroying their fixed incomes with inflationary regulations. Ladies and gentlemen, there is an old song the union organizers used to bring the people together in our very industry. I say we have the need to use those very words now to speak to the government in Washington. I say we have to shout and sing and write those words to them until the message gets through. And we have to do it fast before we give this country away to foreign nations. Join me in asking those people in Washington: Whose side are you on?

The chief of engineering read over the chairman's speech several times. He felt a tightness in his chest, as if he were having stomach trouble again or suffering from flu. He telephoned the chairman's office and was told that the chairman was out of town until the beginning of the following week. He attached a copy of his testimony to the speech and sent it back to the chairman's assistant with a note asking him to consider the discrepancies. There was a history of heart disease in his family. He thought about his pension. There was time before he went to Washington. The figures could be re-examined, the data could be reinterpreted. But the chairman had read his testimony. There had been no comment.

To maintain perfect control of an organization success must reflect on the leader and failure must reflect on those who are led. Any other arrangement jeopardizes the position of the leader. To accomplish this security of leadership both business and government use a totalitarian tactic: the issuing of orders that are both arbitrary and equivocal. When members of the organization fail in their tasks, they can be criticized for misinterpretation of orders or failure to carry out orders; when they succeed, they can be said to have correctly carried out the directives of the leader.

History holds innumerable examples. Montesquieu spoke of Rome: "On occasion they took advantage of their language's subtlety. They destroyed Carthage, saying that they had promised to preserve the state, but not the city." Stalin's sudden switch to the idea of socialism in one country, in 1924, the year of the publication of his conclusion that socialism in one country was impossible, put him in an ideal position to destroy Trotsky and the other internationalists. Hitler was able to give contradictory orders about practically anything, including his own role as leader, which he revised in a late edition of *Mein Kampf*. Arendt describes the Nazi "language rule" as "a code name; it meant what in ordinary language would be called a lie." Machiavelli delivered corollary advice to the Prince with frightening clarity: ". . . Princes should let the carrying out of unpopular orders devolve on others, and bestow favors themselves."

Business uses the tactic to defend the corporation itself, which never admits to error: all errors are committed by individuals within the corporation, benighted souls who have failed to understand the ethical stance of the leaders of the organization. Since the orders are arbitrary, the freedom of the middle manager or technician is abolished; and since the orders are equivocal (unclear or changeable), the one who carries out the orders can never be certain that he will not suffer for doing what he was told.

The moral disruption of living inside a puzzle that cannot be solved leaves men with no choice but to exist as things, without the power to initiate action, unable to think of the meaning of action. They grow old. Knowing that they can never be certain of doing anything right, they can never be certain of doing anything wrong. In that situation, moral values lose their relevance, leaving men without any place from which to launch rebellion. They learn to love beefsteaks and shrimp cocktails more than they love freedom. They are as docile as oxen, taking their comfort in the yoke and the prod.

SIMPLE

> They will be glad to believe our answer, for it will save them from the great anxiety and terrible agony they must endure at present in making a free decision for themselves.
>
> The Grand Inquisitor

The engineer and the public relations man had grown up together in the company. They were enemies in business, they had no respect for each other's work, and they were friends. In twenty years their differences had become institutionalized: the engineer wanted, quite naturally, to speak in the language of engineers, giving details and important qualifications; the public relations man, quite naturally, wanted to speak in the language of public relations, which he described as composed of clear, brief statements that could be understood by any normal twelve-year-old; in other words, the language of the daily newspaper.

Every encounter resulted in a compromise. But as the years passed, the compromises moved slowly over to the viewpoint of the public relations man, for he demonstrated with perfect regularity that complicated statements were either ignored by the press or rewritten into simple language less accurate than that originally proposed by the public relations man. What more evidence do you want? he argued to the engineer. The experiment is repeatable and reproducible. Gravity is less certain than the simplemindedness of the American public.

I am an engineer, said the engineer. We have professional standards, ethics. That's something a public relations man can't even begin to understand.

And if it weren't for public relations, said the public relations man, some goddamn engineer would still be trying to sell the world on the utility of the wheel.

The two men aged in different ways: the public relations man inherited his family tendency to heart disease, so he kept himself thin, exercised regularly, did not smoke, and rarely drank hard liquor, making himself into the kind of ruddy ascetic one finds so often at the higher levels of corporations; the engineer grew sleek, he became confident, taking on more and more responsibility, practicing charm, developing a firm will and a protective coldness that frightened those who were able to see beyond his charm.

The public relations man was loyal to old friends, the engineer was not. The public relations man became the head of the news relations department, reporting to the vice-president, public relations. The engineer became president of the company. Shortly after becoming president, the engineer gathered the senior staff members in the headquarters office for dinner and what some called conversation. He told them, speaking extemporaneously, that he believed the company should act a bit less like a business, less like accountants and more like a high technology engineering firm. The future, he said, was not in work, it was in intelligence. He called for a great change, for a revolution inside the company to put them in the forefront of the second industrial revolution, the tide that was going to sweep the world.

He was applauded. The dinner was excellent. The evening was a success. The public relations man told his staff the next day that the handwriting was on the wall. Under the new regime they would begin writing in more detail, explaining, qualifying, speaking more like engineers and less like Hearst police reporters. He received no argument from his staff; instead, they applauded him.

Less than a week later, he was called to the president's office. This first meeting was awkward for him: he did not know whether to be deferential or to retain the old adversary relationship. The engineer quickly clarified the situation. He said, I just read a press release on the new high-efficiency electric motors. It looks to me like you've lost your mind. The release could be presented as a paper before the society of electrical engineers. Who in the hell can understand that stuff? We don't have one customer in a thousand who'll know what you're talking about.

The engineer pulled a yellow pad out from under a pile of papers. Now, listen to me carefully, he said. There are three points to make about these motors: they're new, they're better, and they cost less to operate. That's what people want to know. They don't care about resistances and low alloy steels. Furthermore, I want to sell this company to our customers and to the stockholders in the same clear way: we're the high company; high technology, high profitability, and high growth.

Is that the end of the discussion? the public relations man asked.

We don't get paid for holding discussions.

The public relations man could not help but laugh. May I tell you something? he asked, and went on without waiting for permission. Until this moment I didn't understand why you got the job. Congratulations. I think you're going to make one hell of a president.

Don't be facetious, the president said.

The public relations man shook his head in disbelief. Come on, he said, would I try to con a colleague?

What is the use? Wittgenstein asked whenever he thought of the meaning of words, phrasing the moral question more profoundly than did Orwell or even Heidegger, who saw in "one-track thinking" a similarity to technological progress and asked what kind of order was heralded in the spread of this kind of language? If language has meaning only as determined by its use, our choice of words and their order is a moral act—each word we use is included; none escapes judgment.

Speaking is acting. Words may not only incite violence, words themselves may do violence, according to the way in which they are used. A lie does violence to the listener, but one need not lie to do violence with language. Words may be used to impose one's will upon another, not to command, but to create a dysfunction, to weaken the listener's ability to understand, to think of meaning.

Simplification wreaks violence upon the listener more certainly than lying. One may discover a lie, but simplifications are perfectly opaque: the will of the speaker cannot be challenged. Simplifications impose "one-track thinking" upon the listener; they cannot be considered.

All messianic movements—religious, social, or economic—speak in simplifications. Messianism wills; it is not political in that it does not speak in a human voice. Paradise cannot be submitted for examination lest it lose the character of paradise.

Hitler urged simplicity in every statement of the Nazi Party, admiring and wishing to emulate the force of will in Luther's program nailed to the gates of Wittenberg. Propaganda, as it developed under the Nazi Party, became the ultimate expression of will in language—simplistic, repetitive, utterly opaque, and devoid of human content. The purpose of this propaganda was to move people as if they were things, to make their every movement acquiescence in life as a thing.

In its use as propaganda, language passes from the human sphere to that of technology. Like technology, it permits no resistance, it does not recognize the right to autonomous existence of any person but the speaker. To disagree with the language of the technological will is to disobey.

Simplification, jargon, and acronyms are so common in the language of business that any deviation from language as technological will in business communication surprises the listener. If speech is the distinguishing quality of human existence, then the disappearance of human speech from business is the most to be feared of all the totalitarian tactics used by business.

IDENTITY

> There are three powers, three powers alone, able to conquer and to hold captive forever the conscience of these impotent rebels for their happiness—those forces are miracle, mystery and authority.
>
> The Grand Inquisitor

Joyfully he retired. Overwhelmed with gifts and good wishes, stuffed with prime rib and awash in scotch and champagne, he said good-by, farewell, good luck, so long, and I've been waiting for this day since I was forty years old.

Good-by to our treasurer, to a man who knew money intimately. We'll miss the guy who picked up seventeen million dollars on the float in a single year. So long, moneybags, may you enjoy some of your own.

He took away fishing rods, a television set, two pairs of

waders, a rocking chair, subscriptions to magazines, three suit-
cases, and a set of The Great Books for a guy who really
knows how to keep the books.

Keep in touch. I'll call you. Don't forget to write. Confi-
dentially, for the next year or two, if you don't mind, we may
need to call on you every now and then to help us with a little
problem or just to give a bit of general advice.

He and his wife packed their belongings, directed the men
in the white coveralls from the moving company to do the
heavy work, and drove west and south to the place they had
bought six years before in Scottsdale. In a month they were
setttled into their new house, members of the country club,
suntanned Southwesterners. There were no calls from Cleveland. There was no mail from Cleveland but the retirees
newsletter. He gardened. She gardened. In May, the Arizona
summer arrived and everything in the garden turned brown
and died.

They drove to Flagstaff to get away from the heat. She
caught cold. He drove her home to Scottsdale. There was
nothing in the mailbox but bills and magazines and an advertisement for life insurance for people over sixty-five.

He swam. She swam. He played golf. She played bridge. He
swam. She swam.

No one held the door for him. There were no parades of
people to say, Good morning. There were no parades of people to say, Good night. No one was afraid of him.

He developed a cough. Probably the damn Arizona dust, he
said. He developed prostate trouble. Not enough sex, he told
her. He treated the cough and the prostate trouble with vodka.

He telephoned Cleveland. A new voice answered. She said,
And what is this in regard to, sir? He hung up the telephone.

In the restaurants they visited no one knew his name. They
had trouble pronouncing it when he told them. No table was
his table. No one asked if he had any new pictures of his
grandchildren.

At the country club he had little to say. He talked about the stock market, he complained about the Democrats, but he had no business. There were no events, no one wanted to know his secrets, no one wanted to buy anything from him or sell anything to him. The days were without distinction. The sales figures did not change, the interest rates did not concern him, he could not promote or reward or demote or dismiss anyone. He did nothing. His belly grew. He awakened, as he had for the past forty-one years, at six in the morning. Then he showered, shaved, ate breakfast, dressed, and went nowhere.

He developed shingles, an abscess in the lung, and the need for his prostate gland to be removed. When he was ready to leave the hospital a blood clot was found in a vein in his right leg. He remained in the hospital for six weeks. No calls and no mail came from Cleveland. It did not matter how long he stayed in the hospital. He had nowhere to go, no one missed him, nothing waited for him. In the year since his retirement, he noted, he had not signed a check worth more than a hundred dollars.

His recuperation was very slow. After he came home from the hospital he did not leave the house. When his wife asked him why he would not go out, he said: I'm not properly dressed. Can't you see, I'm not wearing the right clothes?

She did not press him. He had been ill. The anesthetic had caused much of his hair to fall out. His face was baggy from loss of weight. He was very pale and he trembled, like an old man.

He made two more telephone calls to Cleveland. Neither of the men he called was available to take his call: one was said to be in court and the other was said to have left only the day before on his annual vacation. He told his wife that they were avoiding him, that they wished he was dead.

Don't be silly, she said. They're your friends, your co-workers. They only wish you the best.

Of course, dear, you're probably right. It's just a mistake.

They don't want me to die. They know I'm dead. They must know it. They came to my funeral, didn't they?

The next morning he awakened at six o'clock as usual, showered and shaved, dressed himself in a suit, white shirt, and tie, and sat in the easy chair next to the bed. He did not go out to the kitchen to eat his breakfast.

His wife called to him from the kitchen: Hurry up, dear, the coffee's getting cold.

I can't come out, he answered.

She ran to the bedroom, afraid that something might have happened to him. She was astonished to find him sitting fully clothed in the easy chair. Why won't you come out to breakfast? she asked.

I can't leave the bedroom, not this way, he said. It would be shameful to walk around the house this way.

Which way?

Naked, he said.

———◆———

J. L. Talmon, describing the utter cession of the self required by Babouvism, wrote: "The nation is not the aggregate of men, women and children, but a cofraternity of faith. Moreover, in the true Rousseauist tradition, the individual receives his very personality, and any rights he may possess, from the Social Contract alone."

8

The Promethean
Task

1. Participatory Totalitarianism

If men were happy, brave, and true rebels, the grand inquisitors would be powerless in the world. But we are not happy, for we are not brave and life is complex and often out of keeping with reason. Unlike the immortal gods of the ancient Greeks, we know that we will sicken and die. We are so alone in the world that philosophers from Plato onward have thought it worth considering the question of whether we can understand other men's minds well enough to escape loneliness at all. Dostoevski suggested one result of this sense of loneliness:

> All that man seeks on earth . . . is some one to worship, some one to keep his conscience, and some means of uniting all in one unanimous and harmonious ant-heap, for the craving for universal unity is the third and last anguish of men.
>
> The Grand Inquisitor

And Aristotle tells us:

> The nature of a state is to be a plurality, and in tending to greater unity, from being a state, it becomes a family, and from being a family, an individual; for the family may be said to be more than the state, and the individual more than the family. So that we ought not to attain this greatest unity even if we could, for it would be the destruction of the state.

Loneliness, terrible, impenetrable, and as fearsome as death, incites men to cede themselves to some unifying force: the party, the state, the corporation. All lonely creatures are frightened; to be included provides the delusion of safety, to cede oneself masks the terror of loneliness, to abandon autonomy avoids the risk of beginnings. In the General Will, Rousseau invented a unity to satisfy the human craving. It may also be called communism or national socialism or company loyalty. J. L. Talmon deals with the passage from a democratic society to despotism in *Totalitarian Democracy,* using the failure of the French Revolution for his subject.

Talmon concentrates upon the philosophical power of Rousseau, Babeuf, et al. And there he seems to have been carried away by an intellectual construct, for totalitarianism has no philosophy to guide it. Organizations do not set out to be totalitarian; if they did, they would attract no more than a few lunatics to their membership. Totalitarianism evolves. Hannah Arendt complained of her own work in *The Origins of Totalitarianism* that she had not written an account of its origins, only of some elements. A systematic description of a movement that is not a system would describe something other than the movement. Totalitarianism is only a process in which autonomy is destroyed. The process follows certain patterns, but they are vague, known subjectively long before objective analysis identifies them.

The most distressing realization one comes to after con-

sidering totalitarianism is that while the imposition of a definition of happiness may lie at the root of it, the organization itself cannot be imposed from without. Men do not merely
acquiesce, they choose to live under totalitarian conditions.
Not all men choose totalitarianism, of course, but in a raw
democracy, one without the limits of law, only a majority of
the active members need choose totalitarianism to impose it
upon the active minority and the great mass of inactive
members of the society.

Reasons for this choice have interested philosophers and
psychologists since Plato. Many hypotheses have been offered,
and yet another will be offered in the next section of this chapter. They range from the natural progression of political organization of a state to anti-Semitism to original sin to economic necessity to technological will to the herd instinct to
imperialistic tendencies. One theory has it that men are born
monsters and want only for the opportunity to become despots.

In *The Authoritarian Personality,* Adorno, Frenkel-Brunswick, Levinson, and Sanford conclude that ethnocentrism and
the desire to live under the power of some unmitigated authority are patterns that develop in early childhood. Parent–child
relationships, neurotic and psychotic behavior are discussed at
length in their massive work of research into the psychology of
the authoritarian personality. But parent–child relationships
do not account satisfactorily for Nazi Germany, Stalinist Russia, Maoist China, or Cambodia under the Pol Pot regime.
Neither can such early relationships account for the widespread use of totalitarian tactics in business organizations. Despotic authority may, as they suggest, be a satisfying way to resolve conflicts in neurotic individuals, but enormous numbers
of neurotic people find other means to resolve inner conflicts,
including learning to live with them or even turning them to
constructive use through some form of sublimation. Finally,
the authors concede that the fascist pattern is to a large extent

imposed from above, which, in effect, negates most of what they have said previously about the kind of personality that chooses fascism.

Furthermore, the hypothesis that dilutes the personality hypothesis makes no sense on the face of it: no one may simply declare himself above; he must have the power of adherents, he must be elevated to that position by his subjects.

Totalitarianism can never come to power under the banner of atomization, moral disruption, secrecy, and terror; it comes in other guises, evolving like a river's course, finding the weakness of the territory and cutting into it. Men choose totalitarianism out of fear, mistaking its effect upon them because they do not think of the meaning of their actions. Totalitarianism begins in compromise and ends in murder; it progresses from small gains to irremediable losses.

By definition, the offer of totalitarianism is messianic, holding out to man an end to suffering and loneliness in all the world and time. In return, it asks that he give nothing but himself. It relieves him of the unbearable burden of setting his own course in the world, of the awesome responsibility of beginning anything, and of the weight of dignity. In the beginning of the process men feel a giddy relief, like anoxia, but as the assumption by the organization increases in intensity they begin to apprehend the loss of their autonomy, and they must choose whether to rebel or to succumb. The tactics of totalitarianism ensure that men will succumb.

Men choose a leader for the herd out of instinct, as Freud says, but totalitarianism also bears a great resemblance to Aristotelian comedy, the difference being that when the curtain comes down at the happy ending of a comedy the implication is that happiness will last forever. At that point in the development of a totalitarian organization happiness ends. Men have chosen totalitarianism to find a way out of loneliness. The thorough control and early efficiency of the organization enable the group to move from a lower to a higher position, as in comedy and social revolution. But then the comedy ends: the organization cannot stop expanding, it cannot relinquish control, and the unity of men choosing to work together for their common good becomes the solid, undifferentiated mass of atomized men crushed together by overwhelming force. After the curtain goes down on the comedy, the darkness remains and grows. Happiness and sadness no longer exist; men do what they are told. The participatory stage of totalitarianism ends with the last rebellious act of dignity or beginning.

When societies turn to the messianic promises of totalitarianism, they do not do so overnight. The conditions in the society must be right, there must be crisis. There must also be a cadre of men conditioned to life without dignity or independence, a cadre of atoms whose moral system has been destroyed, men who are accustomed to being deceived by lies and simplifications, a cadre for whom freedom lost all meaning as they became absorbed by an irresistible movement. It is in the creation of such a cadre that the use of totalitarian tactics by business endangers all of society. The waste of men's lives and labors by oppression can barely be tolerated in a society that at most hopes to survive. But when that society makes of its best educated and potentially most able men a cadre inured to oppression, it may, in the grip of a crisis, abandon the rules of civil society and seek its salvation in totalitarianism.

2. A Republic in the Mind

> We must admit that the same elements
> and characters that appear in the state
> must exist in every one of us; where else
> would they have come from?
>
> Plato

Exegetical writing about Plato abounds. In the *Theaetetus* he asks

> Would you be prepared to maintain that every color appears to a dog or any other creature just such as it appears to you?
>
> Or to another man? Does anything you please appear to him such as it appears to you?

And philosophers, particularly those of the analytical school, have been arguing the question and its implications ever since.

The philosopher's fascination with the problem is not difficult to fathom. If the question could be answered with an unqualified no, human society would be improbable if not impossible. If the answer to the question were the opposite, men would be so alike that diversity would not exist in the world and life would have a mechanical sameness that would make all but the simplest interactions among men superfluous. The answer must lie in some middle ground, and it most likely varies according to which men are considered among the observers.

Both the similarities and the differences among men are ostensible. But the similarities are broad while the differences are subtle. Based upon the similarities, a group of anthropologists, particularly Claude Lévi-Strauss, hypothesize that the mind has a definite structure which is similar in all men of all races and societies. He brings a vast knowledge of myths of various cultures to his argument, attempting to prove the hypothesis by showing the structural similarities of myths invented by men of many cultures, both modern and neolithic.

Surely, the mind has a structure; it is not a chaotic mass. The anatomy of the brain shows a similar gross structure among all humans. Several of the characteristics we commonly use to define the species itself—speech, grammar, imagination

—show some deeper similarity. Whether the similarity is as great as Lévi-Strauss hypothesizes remains to be proved, but that the mind has some structure and that there are similarities between all human minds is clear on the face of it.

Assuming that what passes the test of reason for contemporary man also occurred to Plato, is it not possible that Plato meant to say what he said in the *Republic?* No one reckons Plato to have been a satirist, but neither does anyone take him at his word when he says that the republic he is about to describe is an analogy and that he wishes to use his description of an ideal state to explain the composition of a just man. It is, of course, a bit farfetched to take a philosopher at his word, but Plato was an extraordinary fellow; it is worth following this presumption of clarity to find out where it will lead.

If an individual's mind were organized along the lines of Plato's ideal state, it would be an unemotional mind, but a very clear one, ruled by philosophy, with the liars expelled, constantly educating itself in an orderly fashion, wondrously stable, always on guard against deceit and unclear thinking, but totalitarian.

In a single mind the organization described by Plato would seem to pose but little danger. Some aspects of modern totalitarianism, however, would not be acceptable in the mind: one would not want the mind to terrorize the body, although it often does so; the estrangement of the parts of the mind from each other would be unfortunate; the lies and deceitful simplifications would inhibit doing philosophy; the moral disruptions would confuse the urge to do the good; crowding would seriously reduce the ability of the mind to function; and so on; but none of these aspects of modern totalitarianism appear in Plato's ideal state or state of mind. In fact, when Popper accuses Plato of describing a totalitarian state, Popper mistakes tribalism for totalitarianism—the tribal organizations of neolithic man more closely resemble the structure of the mind in

Plato's analogy than do any of the modern totalitarian states or corporations.

The danger of the organization of the mind occurs when it serves as a model: what works for the organization of man does not work for the organization of men. When man creates society in his own image, he repeats the past and he makes something less than himself, because the mechanical society based on the mechanical structure of the mind lacks the capacity to transcend itself. It is this capacity of transcendence that separates the human mind from all other natural and technological creations.

History proves the tendency to follow the model, for there have been innumerable tribal societies, and with the invention of writing and technology, there have been a great many totalitarian organizations. However, nothing in nature demands that man make societies homologous to his own mind. There is no totalitarian imperative, but neither is there a human imperative. Men must choose to be human, just as men must choose to live.

Memory draws us toward death and the return to the inanimate matter from which we arose to become men, according to Freud. Perhaps. If not memory, perhaps the knowledge of history draws us backward. Or is it the knowledge of our mortality? We are not Greek gods, we know our biological destiny. Death, like the structure of the mind, is a model from the past. Like every model, it is a form of will. By its very existence as a model the model wills. And since it is but a mechanical construction, like a technology, the model lacks limits in its willing; it cannot be satisfied until the work of its will has been accomplished totally, until the model is repeated.

In all human activities the will of the model carried within man competes for the organization of the society of men, drawing men backward toward the life of the ancestor ant, away from human life to a lesser existence. What separates us from other creatures, which have no defense against the model, is our capacity for alienation, the quality the Greeks called wonder, that uniquely human capability to stand away from nature, including the nature within ourselves, and think.

Totalitarianism occurs only when men do not think. It is a retreat from human existence toward the mechanical model, a descent toward death. We live all the large and small acts of social life in the struggle between the will of the subhuman model and the will of man to dare to think, to leap into autonomy.

3. Human Fire

Against the will of the model to draw man back toward his mechanical past stands the beckoning of human autonomy, with its promise of the joy of beginnings and the adventure of contingency. Man lives in opposition to the gods, building cultures in defiance of nature, struggling against his fate. Tragedy, in the view of the Greeks, is the inability of man to triumph in his opposition to fate. It is an opposition recognized by all cultures, for this hubris separates what is truly human from all other ways of living. Only man dares to oppose the violent determinism of the force that created him. Only man, of all the creatures on earth, can alienate himself from nature and so transcend himself.

All men know this. All men have always known. To oppose the will of the model is as much a part of the definition of man as is the ability to make language.

Human hubris, the opposition of man to the gods, was known to the ancient Mexica as one of the salient differences between man and all other creatures. In Teotihuacán, the god Quetzalcóatl descended into the Place of the Dead to rescue the bones of man so that men might inhabit the earth. The other gods were angry. They made a pit and Quetzalcóatl fell into the pit and died. But he came to life again, and took the bones and ground them up and gave them life by sprinkling them with blood let from his penis. Quetzalcóatl the god is also the monk who lived in Tula, the city of artisans and poets. He is the culture-bearer.

Our own culture is founded in a similar act of hubris: the theft of fire by Prometheus. The opposition here is more clearly between man and the totalitarian power of Zeus, as Aeschylus tells us:

> All toil alike in sorrow, unless one were lord of heaven; none is truly free, save only Zeus.
>
> . . . Zeus unlawfully rules with new laws . . .
>
> But he, ever savage of soul,
> Swayeth the children of heaven;
> Nor ever will cease till his heart
> Is satiate grown, or another
> Snatches his empire by guile.
>
> No sooner was he established on his father's throne than he began to award various offices to the different gods, ordering his government throughout. Yet no care was in his heart for miserable men, and he was fain to blot out the whole race and in their stead create another.
>
> . . . his will is immutable . . .
> What is destined for Zeus but endless rule?

Prometheus steals fire and gives it to man, raising up man from his life in caves to a new life sufficiently alienated from nature to make possible wonder and all that flows from it. To punish Prometheus for disturbing the "harmony" of his government Zeus instructs Power to have him chained to a rock, where he will suffer an eagle tearing all day at his liver, which will be renewed during the freezing night, in a round of endless torment.

But like Quetzalcóatl, who was made to live again, Prometheus survives. He knows a secret that he can trade to Zeus for his freedom, he knows that the government of Zeus can be destroyed and by whom. The myths of two hemispheres hold the same optimism for man in his opposition to the gods: they promise that the leap to autonomy, although it will cause man to suffer, will succeed.

The opposition that Lévi-Strauss finds in all human thinking exists—and has existed at least since Hesiod—in the way men think of freedom. In business and government we are constantly torn between the will of the totalitarian model and the beckoning of autonomy. By succumbing to the will of the model we expect to find the peace of totality, the resolution of all conflict in a single, mechanical structure, perfect, endless, the future without past or future, devoid of the problems of erroneous thinking, beset by no flaws but those of machines.

By answering the call of autonomy we expect to achieve human life, independent of other wills, without repetitions, but fraught with contingency and the conflicts of pluralism and politics, burdened by compassion, and filled with the agonies of ethics and meaning.

The model promises perfection and delivers the horrors and inefficiencies of a machine that cannot repair its failures because it has no means for recognizing them. Yet men have chosen the model throughout most of their history, and today most governments and corporations are to a large extent imitations of the model. Men who cannot conceive a happiness of their own accept a definition imposed upon them by others. Unable to think of themselves as ends, they consent to being the means to other ends, accepting impossible doctrines of movement toward paradise to put the blessing of rationality upon their cession to the model and to rationalize their existence as mere means.

The power of the model grows out of the failure of men to know that every act, no matter how insignificant it seems beside the velocity of life and business, has meaning and therefore chooses between freedom and death. When men fail in this way, they cede themselves to the totalitarian will, and in that prehuman darkness, they die. The oppressors and the oppressed die alike, for they retreat from humanity alike. These men do not know until very late in their lives, if ever, that they have suffered. They do not apprehend the effect upon themselves of causing others to suffer. They do not think. In the confusion of meanings in their lives, they believe that the retreat from human life is the pursuit of happiness.

The alternative is to accept the Promethean task, to prefer the difficulties of now to the deceit of forever, to admit that men who act autonomously may suffer, and nevertheless to begin. It is not an unfair task that the pursuit of humanity sets for man. All rational men know that no matter how they choose they cannot eliminate unhappiness or achieve perfection in the world. If they choose the tactics of totalitarianism, they suffer and die; if they choose autonomy, they suffer and live.

Afterword:

A Scrivener's Choice

At the end of this book the reader must be tempted to ask, "Then how shall I live? What shall I do?" The writer is tempted to answer that prescriptions are always dangerous; happiness defined by a book subverts autonomous human life no less than happiness defined by the merchant, the manager, or the despot.

Other answers appear in the preceding pages: to be human, to be able to seek one's own happiness, requires a certain sense of alienation, sufficient to distinguish oneself from the rest of the world, but not so great as to leave the person in a state of lawless loneliness.

In the *Apology* Socrates offered sound advice on how to live and how to die: to examine life requires wonder, which devolves from alienation. "This sense of wonder is the mark of the philosopher," said Plato in the *Theaetetus*. "Philosophy indeed has no other origin. . . ."

Yet there are many who oppose alienation, who claim that happiness lies in the opposite direction: in a sense of loyalty, in oneness with the organization, in belonging. They argue that many middle managers and technicians and white collar workers enjoy long and happy careers in business or government without ever having a sense of alienation from the organization. It is a natural response they make, for many do live contentedly inside the organization; having accepted an externally imposed definition of happiness, they live by it, and call themselves happy.

The wounds of those who pass their lives contentedly enduring totalitarian tactics often show most clearly in their families, in ruined children, in desperate wives. The other wounds are less obvious, for who can say what a man might have been if he had lived a human life?

Contentment does not obviate the question of how to survive, for mere contentment is no proof of survival. If totalitarian tactics did not leave most men feeling content, no society would ever have permitted them. If men are deceived into feeling content, into believing they have exhausted their choices, how may they be awakened? To what end? Why should they endure the dangers of the struggle for autonomy? The practical questions are the political questions.

Bruno Bettelheim tells in *Surviving* of his life in Nazi concentration camps. Using the affecting mixture of analysis and feeling that distinguishes his work, he describes the physical beating he endured, the dehumanizing brutality of the camp, and the method he used to save himself from the "disintegration of his personality." Bettelheim's defense was to separate himself from the experience by observing it in himself and others. He practiced his discipline in the camps, he lived in his work. How could the Nazis "break the spirit" of a psychoanalyst psychoanalyzing?

Perhaps a man of Bettelheim's character and intelligence could have survived even if he were a shoemaker. But shoemakers did not survive so well. It is more likely that the nature of his work helped to save him. A writer, whether he is as disciplined and talented as Bettelheim or a fellow of more ordinary means, has available to him protective devices that are denied other men. He may, for example, think of himself as a collector of material for his work or he may think of his job as distinct from his work or he may amuse himself by imagining that he plays the role of both spectator and actor or he may simply have goals that do not make him vulnerable to the definition of happiness pressed upon him by the corporation and the society.

Bettelheim and the more ordinary writer have a common defense—they think. Perhaps their thinking is not of the same quality, but it is thinking, it is "out of this world," alienation from the destructive force of the moment and union with culture and the authority of human history. Happiness—the terms of survival—cannot be defined for them; they are being and watching, they know what they are doing. Similarly Franz Kafka, Simone Weil, and Harvey Swados watched themselves at work. No one watched himself more closely or from a greater distance than the banker of St. Louis and London, T. S. Eliot.

Weil, seeking a prescription in essay after essay, asks, ". . . what can those do who still persist, against all eventualities, in honoring human dignity both in themselves and in others? Nothing, except endeavor to introduce a little play into the cogs of the machine that is grinding us down; seize every opportunity of awakening a little thought whenever they are able; encourage whatever is capable, in the sphere of politics, economics or technique, of leaving the individual here and there a certain freedom of movement amid the trammels cast around him by the social organization." She wrote that in her *Sketch of Contemporary Social Life*.

She found another prescription in *Factory Work:* "A cook says, 'My kitchen,' a gardener, 'My lawn,' and this is as it should be. Juridical proprietorship is but one of the means to achieve such a feeling. *The perfect social organization would be one which, by that and other means, would give a proprietary feeling to all men.*"

Marx tells us, "Human emancipation will only be complete when the real individual man has absorbed into himself the abstract citizen. . . ." Kant also has his prescription and Rousseau his. The difficulty in all of these prescriptions is that they are spoken in the language of analysis. Neither poets nor philosophers tell us what to eat for breakfast or how much to pay for bacon or how to deal with the butcher. The translation to quotidian life poses enormous difficulties. We may ask Kant, for example, if a man who arrives at his place of work on time is less autonomous than one who is late. Or early. We may ask Weil whether the man who says of the giant corporation that employs him, "My company," has the proprietary feeling she desires for all men.

Can the writer, the one who survives by living at the remove of thinking, properly advise the shoemaker? Is there a middle ground of language between crude specificity and eloquent generality? In solitude men may find that language: on airplanes or fishing trips, walking to the office or sitting in church. Philosophy and poetry enter the culture through men when they are alone or alone in conversation with philosophers and poets, as Proust described his time with the classics.

The middle manager who does not succumb to velocity, but finds time in his life for contemplation and conversations with philosophers, has the opportunity to define happiness for himself. A man alone but not lonely may reach the ideal level of alienation that permits thinking. Thinking has neither time nor place; it can have no price; it has dignity. In such moments men learn that they are ends, not means, for both thinking and the thinker are invulnerable to powers that seek to use them, they are autonomous beginners.

Only in thinking can man recognize his own life. In that alienated moment he is the subject who knows his own subjectivity. If he attempts to know his life while moving at the velocity of the business world, he can only be confused, vacillating between subject and object, means and end, like the

Chinese dreamer who did not know whether sleeping he dreamed of waking or waking he dreamed of sleeping. Recognitions come only in the extended space between moments that we call thinking, when we step away from the world to be struck with wonder. Only the thinking subject, who cannot be a means, can know when he has been made a means in spite of himself.

The relation among men that makes a means of one depends upon the delusion of the middle manager, who must consider himself greater than those he manages, the end for which they are but a means. The same delusion tells him that he is not merely a means for those who manage him. The destructive chain of use proceeds in that manner through the organization's layers and pyramidal steps. Only the manager who perceives his subordinates as ends in themselves, autonomous and with dignity, has the opportunity to escape the delusion by which he is made into a means. His autonomy depends upon the autonomy of those below him or outside him.

Egalitarianism, which defines the relation among men in a union, makes the use of totalitarian tactics nearly impossible. Managers, who lack unions, and technicians and white collar workers, who spurn the idea of a union, can protect themselves against totalitarian tactics by recognizing that the two structures of the organization, however powerful, cannot change the true value of men. A manager who knows that his subordinates are his equals becomes the equal of his superiors. If he does not teach his subordinates to fear him, he may not learn to fear his superiors. If he respects their lives, he may learn to respect his own. If he permits them dissent, he may arrogate dissent to himself. Unfortunately, one cannot assign values to men outside the organization until he understands that the organization is not the world and has no right to define the world. Only then, alienated from the organization, can he begin to value men as ends.

No view of the world is more difficult than this, for it requires that a man see himself and all others as subjects, creatures who began the world when they came into it and continue to be potential beginners. At the same time he must
believe himself, although a subject and a beginning, a part of
the whole of equals connected in society. Ends are not atoms;
they have an organic connection to other men; they are connected by the endless activity of dignified conflict—politics.

Political men bargain with each other to secure the good.
They do not expect gifts; they thrive on conflict; they are disagreeable, for the world they live in is real and imperfect, and
they do not expect that it will ever be perfect. This disagreeableness of men reached its peak in America. Now it
suffers the forces of conflation: mass media, opinion polling,
the presumed efficiency of monolithic organizations, mass
production, expansionist dreams, xenophobia, and decline.
America seems to be on its way to becoming the state Plato
called timocracy, the rule of the greedy children of the great,
the first degeneration from the rule of reason, the political
stage of a republic marked by the competitiveness and pleasure seeking of its leading citizens.

Timocrats are "like truant children," according to Plato. It
does not take long for them to fall under the rule of an oligarchy. They lack the disagreeable character of their political
fathers; they compete, but for things, not for freedom, not for
reason, not for the good. Justice to a timocrat is the satisfaction of himself.

Shall we speak of America *mutatis mutandis?* Not yet. The
change proceeds, but it is not yet complete; the capability to
be disagreeable that sent Roger Williams out of Massachusetts
to Rhode Island and moved thousands of families west out of
Virginia and then Kentucky and Tennessee remains, although
it is neither as common nor as strong as it has been. Sam
Adams was not the last feisty American. Emerson and
Thoreau were not the last two Americans who could spend

much of their friendship in political and philosophical disagreement. The disagreeableness of Americans emerged during the Vietnam War, although it was mixed with self-interest for many. The spirit of disagreeableness fails now mainly inside organizations, and the failure spreads from there into the general society.

A cautionary fable about the disagreeable nature of Americans was published by Herman Melville in the middle of the nineteenth century. "Bartleby," tells of a scrivener or law-copyist who epitomizes the spirit of disagreeableness. The fable is narrated by Bartleby's employer, a "rather elderly man," who operates a small business "among rich men's bonds, and mortgages, and title deeds" in Wall Street. The narrator says of himself, "I am a man who, from his youth upwards, has been filled with a profound conviction that the easiest way of life is the best," and, "All who know me, consider me an eminently *safe* man."

The fable tells first of two other scriveners and an office boy, three loyal but quirky helots, and then of Bartleby, who at first did a prodigious amount of copying. "I should have been quite delighted with his application," says the narrator, "had he been cheerfully industrious. But he wrote on silently, palely, mechanically."

When the narrator asks Bartleby to proofread a document with him, he is surprised by the scrivener's answer: "I would prefer not to." A second request elicits the same reply. The narrator describes this as "passive resistance." When he consults with the other scriveners about it, one offers to "black his [Bartleby's] eyes." The narrator declines the offer, and goes on with his work.

He discovers that Bartleby lives in the office, spends practically nothing on food, and generally lives an empty life. When he attempts to reason with Bartleby, the scrivener tells him, "I would prefer not to." The narrator dismisses Bartleby, who does not leave. Finally, the narrator moves his offices, leaving

Bartleby behind. The landlord has Bartleby arrested and carried off to the Tombs, the grim prison of lower Manhattan, where the scrivener dies. The description of the scrivener's choice is complete.

The scrivener was not a safe man, he did not think that the easiest way of life was the best, he refused. Had he not refused, he would have been like the helots who worked in the narrator's office, had he accepted ease and safety with enthusiasm he might have been like the narrator. Instead, he insisted upon maintaining his disagreeableness. He had made a bargain for his wages—to copy documents. He would not read proof or run errands. He stayed with his bargain, he did nothing more, until the bargain overtook him. Refusing became his life, and he died.

Nowhere in literature is the cost of autonomy in the seemingly benign but actually unforgiving world made more clear. The scrivener's choice is the unspoken threat made to everyone who enters business. No union will defend the scrivener, no law will protect him, and he has not been trained by society to endure a life of resistance. He will be more than alone, he will be unbearably lonely. His co-workers will be anxious to betray him, his paternalistic employer will not indulge him for long, and the state will presume him to be a criminal, all that for the cool glory of saying, "I would prefer not to."

How unromantic! To answer the call of autonomy when all around him have succumbed to the pull of the totalitarian model wastes a man. Or so it seems. How would he have been otherwise? For the middle manager the choice is to be both oppressed and an oppressor or to say when the defense of his autonomy requires it: "I would prefer not to." When only one man disagrees, he faces the scrivener's choice. He wins the freedom of Boethius in his cell awaiting death.

When many disagree, they become political men, and the freedom they know enlivens the real world. The task of the first to disagree is to persuade the next, as Prometheus brought fire. The danger is that he will not be like Prometheus, but like Bartleby.

To dare to answer the call of autonomy a man must prepare himself by learning to love reason. Then he will be thrilled by justice and even the smallest instance of the rule of law will set him trembling with emotion. The recognition of dignity in the priceless equality of men will bring him the kind of joy he expected only from the birth of a perfect child. He will think of freedom as an exultation, for he will know that it is the only heaven men can make.

Index

Cambodia. *See* Pol Pot
Camus, Albert, 67, 80, 92, 237, 327
Capital (Marx), 52, 110 ff.
Capitalism, 31, 59, 109 ff., 120–21, 182, 214. *See also* Dividends; specific writers
Capitalism, Socialism, and Democracy. *See* Schumpeter, Joseph
Carlyle, Thomas, 59, 269
Carnegie, Andrew, 129
Cars. *See* Automobiles
Carthage, 348
Castle, The, 28, 85
Castro, Fidel, 186
Categorical imperative, 66
Catholicism. *See also* Christianity; Religion
  Machiavelli and Roman Church, 100
Cato, 82, 180
Cession, 123–24 ff., 148–49, 192–93, 327. *See also* Justice; specific writers
Chicago, University of, 2
Chile, 310
China (Chinese Maoists), 60, 83, 259
  and deportation, 279
Chou En-lai, 29
Christianity, 54, 88. *See also* Catholicism; Protestantism; Religion
  Cicero, 76, 210
  Inquisition, 9, 10
Civil rights, 133–34
Classes, 70, 145–46, 147, 151, 187–93. *See also* Mass man; Middle class; specific writers
  exurban atoms, 320–25
Clausewitz, Karl von, 198
Collectives; collective bargaining, 148–49
Comedy, 360, 361
Coming of the Post-Industrial Society, The, 46
Communism. *See* Marx, Karl (Marxism); specific countries
Communist Manifesto, 7
Company towns, 146
Competition, 36, 38–40, 53 ff., 181, 182, 230–34. *See also* Crowding; Expansion (growth); Movement; Size
  and negative inclusion, 306
  placed loyalties, 211–17
Computers, 50, 64, 126
Concentration camps (death camps), 3, 79 ff., 280, 332
  Bettelheim and, 370
Confessions. *See* Rousseau, Jean-Jacques
Conformity, 15
Consciousness, 119, 121
Consent, free, 72–73
Consolation of Philosophy, The, 81
Conspicuous consumption, 25
Consumption, 25. *See also* Productivity
Contemplation. *See* Thinking (contemplation)
Coulanges, Fustel de. *See* Fustel de Coulanges, Numa Denis
Cowan, John, 135
Cowardice, not, 280–89
Critias, 96
Croesus, 86
Crowding, 81, 328–33
Cuba, 186
Culture, 20. *See also* Autonomy; Language; Rootlessness
Cybernation, 43

Darwin, Charles, 110

Earl Shorris is a contributing editor to *Harper's Magazine*. He is also the author of *The Death of the Great Spirit, Ofay, The Boots of the Virgin,* and *Under the Fifth Sun.*